ROUTLEDGE LIBRARY EDITIONS:
ACCOUNTING HISTORY

Volume 22

FEDERAL SECURITIES LAW AND ACCOUNTING 1933–1970: SELECTED ADDRESSES

FEDERAL SECURITIES LAW AND ACCOUNTING 1933–1970: SELECTED ADDRESSES

Edited by
GARY JOHN PREVITS AND
ALFRED R. ROBERTS

Routledge
Taylor & Francis Group
LONDON AND NEW YORK

First published in 1986 by Garland Publishing, Inc.

This edition first published in 2021
by Routledge
2 Park Square, Milton Park, Abingdon, Oxon OX14 4RN

and by Routledge
52 Vanderbilt Avenue, New York, NY 10017

Routledge is an imprint of the Taylor & Francis Group, an informa business

British Library Cataloguing in Publication Data
A catalogue record for this book is available from the British Library

ISBN: 978-0-367-33564-9 (Set)
ISBN: 978-1-00-304636-3 (Set) (ebk)
ISBN: 978-0-367-51589-8 (Volume 22) (hbk)
ISBN: 978-1-00-305456-6 (Volume 22) (ebk)

Publisher's Note
The publisher has gone to great lengths to ensure the quality of this reprint but points out that some imperfections in the original copies may be apparent.

Disclaimer
The publisher has made every effort to trace copyright holders and would welcome correspondence from those they have been unable to trace.

Foreword

When Professor Al Roberts and I undertook the assembly of this book for its original publication in 1978, the interest in regulatory materials relating to the discipline of accounting were at a low ebb and market based literature had become exclusively dominant. Therefore, in an entrepreneurial fashion, we assessed that it was time to support a new and growing movement to recognize the historical structure of regulatory materials that affected our discipline. As we were among the first elected Presidents of the Academy of Accounting Historians, now a section of the American Accounting Association, Al and I took advantage of a relationship he had developed with the Atlanta Office of the Securities and Exchange Commission. He had identified a treasure trove of past speeches of early SEC leaders, including a 1933 presentation by James Landis, who as instrumental in drafting the securities laws. That speech was given during the period the Federal Trade Commission administered the 1933 Securities Act, prior to the 1934 Act that established the SEC itself and created the Commissioners role and the role for a Chief Accountant. What better place to begin developing a literature than the beginning!

The first person to technically serve as Chief Accountant was Commissioner Robert Healy, one of the original five SEC Commissioners, who also held the title acting Chief Accountant from July 1934 to December 1935. Thereafter Carman Blough, William Werntz, Earle King and Andrew Barr filled the position through January 1972... covering one of the most important eras in American Accounting History.

The original Foreword to this volume was prepared by Andrew Barr, the longest serving Chief Accountant. In it he profiles the SEC Commissioners whose speeches are included. The last serving of these Commissions held a term into 1972. Altogether the Commissioners include those who served terms under the administrations of Presidents Roosevelt, Truman, Eisenhower, Kennedy, Johnson and Nixon.

The volume's unique value is its overview of the unofficial individual expressions of policy as issues emerged, matured and met changing capital market circumstances. It should be recalled therefore that such addresses were not official statements of position of the Commissioner per se and were undertaken under the guide of a disclaimer, so that the addresses represent personal and not Commission views.

Professor Roberts passed away in 2007. I am grateful to his son, Mark Roberts, and his daughter, Margaret Pruitt, for their kind support in undertaking this Reissue.

Gary John Previts
Case Western Reserve University
February, 2020

U.S. Securities and Exchange Commission Office of the Chief Accountant—Chief Accountants

Name	*Dates Served*	*Duration*	*Prior Affiliation*
R. Healy (SEC Comm/Acting)	July 1934 – Dec. 1935	1 Yr. 5 Mos.	Fed. Trade Comm.
Carman G. Blough	Dec. 1935 – May 1938	2 Yrs. 5 Mos.	State of Wisconsin
William W. Werntz	May 1938 – Apr. 1947	8 Yrs. 11 Mos.	Yale University
Earle C. King	Apr. 1947 – Nov. 1956	9 Yrs. 7 Mos.	Arthur Andersen
Andrew Barr	Nov. 1956 – Jan. 1972	15 Yrs. 2 Mos.	Yale University
A. Clarence Sampson (Acting)	Feb. 1972 – May 1972	0 Yrs. 3 Mos.	Arthur Young
John. C. "Sandy" Burton	June 1972 – Sept. 1976	4 Yrs. 3 Mos.	Columbia University
A. Clarence Sampson (Acting)	Sept. 1976 – Aug. 1978	1 Yr. 11 Mos.	Arthur Young
A. Clarence Sampson	Aug. 1978 – Dec. 1987	9 Yrs. 4 Mos.	Arthur Young
Edmund Coulson	Jan. 1988 – Jan. 1991	3 Yrs. 0 Mos.	RSM-McGladrey
George Diacont (Acting)	Feb. 1991 – Dec. 1991	0 Yrs. 10 Mos.	Chief Acct SEC/Enf
Walter P. Schuetze	Jan. 1992 – Mar. 1995	3 Yrs. 2 Mos.	KPMG
John Riley (Acting)	Apr. 1995 – June 1995	0 Yrs. 2 Mos.	Arthur Andersen
Michael H. Sutton	June 1995 – Dec. 1997	2 Yrs. 6 Mos.	Deloitte
Jane B. Adams (Acting)	Jan. 1998 – June 1998	0 Yrs. 5 Mos.	AICPA/FASB
Lynn E. Turner	July 1998 – Aug. 2001	3 Yrs. 1 Mo.	PwC
Robert K. Herdman	Oct. 2001 – Nov. 2002	1 Yr. 1 Mo.	EY
Jackson M. Day (Acting)	Nov. 2002 – Mar. 2003	0 Yrs. 4 Mos.	EY
Donald T. Nicolaisen	Aug. 2003 – Oct. 2005	2 Yrs. 2 Mos.	PwC
Scott Taub (Acting)	Oct. 2005 – Aug. 2006	0 Yrs. 10 Mos.	Arthur Andersen
Conrad W. Hewitt	Aug. 2006 – Jan. 2009	2 Yrs. 5 Mos.	EY
James L. Kroeker (Acting)	Jan. 2009 – Aug. 2009	0 Yrs. 7 Mos	Deloitte
James L. Kroeker	Aug. 2009 – July 2012	2 Yrs. 11 Mos.	Deloitte
Paul Beswick (Acting)	July 2012 – Dec. 2012	0 Yrs. 5 Mos.	EY
Paul Beswick	Dec. 2012 – May 2014	1 Yr. 5 Mos.	EY
James Schnurr	Aug. 2014 – July 2016	1 Yr. 11 Mos.	Deloitte
Wesley R. Bricker (Acting)	July 2016 – Nov. 2016	0 Yrs. 4 Mos.	PwC
Wesley R. Bricker	Nov. 2016 – June 2019	2 Yrs. 7 Mos.	PwC
Sagar Teotia (Acting)	June 2019 – July 2019	0 Yrs. 1 Mo.	Deloitte
Sagar Teotia	July 2019 – Present		Deloitte

GJP-2/2020

FEDERAL SECURITIES LAW AND ACCOUNTING 1933–1970

Selected Addresses

Gary John Previts
and Alfred R. Roberts, editors

Garland Publishing, Inc.
New York and London
1986

For a complete list of Garland's publications in accounting,
please see the final pages of this volume.

Library of Congress Cataloging-in-Publication Data

Federal securities law and accounting, 1933–1970.

(Accounting thought and practice through the years)
Includes index.
1. Securities—United States—History. 2. United States. Securities and Exchange Commission—History. 3. Disclosure of information (Securities law)—United States—History. 4. Accounting—Law and legislation—United States—History. I. Previts, Gary John. II. Roberts, Alfred Robert. III. Series.
KF1439.F45 1986 346.73'092 86-9989
ISBN 0-8240-7870-5 347.30692

Design by Bonnie Goldsmith

The volumes in this series are printed on acid-free, 250-year-life paper.

Printed in the United States of America

To our daughters,
Joanne Louise Previts
K. T. Roberts
Magee Roberts
Susan Beth Previts

FOREWORD

On the evening of June 29, 1984, the SEC celebrated its first fifty years with a dinner and speeches and distribution of a brief anecdotal history of those years. The title of the brochure used the last eight words of a quotation from former chairman Donald C. Cook's speech at the thirtieth anniversary celebration:

> If there is a single solid tradition of the great agency, if there is a unifying thread of continuity that kept the Commission—and still keeps the Commission—an integrated part of America's economic destiny, it is this fusion of good people, important problems and workable laws.

This selection of addresses covers the developments of the first thirty-seven years of the Securities Acts and, I believe, supports appraisals made from time to time of the commission's performance. In its twenty-fifth annual report the SEC cited as having continuing applicability the 1949 Task Force Report on "Regulatory Commissions" by the first Hoover commission where the SEC was characterized as "an outstanding example of the independent Commission at its best."

The commissioners, especially the chairmen, and senior staff members were in great demand by professional and business groups to interpret the securities laws. Lawyers, accountants in public and private practice, financial executives, investment bankers, and brokers and dealers all had a compelling interest to get acquainted with the securities laws. I have called this missionary work—an opportunity to assist those who would carry the burden of compliance with the new laws.

Some comment on the addresses appears to be in order:

James M. Landis: This is the first of several forceful alerts to the requirements of the Securities Acts. John L. Carey in his book *The Rise of the Accounting Profession* describes this period and that of Commissioner Mathews in a chapter entitled "Government Intervention in Accounting."

George C. Mathews: One of his duties was to oversee the work of the staff accountants. He was responsible for bringing Carman G. Blough, who later became the first chief accountant, to the commission. Blough's effectiveness and influence in accounting are well known.

William O. Douglas: Douglas began work on the study of protective and reorganization committees while a professor of law at Yale University, where, with Werntz's assistance, he introduced a course in accounting in the law school. When Werntz went to the SEC as a lawyer, he was assigned to the Forms and Regulations Division, where he developed the first draft of Regulation S-X exposed for comment as Regulation Z. This work prepared him for his appointment as chief accountant when Blough resigned.

Robert E. Kline, Jr.: Cooperation between attorney and accountant forms the basis of much of the commission's work in all divisions.

William W. Werntz: Werntz's papers have been edited by Robert M. Trueblood and George H. Sorter and published by the American Institute of Certified Public Accountants, Inc. As noted above, he was associated with and followed Douglas to the SEC.

Andrew J. Cavanaugh: In his work in the Registration Division, Cavanaugh could be compared with the regimental commander of troops in combat.

James J. Caffrey: Caffrey was regional administrator in the New York office of the SEC at the time of the McKesson & Robbins, Inc. investigation.

Harry A. McDonald: McDonald was one of the few commissioners to bring a strictly business background to the SEC.

Donald C. Cook: For this paper the staff was directed to prepare a thorough study of accountants' independence.

Ralph H. Demmler: Demmler was the first Republican to be appointed to the commission and designated chairman by a Republican President—Eisenhower.

Byron D. Woodside: The first address was delivered when Woodside was director of the Division of Corporation Finance. He came to the SEC when the staff of the 33 Act was transferred from the Federal Trade Commission. His background was Wharton School, then law, and with this combination he developed into an outstanding expert on the securities acts. He became a commissioner in 1960. When the Securities Investor Protection Act was passed, he was named its first chairman.

Sydney C. Orbach: Orbach was chief accountant of the Division of Corporation Finance. In this capacity he supervised the front-line accounting review and provided consultation and advice for registrants and their independent accountants.

Manuel F. Cohen: Cohen was chairman of the Commission during a period when acquisitions resulting in conglomerates were a prominent feature of corporate financing. He expressed his view of the results by saying consolidation of financial statements conceals more than it reveals.

James J. Needham: Needham is the only practicing CPA so far appointed to the commission. This paper contains a warning against shopping around for accounting principles.

Andrew Barr
The University Club
Washington, D.C.

December 23, 1985

PREFACE

For several years we have had access to the file of speeches from which these papers have been drawn. Through the thoughtful efforts of Mrs. Evelyn Taylor, who maintained the file at the Atlanta Regional Office of the Securities and Exchange Commission, the materials were donated to the collection of the Accounting History Research Center. Our early use of this material was limited, but as the interest in the evolution of regulatory policy increases, we became convinced that those principal papers that had not been previously published or widely distributed warranted new attention. Thus we have set forth those papers as the contents of this volume, *Federal Securities Law and Accounting*.

The appendix contains the complete file listing available at the research center at Georgia State University's School of Accountancy.

We are indebted to student assistants Hudy Mulia and Suzanne Redmond for their important efforts in support of the production of the volume and also especially to Betty Tracy of the staff of the Weatherhead School of Management, Case Western Reserve University, for her efforts in preparing the manuscript.

Alfred R. Roberts
Atlanta, Georgia

Gary John Previts
Cleveland, Ohio

January 16, 1986

Contents

FEDERAL SECURITIES LAW AND ACCOUNTING

1933-1970

Selected addresses by members of the Securities and Exchange Commission and members of the staff

Edited with abstracts prepared

by

Gary John Previts
Professor of Accountancy
Weatherhead School of Management
Case Western Reserve University

and

Alfred R. Roberts
Professor of Accountancy
School of Accountancy
Georgia State University

#1 James M. Landis

October 30, 1933

Principles of Federal Securities Legislation

Abstract

Landis, an attorney who later became a member and chairman of the Securities and Exchange Commission (SEC) was Commissioner of the Federal Trade Commission at the time of this address. He emphasized the standards of conduct that would reduce the perils of liability under the Securities Act of 1933. The standards relate to three areas: (1) civil and criminal liabilities consequent upon misstatements or omissions of facts in a registration statement; (2) the idea of materiality; and (3) the fiduciary concept of reasonable care.

Considerable hesitation accompanied my first decision to accept your kind invitation to talk to you upon some phases of the Securities Act of 1933. You people represent a profession of competence in a field different than that of mine, and a field which, despite efforts of mine to understand, still remains much of a heathenish mystery. True, sometimes I have wondered whether you,

---

Address before the New York State Society of Certified Public Accountants.

just like the members of my profession, do not tend to make more mysterious your own knowledge so as to widen the gulf that separates you and us from the ordinary unsuspecting laymen. But after all, a profession must have some excuse to regard itself as such. Recognizing then that I have no ambition to speak to you from the accounting angle, I shall ask you to bear in mind that what I may say represents only the limitations of the lawyer having had some familiarity with the type of problems presented by financing.

Misconceptions about the Securities Act and its effects seem to abound. Like the passions aroused by some of our causes celebre in this country, the Securities Act is tending to divide its opponents and adherents into separate camps. Studied and colorless consideration of the nature of the Act and the character of its effects has, in the main, been lacking. Such intemperate attitudes to this most complex problem of the control of corporate financing are nothing short of a tragedy. And if the issue develops, as it now threatens to develop, into one of the public against the bankers, instead of that of a consideration of the best interests of the public--a concept which still includes the banking group--what legislation will evolve out of such an emotional tempest is certain to be both unwise and impractical.

This attitude that now threatens is so different from that which prevailed as of the time of the birth and passage of the Securities Act. The President's message calling for federal security legislation and outlining the basic principles that should be embodied in such legislation has yet to find any critic. No opposition to the President's aims was voiced at the hearings on the bill, which were wholly devoid of any sensationalism. Some five weeks of what might properly be termed unremitting labor by a subcommittee of the House were spent in working over the details of the legislation before the bill emerged from committee. With one exception, its passage through the House as well as the passage of the companion bill through the Senate evoked no dramatic speeches, no threat of retaliation against a class. No member of either House at any time voted against the passage of the bill, nor took occasion to criticize any provision that the bill contained. Those who had the opportunity to watch the progress of this bill at close range could not fail but to be impressed with the earnestness, sincerity and competence of those members of the House and of the Senate who had the bill in charge. I cite these facts merely as illustrative of a Congress with its emotions unaroused but deeply conscious of the evils which unrestrained exploitation of our capital resources had brought into existence.

One other characteristic of the framing of the Securities Act deserves notice. It is customary for some critics to regard the Act as the product of a single session of Congress, to attribute its authorship to individuals, to think of it as new and hastily drawn legislation. Nothing is farther from the facts. The experience of many years and of many nations is epitomized in the provisions of the Securities Act. Many of its features, with variations suitable to the form of financing in this country and to the constitutional limitations upon federal power, have been drawn from the English Companies Act, which represents the culmination of almost a hundred years of struggling with this problem abroad. Since 1911 most of our 48 states have been developing forms of security legislation and much of the experience of these states has gone into the federal act. More specifically, the work of the Capital Issues Committee during the War led to the introduction of a bill in Congress, known as the Taylor Bill, whose basic outlines are essentially similar to those of the Securities Act. Later, the Denison Bill, devised primarily to make more effective state security regulation, actually passed the House but failed of action in the Senate. In other words, the Securities Act embodied little that was novel in conception, nor did it emanate from a Congress that for the first time had been called upon to consider the problem of security regulation.

For this audience I need spend little time in outlining the principal features of the Securities Act. Rather I shall assume a knowledge of its basic features and use my time in discussing a problem that seems to give the most concern. This is the problem of civil liability. What liability there exists for damages for violation of the Act comes as a result of the provisions embodied in Sections 11 and 12, but I intend on this occasion to limit myself merely to a discussion of Section 11, the section that imposes liabilities consequent upon misstatements in a registration statement.

The suggestion has been made on occasion that civil liabilities arise also from a violation of Section 17, the first sub-section of which makes unlawful the circulation of falsehoods and untruths in connection with the sale of a security in interstate commerce or through the mails. But a reading of this section in the light of the entire Act leaves no doubt but that violations of its provisions give rise only to a liability to be restrained by injunctive action or, if wilfully done, to a liability to be punished criminally. That such a conclusion alone is justifiably to be drawn from its provisions is a matter upon which the Commission has already made a pronouncement, the authoritative quality of which I shall have occasion to consider later.

Turning now to Section 11, - the section from which liability arises as a result of misstatements in the registration statement - it is worth our while carefully to analyze its content from several angles; (1) the persons upon whom it imposes liability; (2) the standards of conduct that it insists these persons shall observe in order to be immune from liability; (3) the damages that flow from a violation of its provisions.

Broadly speaking, the persons upon whom liability may be imposed can be divided into five groups: (1) the issuer; (2) the directors of the company, whether or not they have signed the registration statement; (3) the chief officials of the company; (4) experts, such as accountants, engineers, appraisers, and any person whose profession gives authority to a statement made by him -- a phrase which, as a matter of pride for the profession, would, I hope, include the lawyer; and (5) the underwriters of the issue, remembering always that the legal and not the dictionary meaning of that term is involved. Though all these persons may be liable for misstatements in a registration statement, it is utterly erroneous to assume that because there is a misstatement all these groups of persons are liable. To make that apothegm clear, it becomes necessary to examine the standards of conduct required to be observed by these groups of persons.

An understanding of that standard seems to me essential to a clear picture of this liability. It must be understood from three standpoints, or, in other words, three questions must separately be asked. The first is this: Was there the required misstatement or the required omission? No difficulty is raised in determining whether or not a misstatement has been made, but the requirements of the Act relative to omissions have been the source of much -- I am tempted to say -- ingenious confusion. Omissions in order to be a ground for liability must, in the language of the statute, be omissions to state facts required to be stated in the registration statement or necessary to make the statements in the registration statement not misleading. In non-technical language, this, as the history of the Act amply demonstrates, means simply that a half-truth is an untruth, a fact that Congress, in its wisdom and with some experience in such matters, thought best to put beyond the power of sophist lawyers and judges to dispute. It is impossible, especially in the light of the Federal Trade Commission's exposition of this matter, to interpret this language to require an issuer at the peril of liability to state every fact which may be relevant to gauging the value of a security.

Cases of this character have commonly been put to develop the supposed dangers of that phraseology. Suppose that those associated with an issue are aware of a competitive process in the same field of manufacture as that of the issuer, but at the time reach a perfectly proper business judgment that the danger from the rival process is so slight that it can be ignored and therefore make no mention of that danger. A few years later it develops, however, that the competitive process proves its value and the issuer is driven to the wall. Is the business judgment of the directors and the officers to be reviewed some years hence by a jury viewing the situation from the hindsight of what happened rather than the foresight of what might happen? The answer to such and similar questions, whether fortunately so or not, is in the negative. Nothing in the registration statement calls for a statement of the position of the issuer in the general competitive structure of its industry and consequently omissions to state facts descriptive of this situation afford no basis for liability. The requirements of the registration statement alone are the basis for determining what statements must be made and therefore what omissions dare not be made. Beyond these requirements an issuer may, of course, go, but no requirement now calls for such statements to be made at the peril of liability.

I hope that during this discussion you have been aware that I have talked simply of misstatements and omissions of facts without reference to the question of their materiality. Indeed, I have purposely done so, because this question seems to me the second of those that should be asked in connection with the standards of conduct that the Act requires should be observed, namely, assuming that there was a misstatement of fact or the required omission, did such misstatement or omission relate to a material fact? Let me repeat the phrase "material fact" again. It embraces two conceptions, that of fact and that of materiality. It may seem to you that the problem of what is a fact is one that has been unanswered by philosophers since the days of Plato. Though some may be true of philosophy, law in its ignorance has been called upon from time memorial to distinguish between representations of fact and representation of opinion. The guiding line between these two conceptions rests upon the possibility of subjecting the conclusions in the respective realms of fact and opinion to definiteness of ascertainment. Much also depends upon the method of expression for what should appropriately be expressed as inferences or deductions from facts and hence as opinions, are too often expressed as facts themselves and hence for the purposes of legal liability, whether at common law or under the Act, become facts. It has been said, and very rightly in my humble opinion, that most of accounting is after all a matter of opinion. But though this may be true, I have still to see the case of a prospective invester being offered a balance sheet and having it carefully explained to him that this or that item is merely an opinion or deduction from a series of other opinions mixed in with a few acknowledged facts. Accounting, as distinguished from law, has generally been portrayed as an exact science, and its representations have been proffered to the unlearned as representations of fact and not of opinion. If it insists upon such fact representations, it is, of course, fair that it should be burdened with the responsibility attendant upon such a portrayal of its results.

I turn now to the problem of materiality, for it is obvious that liability under Section 11 does not follow as a result of every misstatement. The misspelling of a director's name and other such matters could not conceivably carry liability. But what is material? Clearly materiality must be gauged with reference to purpose, and, recognizing that the purposes of the Act are the protection of the investing public, it does not become difficult to depict the standard of materiality. In other words, facts become material for the purpose of omissions and misstatements when, as a consequence of such omissions and misstatements, non-existent values are attributed to a security.

The third of the questions that I suggest must be asked in order to determine whether the standard of conduct prescribed by the Act predicates that answer to the other two questions has been in the affirmative. That is, assuming that there has been a misstatement or omission and that such a misstatement or omission has had reference to a material fact, is the person to be excused from liability because he exercised reasonable care under all the circumstances and entertained a reasonable belief that the statements he made were true? Reasonability, it should be borne in mind, will differ widely according to the person involved. Under some circumstances such a standard would require personal kowledge of the facts assumed to be true. Delegation to others of the duty to verify the facts would under other circumstances suffice to meet the requirement. A director, for example, would have little excuse for not having personal knowledge of what his stock holdings in the issuer and its subsidiaries were, but he should obviously be entitled to rely upon the statements of his fellow directors, as checked by the stock books, as to what their stockholdings were. Furthermore, the director, who is also chairman of the board or chairman of some special committee, will stand in a different relationship as to the knowledge which is the special concern of his committee. Or take the situation of the underwriters. The type of investigation which can reasonably be demanded of the sponsoring or principal underwriters is one thing; that which the Act requires of the small participating underwriter in order that he shall satisfy its requirements is another thing, while an even less standard of investigation would be demanded of the dealer selling on commission who, because of his relationship to the issuer, is considered as an underwriter by the Act.

These conceptions permitting a reasonable delegation of duties by the various parties connected with the flotation of an issue, are not interfered with by that provision of Section 11 which likens the standard of reasonableness to be applied, to that which the law commonly requires of a person occupying a fiduciary relationship. That section does not make these individuals fiduciaries in and of themselves, but simply refers to that standard which, briefly stated, requires the exercise of a degree of care that a prudent man would exercise in his own affairs, as a measure of the type of conduct that in decency can be expected of those soliciting other peoples' money for investment.

Thus far we have discussed the persons made responsible for misstatements in the registration statement, and the standards of conduct that the Act calls upon them to observe. There remains the question of the nature of the damages for which these persons are responsible in the event that their liability otherwise is established. The first measure is what might be termed, somewhat inaccurately, the right of rescission. This is the duty to respond in damages equivalent to the price paid by the purchaser, never, however, exceeding the offering price, upon the tender of the security. Two illustrations will make this clear. The offering price of a bond is $100. Purchaser A buys it on the market at $75; purchaser B at $125. A, upon tendering back the bond, could only recover $75, whereas B could only recover $100.

The Act also grants another right, which might appropriately be termed the strict right to damages. This can only be availed of by a purchaser who has disposed of the security. It is a right derivative in nature from the right of rescission. To illustrate its operation, we may turn to the case originally put and assume that A and B have disposed of their bonds on the market at $60. A, who had paid $75 for his bond, could recover $15, whereas B who had paid $125 for his bond recovers not $65 but $40.

It should be observed that each person whose liability on the registration statement has been established is responsible in damages to any purchaser of the security, whether such person shall have purchased from him or from some other person. Theoretically this means that each person so liable can be held to a liability equivalent t that of the total offering price of the issue. Practically, of course, no such large liability exists. Several factors will operate to keep the liability within much smaller bounds. For one thing, the value of a carefully floated issue can hardly be assumed to reach zero. For another, every purchaser would hardly be likely to bring suit. Again, the issue of liability--generally, a complicated question of fact--would be retriable in every suit, and it beggars the imagination to assume that every jury faced with such an issue would come to the same conclusion. Furthermore, each person liable has a right of contribution against every other person liable, unless the one suing is guilty of fraud and the other is not. So that even eliminating the other practical factors that I have mentioned, it would be necessary for every other person liable on the registration statement to be insolvent in order that one of them would be affixed with the large theoretical responsibility.

In elaborating upon these damages--of which I shall have more to say--I have not, I believe, unduly minimized their character. But I have tried to look at them with some degree of reality rather than in the fanciful and unreal fashion that has characterized their exposition by some members of the legal profession in this and other cities. To pretend that they are insignificant is wrong; but as equally vicious is the practice, unfortunately too common, of conjuring up bogey men to frighten those who may wish to seek new financing through public issues. Not only does it discourage operation under the Act; but the bar when later faced with the task of defending those who may nevertheless register under the Act will be forced to do one of those volte-faces so humiliating to the legal profession. Its opinions upon matters such as this are too often dictated by the interests of its clients. In other words,--and here I voice a thought that I am afraid is likely to be misinterpreted, though the origins of this belief are of many years standing--the opinion of the bar reflects too accurately the condition of the capital market. Were it booming, were the bond market boiling, were there bankers eager to handle issues, the tendency of the bar, I suspect, would be to minimize the liabilities of the Securities Act. A leader of the New York bar, only recently dead, respected by all my generation for his refusal to think of his clients' causes as just when they were not, once remarked: "When a client asks for my opinion he gets <u>my</u> opinion; if he wants a brief to uphold his interests, let him ask for a brief and not an opinion." Were that attitude to characterize the legal advice now being given with respect to the Securities Act, many of the headaches of today and the heartaches of tomorrow might be avoided.

If, in the discussion of the question of damages, I have led you to believes that damages against the persons liable on the registration statement are compensatory in character, that is, that they compensate only for what damages may flow from the misstatements, let me disabuse you of that fact. Let me illustrate their non-compensatory character by a simple illustration. A careless misstatement of the quick asset position of a corporation justifies, let us say, the conclusion that had the facts been properly stated the offering price of a bond should have been 90 instead of the 100 at which it was actually offered. For reasons utterly foreign to this misstatement and even beyond the possibility of conjecture at the time of the offering, the price of the bond declines to 30. A purchaser who bought at 100 could nevertheless, if he sold the bond at 30, recover from those liable on the registration statement the difference between 100 and 30, or 70.

This result, you may say, is unjustifiable. To that let me answer first that it represents no extraordinary principle of legal liability. Suppose that I buy an ordinary chattel from you for $100 upon your representation that it has certain qualities. It does not possess these qualities but the difference between the type of chattel that I bought and the type that you represented to me I was buying, can be measured by the sum of $10. Because of conditions that neither of us could have foreseen and over which neither of us had control, the market value of these chattels falls to $30. I can, nevertheless, as a matter of law, tender you back the chattel and recover $100. In other words, the general market loss of $60 falls not upon me as purchaser but upon you as seller.

A second justification for the principle of non-compensatory damages in the Securities Act is their <u>in terrorem</u> quality. If recent history teaches us anything, it discloses that some groups of persons associated with security flotations are not induced to refrain from material non-disclosures by fear either of the very real liability for compensatory damages at common law or fear of prosecution under the criminal law. True, my good friends tell me of a reformed investment profession, that refuses to take secret profits or refuses to manipulate a market to unload its own securities under the excuse of maintaining the market during the period of secondary distribution, or refuses to engage in practices that were too current during the boom times of another era. I devoutly hope that this is true. But the evidence of even a sudden conversion is lacking, wholly irrespective of its permanency. Examination of some of the security issues, both new and of the type that seek to effect readjustments of corporate capital structures, that hurriedly preceded the effective date of the Securities Act indicates that little change from earlier methods has taken place. Nor can anyone, who has watched carefully the amendments that have been made to registration statements now on file with the Commission, and seen the reluctance that accompanied the recital of certain very relevant but unpleasant facts in those same registration statements--sometimes only upon the threat of stop order proceedings--hold much of a brief for minimizing civil liability. And I speak here not merely of so-called fly-by-night issues, but of those prepared and sponsored by persons generally deemed by the Street to fall well within the bounds of respectability.

With this note, let me close my discussion of civil liability, even though there are aspects of it that are still untouched. But before closing this talk, let me comment upon one other aspect of the Securities Act that I think is of special import to your profession, and this is the Commission's power of moulding the Act through administration, regulation and interpretation. The Comission's powers of regulation have rarely been emphasized in any discussion of the Act and to my mind they are of great consequence. Practically all the accounting regulations are subject to the Commission's jurisdiction. The entire character of the demands that the registration statement makes depend upon the wise exercise of the Commission's powers within the very broad standards laid down by the Act. Relaxation or strengthening of these features of the Act lie within the control of the Commission. Furthermore, the Commission's power to define trade terms gives it extensive control, for hardly a term is not a trade term in view of the fact that its meaning is rightly significant only in relation to the "trade" of floating securities.

Thus far the Commission has been very sparing in its use of these powers and wisely so, for it must learn, as all of us do, under the imparts of experience. But that experience is rapidly accumulating so that the time for close fitting of general expressions of the Act to typical complex situations is about ripe. Such regulations, it should be borne in mind, have the force of law. No right to review general regulations of this character, except to determine whether they fall within the delegated powers of the Commission, exists. They must, of course, supplement the general provisions of the Act, but they can make concrete and definitive the application of the Act to various recurring situations.

Again, the Commission has on occasion exercised the power of interpreting the Act. Such a power is incidental to that of administration. Such interpretative action has not, to be sure, the force of law, but it has always been recognized by courts as having large persuasive powers. Especially true is this under the Securities Act as distinguished from other situations in which administrative agencies exercise interpretative powers. There is an element of estoppel, as lawyers would say, present in this situation which is of great consequence in determining whether or not the courts would follow the Commission's interpretations. This element, to be explicit, consists in the fact of action in reliance upon administrative interpretation. In other words, the only rights created under the Securities Act, whether those rights are enforced by the state or the federal courts, are created by the

United States government. The United States government, speaking this time through the agency of the Federal Trade Commission, says to an issuer--put in such a fashion and no rights, either criminal or civil, will be created against you. It would, indeed, be unusual if action in reliance upon such advice should be treated by another agency of the same government--the courts--as subjecting the party so advised to liability. This recognition of the fact of there being something akin to estoppel present in such action by the Commission, has naturally made the Commission, as distinguished from its divisional officials, chary of the exercise of these powers. Only two Commission opinions have thus far been rendered, and these naturally merely make more explicit what is already implicit within the Act.

I make these remarks upon the Commission's powers of regulation and interpretation not for the sake of emphasizing the powers as such but to illustrate the flexibilities inherent in the Act and its capacities for adaptation to the complexities of the situations it covers. Indeed, if half of the energy that has been expended in fulminating against the Act and propagandizing for amendments were enlisted in the effort to advise the Commission in the wise exercise of its powers, the government and issuers, bankers, lawyers and accountants would be far nearer to a solution of their problems. I cannot urge too strenuously such a course of action. The control of financing inherently bristles with complex situation adaptable far better to particularised administrative action than to the generalities that must of necessity characterize the legislative process. Along this road lies a better understanding between government and finance of their common problems. It presents none of the pitfalls that necessarily attend efforts to open the Act to the attack of selfish and short-sighted interests. I invite you seriously and without bias or passion to essay that road, remembering always, according to the Congressional mandate of the Securities Act, that the public interest and the protection of investors must be the guiding consideration.

#2 Commissioner George C. Mathews

January 18, 1935

Questions Relating to the 1934 Act

Abstract

The inception of the registration forms and procedures for filing under the 1933 and 1934 Securities Acts is discussed in some detail. Form A-2 relates to securities issued by a going concern. Form 10 relates to the permanent registration of securities already listed on a national securities exchange. The address is mainly composed of previously submitted questions from accountants on the current concerns with accounting theory, practice and reporting.

As most of you doubtless know, the Commission shortly before the holidays, issued what is known as Form 10, with an accompanying instruction book, to be used for the registration under the Securities Exchange Act of 1934 of those issues of securities which have been temporarily registered under the provisions of that Act. Within the past week the Commission issued a corresponding form, referred to as Form A-2, and the accompanying instruction book, for

Address before the Illinois Society of Certified Public Accountants.

registration under the Securities Act of 1933 of issues of securities of corporations which file profit and loss statements for three years and which have, in the past fifteen years, paid dividends upon any class of common stock for at least two consecutive years, except such statement as to which a special form is specifically prescribed. The questions which I have been asked to discuss this evening are very largely related to those forms and to the accompanying instructions. Inasmuch as neither form has yet been used by any registrant the Commission has had no occasion to issue interpretations or opinions dealing with either of them.

In order that my discussion this evening might be fully authoritative, it would be necessary that the Commission should have passed upon all the questions to which I shall refer. That has not been done. I cannot speak to you as either an attorney or an accountant and, except as I may indicate otherwise, I hope you will take what I have to say as an expression of my opinion only, which opinion is necessarily in many respects a non-expert one. I believe that the answers which I shall attempt to give are correct answers but they cannot carry the weight of an opinion of counsel nor of an official interpretation by the Commission.

Before I take up the specific questions which I have been asked to answer, I should like to say a few words regarding Form 10 and Form A-2, and regarding the purposes and hopes of the Commission in connection with the use of those forms. First, as to Form 10. It has been the hope and purpose of the Commission that its requirements for permanent registration on national securities exchanges of these securities which have been admitted to temporary registration would not have the effect of causing any delistings but would in fact tend to encourage the permanent registration of these securities. The underlying thought has been that, regardless of what the situation may have been in the past as to the transaction of business on the exchanges, it is desirable to keep, for securities which have already been listed, the free and open market provided by the exchanges. One major objective of the Securities Exchange Act is the prevention of practices which have caused criticism of the exchanges and the limitation of the exchanges to the performance of their functions in furnishing an open market. If the accomplishment of this objective may be anticipated, I think no one would deny that it is generally in the public interest that securities which have heretofore been on the exchanges should become permanently registered so that trading on the exchanges may continue after July 1st. Any course of action which unnecessarily results in failure to secure registration of such securities, including any course of action which might impose unnecessary burdens in connection with registration, we think would be an action opposed to the public interest. Therefore, in the preparation of Form 10 and the accompanying instruction book, the Commission has availed itself freely of the opportunity to consult with corporation executives, with leaders in the accounting and legal professions, and with representatives of the exchanges. I think it is correct to say that the reception which has been given to Form 10 indicates that the requirements are not considered unreasonable or unnecessary.

As to the new form for registration under the Securities Act of securities issued by going concerns, the Commission adopted much the same course of procedure that it did in the preparation of Form 10. The actual drafting of the requirements was done very largely by a committee embodying experience gained by its members in the work of one of the leading investment services, in the analysis of securities for an investment banking house, and in the experience and studies of a member of the faculty of Harvard Business School. Effort has been made as far as possible to make the accounting requirements for registration of securities of going concerns under the Securities Act consistent with those for the registration of securities on the exchanges. The same free use of the criticism and suggestions which could be offered by experts not on the staff of the Commission has been made. We believe that we have accomplished a substantial reduction in the amount of time and expense which will be required in furnishing the information for registration under the Securities Act and that the information which is called for is that which has a real bearing on the question of the merit of the offering.

I should like to point out that the Commission has carefully avoided requiring uniformity of accounting either as to matters of classification or as to matters of principle. It has provided for a degree of uniformity in methods of reporting the results of business operations and the financial condition of the business, but even here its requirements are not rigid. Let me read you from the instructions issued with Form 10, the following:

> "The registrant may file statements and schedules in such form, order and using such generally accepted terminology, as will best indicate their significance and character in the light of the instructions."

and further from the same form let me quote a paragraph:

> "If any change in accounting principle or practice has been made during the period covered by the profit and loss statements and such change substantially affects proper comparison with the preceding accounting period, give the necessary explanation in a note attached to the balance sheet or profit and loss statement and referred to therein."

Those who asked me to speak here this evening have submitted a list of questions with the request that those questions be answered. Before I go into the specific questions which have been submitted, I feel that I should comment upon and explain a rule of the Commission which has just been amended, which rule in its original form caused a great deal of confusion and misunderstanding. As I read the questions which were submitted to me, it became apparent that a great many of them grew out of that rule and the misunderstanding to which I have referred. Section 13 of the Securities Exchange Act deals with the filing of reports with exchanges and with the Commission as referred to in two paragraphs of that section. The important parts of the section, for the purpose of the present discussion, are those which state the general character of the reports which the Commission may require to be filed with the exchanges and with it. The Commission may require such information and documents as are necessary to keep reasonably current the information and documents filed in the applications for registration and it may require the filing also of such annual and quarterly reports as it may prescribe. No direct requirement dealing with these matters has been made, but the Commission did issue what was known as Rule KC1, which, in its original form, read as follows:

> "Reports by issuers of securities registered under Rule JE1. Every security registered pursuant to Rule JE1 (which was the rule providing for temporary registration) and the issuer thereof shall be exempt from the provisions of Section 13 upon condition that the issuer mails to the exchange and, in triplicate, to the Commission copies of all reports and financial statements which are made available to security holders and/or the exchange at the time they are so made available."

Rule KC1in the form which I have just quoted was commonly and erroneously understood to require issuers having securities temporarily registered to file with the Commission copies of all reports and financial statements which were made available to security holders or to the exchange. Actually, that was not the effect of the rule. The rule was issued in anticipation of requirements being promulgated under Section 13 to which I have referred, and provided, as you will have noted, that if issuers filed with the Commission the reports and statements covered by KC1 they would be exempt during the period of temporary registration from Section 13. But no requirements have been made under Section 13 and consequently there have been no requirements from which the filing of information under Rule KC1 could exempt an issuer.

Rule KC1, as I have said, was amended by the Commission yesterday, so that it now reads as follows:

> "Exemption of securities registered pursuant to Rule JE1 and issuers thereof from Section 13. Notwithstanding any provisions contained in applications for registration on Form 2, every security registered pursuant to Rule JE1 and the issuer thereof shall be exempt from the provisions of Section 13 for the duration of the period of temporary registration of such security."

Under the amended form of Rule KC1 there is no longer any doubt that the rule does not require that reports and statements furnished to stockholders be filed with the Commission in the cases of securities which are temporarily registered. Rule KC1 in its amended form also overrides a provision in the applications for temporary registration on Form 2 whereby issuers in substance have agreed to conform with the requirements of the old Rule KC1. In addition to pointing out the clarification of Rule KC1, I might also say that Rule JF4 has been amended so that the exchanges are no longer required to file with the Commission annual reports and other statements of issuers whose securities are admitted to unlisted trading privileges.

The Commission has not yet issued its regulations governing permanent registrations on Form 10 and on the other forms which are contemplated, and therefore there are now no requirements for the filing of reports or other information by issuers whose securities become permanently registered. The Commission, of course, contemplates providing for periodic financial reports under Section 13. With the clear understanding that I am not in a position to express for the Commission its view on this subject, I think I may say that members of the Commission understand quite clearly that to require by rule or regulation, assuming that such power exists, that reports which are furnished to stockholders be filed with it, might result either in corporation concluding that they could not safely furnish to stockholders anything less than the full information required by Form 10, or by such form of annual report based on Form 10 as the Commission may prescribe under Section 13, or that those responsible might expose themselves to liability under Section 18 if they omitted from reports to stockholders information required in the registration statement or in other reports to be filed under Section 13.

Bear in mind that liabilities for misleading statements under the Securities Exchange Act arise only with respect to statements in any application, report or document filed pursuant to the Act or to any rule or regulation thereunder. It seems clear to me, therefore, that, unless the Commission has in effect a rule which requires that reports which are furnished to stockholders be filed with it, no liability can arise under the Act on account of such reports to stockholders. This may be clearer if I make a comparison with requirements under the Securities Act of 1933. As you know, that Act requires not only that a registration statement be filed with the Commission, but also that a prospectus relating to that statement be furnished to the prospective investor. The Exchange Act, however, requires only the filing of certain statements and reports with the Commission. It does not have a further requirement for the actual delivery to investors of any reports or documents relating to the statements or reports so filed. Under the Securities Act liability arises both upon the registration statement and upon the prospectus; under the Exchange Act liability arises only upon the statements required to be filed with the Commission. Irrespective of any question as to the Commission's right to require by rule or regulation that reports which are made to stockholders be filed with it, I think that sound administrative policy obviously would indicate that such reports be not required to be filed with it by rule or regulation until the

Commission should have determined either that those reports must contain all or substantially all of the information which might be required in reports prepared for filing under the provisions of Section 13, or that those who issue a more abbreviated report would not be exposed to liability under Section 18 because of the use of a more condensed form.

I think that what I have said makes it unnecessary to take up the considerable list of individual questions which have been submitted to me regarding what material should be included or might be omitted from reports to stockholders. The general question preceding the statement of the specific inquiries was:

> "Regardless of whether the liabilities of directors and independent accountants are considered to exist under the specific provisions of the Securities Exchange Act or whether only the common law liability is deemed to apply in the case of annual reports to stockholders, does the fact that certain specific information is required to be filed with the Commission under Form 10 of the regulations recently issued by the Securities and Exchange Commission enlarge the scope of the information that should be furnished to stockholders?"

It is my understanding that the common law liability is not affected by the Securities Exchange Act. I think it is clear that there is no liability under the Act as matters stand now with reference to reports to stockholders. If I am correct as to both of these, the answer would be that the scope of the information that should be furnished to stockholders has not been enlarged. Understand that I am answering this question only with reference to the situation created by the Securities Exchange Act. I do not mean to be understood as saying that I think that reports which have actually been furnished to stockholders have always been what they should.

I think we may turn now to more specific questions which have been asked.

The first of these relates to the provision in reference to Form 10 that the information called for in that form is a minimum requirement to which the registrant may add such further information as will contribute to an understanding of its financial condition and operations. First the question is asked whether the use of the word "may" conveys that the disclosure of additional information is optional to the registrant. The answer to that, as far as any requirement of the Commission is concerned, is "Yes." The disclosure of additional information is optional to the registrant. It is true that, aside from any requirement of the commission, there may be instances in which it is necessary to furnish further information in order that that which has been given in response to the requirements of Form 10 is not misleading. I do not think that there should be any substantial difficulty in determining in most cases whether or not additional information ought to be given. It will usually be only that information which is clearly material, and I should say that if the registrant adopts the attitude that it wishes to give the information which is material rather than the attitude that it wishes to give as little information as it can and meet the technical requirements of registration, it should encounter no serious difficulty.

The question is then asked whether, if the registrant so interprets the phraseology, it will be protected under the Securities Exchange Act assuming that it has in good faith furnished in satisfactory form and content all of the information specified by the Commission in the registration form, or must other material facts be disclosed, such as those which I will mention. I do not know whether the framers of this question meant to alter its substance by making the reference to the necessity of including other material facts or not. The first specific question with reference to this is whether the registrant should show a surplus arising from donations by a parent company or by stockholders. I think there is no necessity of showing more as to surplus than the form requires; that is, if the registrant has on its books separate balances in several surplus accounts those separate accounts should be carried forward in the registration statement. If it does not have on its books separate balances but carries all of its surplus in one account, all that it will be expected to do is to utilize that account for the opening balance and furnish an analysis for the year covered by the profit and loss statement. You will bear in mind in connection with this, however, that Form 10 calls for the submission of certain supplemental financial information dealing with investment, property plant and equipment, intangible assets, restatements of capital stock, and writing off of bond discount and expense ahead of the regular amortization program. This requirement will undoubtedly result in many cases in the registrant showing much that is important regarding the history of the surplus account.

The next question is whether the registrant should disclose, in addition to the information called for by the form, write-offs of operating deficits in prior years. I assume that reference is intended here to write-offs against other accounts than earned surplus, and I think the answer which I have just made covers the answer to this question also.

Another question dealing with whether or not additional information should be furnished has to do with the existence of large amounts of abandoned or obsolete property no longer used or useful which have not been eliminated from the property, plant and equipment account of the registrant. I think no all-inclusive answer can be given to that question. If reserves are adequate to take care of depreciation in used and useful property and in addition to absorb the loss which would be accounted for by writing off the abandoned or obsolete property, I should say that the importance of showing the existence of such property would be much less than if reserves were not adequate. I think also that something will depend upon the type of business and the relative importance of the accuracy of a fixed capital statement to the investor. You will remember that the question related to "large amounts" of such property. No one could say as a general thing that the fact that such large amounts exist need not be shown, and certainly if they are of such magnitude as to appear to the registrant matters of importance they should be reported.

The fourth question having to do with the general topic of furnishing information not called for by the form relates to transactions which would require disclosure in accordance with the requirements of item 34, which is the historical survey to which I have referred, except for the fact that they occurred prior to January 1, 1925 and the specific question is whether the fact that the existence of these transactions prior to January 1, 1925 was known to the person certifying to the answers to item 34 would have any bearing with respect to the answer to this question. As a general matter, I do not think that it is necessary to report any of the sort of information called for by item 34 for any period prior to January 1, 1925, although I have no doubt that hypothetical cases might be set up and possibly some actual cases, in which the history of these accounts prior to January 1, 1925 might be of such significance to the investor that additional information should be furnished. I believe, however, that such cases would be quite exceptional and that the general answer to the question is that there is no necessity of reporting as to these accounts more than is called for by item 34.

The next question asked I will read to you as it was presented to me:

> "The instructions accompanying Form 10 with respect to the 'Supplemental Financial Information' (par. 6547-34) provide that the answers may be certified either by (a) the board of directors through its authorized agent or (b) the chief accounting officer of the registrant company or (c) independent public or independent certified public accountants. Assume that in accordance with these instructions the answers are prepared and certified by the chief accounting officer of the registrant and that the answers as thus prepared are later found to be false or misleading with respect to a material fact but that the directors and other officers of the company at the time of the filing had no knowledge of the fact that the answers were false or misleading. Under such circumstances could the directors or other officers be held liable under the Securities Exchange Act?"

I do not feel prepared to give a definite answer to this question but I direct your attention to the fact that under Section 18 of the Act the liabilities for false or misleading information arise "unless the person sued shall prove that he acted in good faith and had no knowledge that such statement was false or misleading." This section refers, among other things, to the liability of persons (such as directors) who cause statements to be made. The answer to the question, therefore, really depends upon the proof that the directors are able to make. If, under the recognized standards of the common law, they acted in good faith without knowledge of the falsity or misleading character of the statement and can so prove, I am sure that they would not be liable. I think that attorneys will agree with me that, under the standards of the common law, it would be only in the most exceptional case that a director who relied in good faith upon such statements prepared by the controller or other chief accounting officer would be charged with knowledge of facts that he did not actually know. Or, to put it more plainly, I think that if directors or officers who took such action in good faith would be held liable in any case, it would be only in a very exceptional one involving gross negligence on their part.

The next question to which an answer is sought is illustrated by the following assumed state of facts: X company's total sales for the year 1934 were $1,000,000. Sales of $900,000 were made under private brand to one customer, which customer is still purchasing substantially the same amount of goods. The question seems directed toward the extent of disclosure required under the Securities Exchange Act by the use in that Act of the words "or misleading with respect to any material fact" as compared with the language of the Securities Act which reads, "or omitted to state a material fact required to be stated therein or necessary to make the statements therein not misleading." Specifically the question is: "Does the Securities Exchange Act of 1934 provide only that the material facts stated be not misleading or, like the Securities Act of 1933, must there be no omission of material facts?" Of course, the Exchange Act lacks the provision imposing liability for omissions of facts required to be stated by the Act or the rules of the Commission, but with respect to omissions to state a material fact necessary to make the statements made not misleading, I believe there is no substantial difference in the provisions of the two laws. The substance of the standards provided in both acts is that a half truth should not be told. In other words, if, under the Securities Act, it appeared necessary to state something in order that the statements made in response to the requirements of the Commission should not be misleading, I believe the same necessity would exist under the Exchange Act.

In the specific instance cited, which has to do with a substantial part of a concern's gross sales being made to one customer, I direct your attention to the fact that the instructions with reference to item 41 of Form A-2, which has to deal with information as to material contracts under the Securities Act, state "any contract for the purchase or sale of current assets for a consideration less than 3% of net sales as shown by the registrant's latest profit and loss statement for an annual period filed with the registration statement, or, if a consolidated statement is filed, in the latest consolidated statement for such period so filed," is to be deemed to have been made in the ordinary course of business. This leaves open the question as to whether contracts for sales in excess of 3% of net sales are made in the ordinary course of business and whether, under the Securities Act, they might therefore have to be summarized as required by item 41 of Form A-2. Not every material contract is required to be summarized but only certain material contracts not made in the ordinary course of business. The standard of the Exchange Act is not the same. Under that Act only material bonus and profit-sharing, management and service contracts, are called for.

The question really is whether it would be necessary to qualify the financial statements by reference to a statement of the situation, or to item 41 in the case of registration under the Securities Act. If it would appear necessary to qualify the financial statements in a registration under the Securities Act, then I believe the statements should be qualified in a registration under the Exchange Act. Assuming that there is no contract covering these sales, there would still be the question as to whether the financial statements should be qualified in either case. Personally, I think that in as extreme a case as the one cited it would always be well to qualify the financial statements, although I believe that necessity for qualification might be affected by the position of the issuer in the business, by the keenness of competition, by the extent to which patents enable the issuer to control his market. I think no one can express a general opinion as to whether the financial statements ought to be qualified in every such case. Certainly the safer policy would be to make the qualification. As extreme a case as that cited in the question would, I think, undoubtedly be brought out by the answer to item 11 of Form 10, which calls for a brief description of the general character of the business. Having in mind the question asked by item 11 and that, in fact, financial statements might be misleading which were not qualified by reference to the condition in question, I should say that the registrant ought not to omit reference to the situation.

The next question directs attention to the fact that the Securities Exchange Act affords remedies both to sellers and purchasers of securities who have sold or purchased the securities in reliance upon a false or misleading statement. The question is whether, where directors in good faith have adopted a policy which they believe to the best interests of stockholders and have been actuated by no ulterior motives but where that policy has been ultra-conservative with reference, for instance, to such items as provision for depreciation, provision for bad debt losses, and provision for inventory losses, the directors and independent accountants (unless they take definite exception to such policies) would be subject to the liabilities provided by the Act. Here again we have a question which is so broad that I doubt if it can be answered flatly. In a given case the policy may be so conservative as to amount to a substantial misstatement of financial condition or of results of operation, or it may be conservative only within such limits as would ordinarily indicate that the officers and directors of the corporation were merely following prudent practices. I think the best answer that can be given is that, if the ultra-conservative accounting policies materially affect the financial statements, the policies followed should be clearly stated and the fact that they affect the financial statements should be brought out. I do not think that such qualifications should be limited only to those cases in which independent accountants might feel justified in taking definite exception to the policies. Let me illustrate. In public utility accounting it is common practice to make provision for retirement of property on a basis which falls far short of accepted depreciation accounting in industry generally. I do not regard it as the accountant's duty to take exception to that policy. I believe he should state what the policy has been and the nature of the effect which that policy has upon the financial statements. If the policy has been ultra-conservative, on the other hand, I think the accountant should likewise state the policy and the nature of its effects. In making this general answer I am not prepared to say that there may not be cases so extreme that the accountant should definitely take exception to the practice followed. I am merely trying to indicate that in my opinion the fact that ultra-conservative accounting policies have been followed and the nature of the effects flowing therefrom should be stated just as should be done if a policy which was not sufficiently conservative with reference to accounting for depreciation had been followed.

Form 10 provides for the furnishing in the application proper of certain schedules, such as schedules dealing with funded debt of the registrant and funded debt of subsidiaries included in the consolidated balance sheet. The question is whether it should be understood that independent accountants should certify to such schedules. There are no specific instructions dealing with this subject in connection with Form 10. We have, however, similar schedules provided in Form A-2 for registration under the Securities Act. In both forms these schedules are really in support of the balance sheet and in the instructions on the use of Form A-2 it is provided that "the certificate of the accountant or accountants shall be applicable to the matter in the registration statement proper to which a reference is required on the balance sheet." Reference to the schedules in question is required on the balance sheet both in the use of Form A-2 and in the use of Form 10, although the instructions as to covering the schedules by the certificate are lacking in connection with Form 10. The instructions ought to be the same on both forms and the schedules in support of the financial statements should be certified by the independent accountants. This includes those schedules which are included in the body of the form and those schedules which are covered in connection with the instructions as to financial statements.

The next question in substance may be stated as follows: Corporation A constructed a building in 1928 at a cost of $5,000,000. Its balance sheet correctly shows the cost of the building. The building today may not be worth a million dollars. What would be the obligation to disclose the fact that the value at which the fixed assets are carried is in excess of present value, provided that the balance sheet states the basis on which the asset is carried? I would say that if the balance sheet shows correctly that the building is carried at cost and if the income statements correctly reflect the decline in earnings which has probably accompanied the decline in value, all the disclosure contemplated by the Act had been made unless there are circumstances not included within the question. As to fixed assets, I do not think that a balance sheet may properly nor practically attempt to reflect current values. Anyone who would attempt to have a balance sheet from year to year reflect the value of fixed assets must indulge in conjecture, must be constantly changing the statement of his fixed capital accounts, and I should say must run a substantial risk of making misleading statements. If the extreme case which I have cited were the typical case, it might appear that the registrant should assume some duty of expressly notifying the public that in its judgment values had declined, but if it is to be expected to assume such a duty I do not know where the line would be drawn. It might even follow that, if in the judgment of the registrant's directors, values had increased above the cost, they would be obliged to so state. My opinion is that nothing of this sort was intended, that we must recognize the limitations on financial statements, and that there is no obligation on the registrant or its officers or directors to express their opinion on the question of value in such cases. Their obligation is to show the basis on which the company has done its accounting and not to attempt to adjust each financial statement, either on its face or by means of accompanying statements, to changes in current value.

The next question has to do with the situation of a corporation having fixed assets of a ledger value of $25,000,000, of which $5,000,000 represents investment in plants not now used and which will not be required until business conditions show a material improvement. Is it necessary that this condition be stated? While I believe that in most instances the accompanying statement of income is normally sufficient to prevent a statement which does not direct specific attention to the facts quoted from being misleading, it may be that under item 11 of Form 10 such information should be furnished. I am inclined to the belief that the registrant would do best to state the situation in his response to item 11, or it might be stated in some instances in response to item 12, which has to do with the general character and location of principal plants. I have no difficulty in thinking of cases where I believe that facts analogous to those stated in the question would be so decidedly material that failure to state them would be misleading. For instance, I know a street railway company which has abandoned the use of tracks and street cars almost entirely and has turned to busses. Its income account has not been very seriously affected by the change. It is possible that it might return to street railway operation under more favorable conditions, as the present situation is largely the result of ruinous taxicab competition. It is true that in such a case item 11 would develop the material information but even if item 11 were not in the form, it seems to me that such a street railway could not think of registering without making a disclosure of the facts. While my answer is, therefore, that in a great many cases I do not believe that disclosure is necessary, I must recognize that there will be cases where the failure to make disclosure would be serious.

The next question relates to a corporation which has an investment of $15,000,000 in fixed assets, of which $5,000,000 represents a plant used in a department that shows a loss for the year. Is this material information that should be disclosed in the statement? I do not regard it as such. It is true that if that same plant were owned by an uncolsolidated subsidiary, the balance sheet and results of operation of that subsidiary would have to be separately disclosed. There is no requirement in the form, however, for such disclosure in case the plant is owned by the registrant or by a consolidated subsidiary. Here again I think one can anticipate that there may be situations where disclosure should be made. If the loss has been due to changes in the industry which make the plant in question unable to keep its place and show a profit, I should think that fact should be shown. For instance, there have been recent developments in the steel industry which have made properties obsolete and, I should assume, have caused large plants to operate at a loss because they could not meet the competition of more modern methods. Here the problem is not merely that of bridging a period of depression but of being permanently out of the field unless new equipment and new methods are adopted.

We come next to a question which has no accounting significance. The question is: Under what conditions does the Commission permit securities to be withdrawn from listing? The answer is that there have been no cases involving questions of policy which have had to be decided. The only questions presented so far have been procedural ones. Consequently I am not able to outline for you anything as to the Commission's opinion regarding the conditions under which securities may be withdrawn from listing where any real issue is raised in connection with an application for withdrawal.

The next question is, in substance, whether the definition of an exchange as included in the Act includes over-the-counter transactions. Obviously it was not intended to do so and I think it does not. It is true that there may be borderline cases in which it is hard to state whether the characteristics of an exchange are or are not present. In such cases the answer probably cannot be obtained by applying any single form.

Coming back now to questions dealing with accounting, we have this one. Many companies maintain a system of internal check but no staff of internal auditors. The Commission's regulations provide that accountants may give due weight to an internal system of audit regularly maintained by means of auditors employed on the registrant's own staff. The question is: May accountants give due weight to a system of internal check where no staff of internal auditors is employed? I do not know what "due weight" would be in such a case and consequently I cannot definitely answer the question. It may be answered in part by the instructions as to the accountants' certificate in connection with Form 10. The language is: "Nothing in these instructions shall be construed to imply authority for the omission of any procedure which independent public accountants would ordinarily employ in the course of a regular annual audit." I do not suppose that any two firms of accountants would have the same definition of the words "due weight" as applied to a system of internal check. I think the question is one of what constitutes due weight to be given to a system of internal check rather than whether or not any weight may be given to such a system.

The question is next asked what constitutes non-recurring income within the meaning of the regulations, and certain specific questions to which I will later refer are asked in connection with it. I cannot attempt a comprehensive definition of what constitutes non-recurring income. My conception of the term, however, is that it was meant to include items which might be passed through the income account but which I think would generally be more properly entered directly in the surplus account. Such items would include profits on sale of capital assets and profits on sale of the corporation's own securities. This statement of my opinion is concurred in by the Commission. I would not classify as non-recurring income income which had been received in the ordinary course of business from a customer, even though a very large customer had been lost.

We come now to the specific questions. The first: Utility A suffered a rate reduction in September 1934. Must this fact be disclosed by the independent public accountants or by the registrant? I should say that there is no obligation on the independent accountants with reference to such a situation. Whether there is an obligation on the registrant I think depends on the circumstances. Many rate reductions are made in the ordinary course of business. The fact that they may have been made by order of public authority does not in my opinion alter that fact. Many such reductions are overcome by increasing business. I think clearly there is a class of rate reductions to which attention would not need to be called. On the other hand, there may be rate reductions of so serious a character that they are likely to have a substantial effect upon the securities of the company. There is no absolute test that I know of that can be set up for such cases and I think a good policy would be for the registrant to sdopt a liberal construction of its obligation to make disclosure and to make such disclosure even though in an individual case the clear necessity therefore might not appear.

The next question I can only answer in about the same way. This relates to the case where a customer was lost at the end of November 1934, which customer's purchases from the registrant amounted to 30% of its total sales and yielded a margin of gross profit commensurate with that of the other business of the registrant.

The next question deals with the obligation to make a disclosure which would probably enhance the value of the securities. Company X operates a gold mine. It has struck a new vein which will greatly increase the productivity of the mine. Should disclosure of this be made? I would say that ordinarily such disclosure should be made if there had been sufficient exploration so that it had been determined that the productivity of the mine would be greatly increased. It is probable that the element of good faith would be involved here. If the information were withheld and, following that, insiders used the information to their own advantage, it may very well be that liability would arise from failure to make the disclosure. On the other hand, if the information were withheld in good faith rather from a desire not to magnify unduly the prospects of the company than from any sinister motive, I would question whether there would be any liability.

Next we turn to the instructions dealing with the disclosure of defaults in principal, interest, or sinking fund provisions. The question is: Is it intended that default in other specific covenants need not be disclosed? In answering this I should like first of all to call your attention to the technical nature of many defaults and the fact that to state whether such defaults exist often calls for conclusions of law. It was not the intention of the Commission to provide that other defaults must be disclosed. The question in the form has reference to the balance sheet only and is obviously intended to elicit information only as to such defaults as to which failure of disclosure might make the balance sheet misleading. The instruction is that the facts and amounts with respect to any default in principal, interest, or siking fund provisions shall be stated in a balance sheet note if not shown in the balance sheet.

In connection with the next question a number of illustrative cases were cited and the question raised as to whether or not certain corporations are subsidiaries of other corporations for the purpose of item 10. I think I can give a general answer to this. The question of whether a corporation is or is not "controlled by" another is not entirely answered on any percentage basis. Where there is a clear majority of voting stock of one corporation owned directly or indirectly by another, I should say that it would be a very unusual case in which there was not actual control, but there may be actual control in many cases accompanying only a minority stock holding. The question is not how large a percentage of the stock is held but whether there is actual control. In all those cases where control may be associated with the ownership of a minority interest in voting stock, the answer must be based upon the realities of the situation and no general answer to hypothetical questions can be given. For determining the necessity of furnishing financial statements under Form 10, and also under A-2, the test is the ownership of more than half of the shares of stock normally entitled to vote.

The next question is one with reference to which I think Form 10 is not entirely clear. The question is stated as follows:

"Many corporations have types of operations which are merely incidental to their principal business and the cost of such operations is often charged to clearing accounts, from which it is distributed to primary operating accounts on some proper basis. An example of the foregoing would be the automobile expense of a public utility operating company. Such expense, of course, would include elements of maintenance, depreciation and taxes. Under the foregoing conditions, is it necessary to attempt to break down both the character of the cost and the distribution thereof to primary accounts for the purpose of complying with Schedule VIII accompanying the financial statements?"

I direct your attention to the difference between Schedule VIII of Form A-2 and Schedule VIII of Form 10, both of which deal with the same subject matter, which is the distribution of the total charges for maintenance and repairs, depreciation, depletion, and amortization, property taxes, management and service contract fees, and rents and royalties. In Form 10, as to each of these major classes, it is required that there be shown the amount charged to costs, the amount charged to profit and loss, and the amount charged to other accounts, naming the accounts and specifying the amounts. In Form A-2, the distribution is among the amounts charged to costs, the amounts charged to profit and loss, and the amounts charged to other accounts, without specifying as to each account the amounts charged. It is my understanding that Form A-2 would be complied with if the total charged to such clearing accounts as those for automobile expense were shown without any further distribution. It is not so clear that such an answer would meet the requirements of Form 10. This may be a defect in Form 10, as A-2, I think, contains all that the Commission considers essential in this respect.

The next questions asked involve the Commission's interpretation of the exemption from the registration requirements of the Securities Act provided by Section 77B of the Bankruptcy Act. I shall take up together the problems involved in soliciting consents to a plan of reorganization under Section 77B as well as those involved in a solicitation of deposits in connection with such a plan. This question is one which has given rise to considerable difficulty and is strictly a matter of legal interpretation upon which I am not fully qualified to speak. The exemption afforded by paragraph (h) of Section 77B of the Bankruptcy Act is believed, with certain immaterial exceptions, to apply only to securities issued subsequent to a court's confirmation of a plan of reorganization, and since a certificate of deposit normally is a security within the meaning of the Securities Act, the exemption is, therefore, not applicable, generally speaking, to certificates of deposit which are offered prior to such confirmation of a plan.

Before a plan may be proposed to the court in 77B proceedings, it must have been proposed by the debtor or approved by a certain percentage of the debtor corporation's creditors and security holders. Confirmation of a plan which has been proposed to the court in accordance with this Section is conditioned upon the acceptance thereof by a larger percentage of creditors and security holders.

Assuming that a plan of reorganization meets the requirements of paragraph (b) of Section 77B, I understand that Judge Burns, General Counsel to the Commission, has stated as his opinion:

1. That a reorganization committee may solicit from creditors and stockholders by mail or by use of interstate commerce, approvals of a plan necessary in order to authorize its proposal to the court pursuant to paragraph (d) of Section 77B, without there being in effect any registration statement in connection with the plan or the securities of the new company to be issued thereunder.

2. That similarly no registration statement is required prior to the solicitation of acceptance of such a proposed plan pursuant to the provisions of paragraph (e)(1) of Section 77B in order that such plan may be confirmed by the court in conformity with the provisions of that paragraph.

Following out these opinions I understand that the General Counsel to the Commission has also rendered his opinion that, assuming a plan of reorganization is one which meets the requirements of paragraph (b) of Section 77B of the Bankruptcy Act, the deposit of outstanding securities, or the presentation of the same for stamping, may be solicited to evidence the approval or acceptance of the plan by the security holders, even though such solicitation takes place prior to confirmation of the plan, provided:

(1) That any general power of the reorganization committee under the plan is or will be limited to the power, subject to the provisions of Section 77B, to take such steps and action as may be incidental to the carrying out of the plan in accordance with the provisions of that Section;

(2) that holders of stamped or deposited securities will not become liable individually, nor their securities be subjected to any lien, to pay any expenses or fees in connection with the reorganization, except to the extent that the court may order payments to be made out of the debtor's assets in accordance with Section 77B; and

(3) that the effect of the deposit or stamping of securities does not create any greater substantive rights, powers or obligations than those involved in the giving of approvals or consents such as I have already outlined.

In other words, any receipts which may be issued prior to the court's confirmation of the plan of reorganization proposed in connection with Section 77B proceedings do not need to be registered if, and only if, their legal effect is equivalent solely to "approval" or "acceptance" of a plan of reorganization in those proceedings.

The next question asked is as follows:

> "In cases where properties are acquired as an entirety for a total consideration payable either in cash or securities it is, of course, impossible for an accountant to segregate the amount of the total consideration which may be applicable to tangible and intangible properties. Under these conditions should the applicant state either in his certificate or in the financial statements that it is impossible to make such a segregation?"

My answer to this question is, generally, "Yes." I anticipate that in some cases it may be difficult if not impossible for the accountant to determine whether or not <u>any</u> part of the purchase price was paid for intangibles. I direct your attention to notes on Schedule IV of the instructions to Form 10. Schedule IV is a schedule of the changes during the period in the asset accounts for intangibles. The note is: "Where, in the accounts of the registrant, it is not practicable to separate intangible assets from property, plant and equipment, the information here required may be included in Schedule II." Schedule II is the schedule for property, plant and equipment. I recognize that there will be a great many cases in which corporations have actually expended money for the acquisition of intangible assets where it will be impracticable to identify the cost of such assets and the practical limitations are, I think, adequately recognized in the form.

The next question is:

> "In cases where a considerable number of companies are involved as well as a very detailed classification of property, plant and equipment, how much detail should be presented in complying with Schedule II accompanying the financial statements? In connection with the foregoing it should also be noted that in a great many instances detailed classifications of properties shown on the company's records will be meaningless due to the fact that there are considerable amounts of unclassified property acquisitions, etc. and also to the fact that retirements of properties which were included in such unclassified balances have been credited to the primary classified accounts rather than to the undistributed balances previously referred to."

It is not intended that Schedule II should be answered with reference to a very detailed subdivision of property. For instance, in the case of public utilities it would be sufficient to show the primary accounts of generation, transmission, distribution, etc., and a corresponding degree of subdivision should be sufficient in the case of other companies. Where there are unclassified balances on the company's books, it will often be impracticable to break them down by primary accounts, and in that event the unclassified balance should be carried into Schedule II as such. I agree that where there are considerable amounts of unclassified property any classification in Schedule II will be necessarily inadequate, both because the classification itself is not comprehensive and because the cost of property retired may have been charged to the unclassified balance or to the primary classified accounts without relationship to whether the property actually retired was included within the one or the other, and in many cases without the possibility of making such determination.

The question is asked whether the exemption which extends under certain circumstances to the exchange of a company's securities with those of its own security holders, extends also to an exchange of the securities of a wholly owned subsidiary with the holders of a company's own securities. Section 3(a)(9) of the Securities Act provides an exemption for "any security exchanged by the issuer with its existing security holders exclusively where no commission or other remuneration is paid or given directly or indirectly for soliciting such exchange." The answer to the specific question is "No."

The next question has to deal with who is an independent accountant within the meaning of the Act. I am asked whether I would consider a public accountant independent if a member of his family or a partner owned a small block of the securities of the registrant. I do not think that an adequate answer can be made to the question as framed. Perhaps the best way to answer the question is to quote from a letter which was sent by the Chief of the Securities Division of the Federal Trade Commission, at the time that that Commission administered the Act, to a firm of accountants. I am quoting from the letter:

> "With respect to the question of stock ownershp, I do not believe that this can be answered categorically either with regard to the amount of stock which may be held or with regard to the persons by whom it may be held. A nominal stock holding which obviously would not influence the judgment of an accountant, would not, I believe, affect the accountant's independence. Certainly an employee of a firm of accountants who has no connection with a particular client might hold considerably more stock in that client without affecting the independence of the firm of accountants than could a partner of the firm directly in charge of the work for that client. In any case, I believe that the stock holdings of all persons, either partners or employes, who are concerned with work for a particular client of an accounting firm, should be taken into consideration and I do not believe

that a firm can be deemed independent if such stock holdings in any case, either directly or indirectly, are more than nominal in amount."

I would like to direct your attention also to a change in Form A-2 from what appeared in Form A-1 which may be taken to indicate something of what the Commission has in mind, although it does not answer the specific question. Item 50 of Form A-1 provided that "If any statement contained herein purporting to have been prepared by an expert has been prepared by a person who has any interest in or is to receive an interest in the issuer as a payment for such statement or has been or is employed by the issuer or a subsidiary or affiliate thereof or has been employed upon a contingent basis, a full explanation of the circumstances." Item 44 of Form A-2, in calling for the corresponding disclosure of relationship, does not call for a statement of facts where the expert has or is to receive any interest, but only where he has or is to receive an interest of a substantial nature.

I think it would be clear that the mere holding of a small interest does not destroy the independence of the accountant or other expert but there may be facts associated with such holding which will destroy his independence for the purposes of the Acts.

#3 George C. Mathews

January 8, 1937

SEC Accounting Issues and Cases

Abstract

This address represents a statement of philosophy by the Commission in regard to the regulation of accounting and reporting methods. While the Securities Acts give the SEC authority to specify accounting methods, the Commission adopted a case by case approach in dealing with problems. Mathews notes, however, that if the professional accountants do not adhere to reasonable standards of full and fair disclosure of material facts, the SEC would have to prescribe them.

To introduce my talk this evening let me say, what at least some of you know, that I am not an accountant. I cannot bring you a message with any such authority as might attach to the statements of one who professes competency in the science of accounting. What knowledge of accounting I have has been obtained by exposure to accounting discussions and to the necessity of forming

---

Address before the Milwaukee Chapter, Wisconsin Society of Certified Public Accountants.

unprofessional judgments rather than by consistent and organized study of this subject.

A layman who voices his opinions on any technical subject or with reference to the application of standards by the members of a profession is always in danger of getting beyond his depth and of merely exposing his ignorance where he is most vocal in criticism. What I have to say this evening may offer no exception, but whether or not you think that what I say in criticism is sound, the relationship between your profession and the administration of the securities legislation is such that you are entitled to have that criticism expressed, even though you may not admit that it is valid.

I might limit myself to a presentation of specific instances which have been considered by the Commission in connection with the application of the program for regulation of the sale of securities--and before I am through I plan to bring to your attention a number of such instances in the hope that I may leave with you some understanding of the Commission's attitude and of the philosophy--if such it may be called--of its approach to these accounting problems. But I think I should attempt to do more than this. I think I should discuss with you some of the difficulties which seem to be fundamental.

The Commission, as you know, has not adopted general regulations governing accounting methods. Rather it has sought to attack each problem as it is presented in an individual case. In this way, case by case, the Commission has been sorting out what seem to it improper accounting practices, securing correction of statements, and criticising methods reflected in statements. This, I think, constitutes a movement in the right direction. Some of the leading accountants of the country report that already there has been a considerable improvement and have urged the Commission to continue this policy of handling each problem as it arises in a particular case as opposed to adopting a set of general accounting rules. Many accountants, on the other hand, have favored the formulation of general rules--feeling that such rules would be helpful to them and their clients.

Section 19(a) of the Securities Act empowers the Commission to prescribe the items or details to be shown in the balance sheet and earnings statement, and the methods to be followed in the preparation of accounts, in the appraisal or valuation of assets and liabilities, in the determination of depreciation and depletion, in the differentiation of recurring and non-recurring income and as to certain other accounting matters. A similar provision in the Securities Exchange Act is contained in Section 13(b). Up to the present the Commission has not issued rules covering these matters but has tried to stake out its path by its handling of individual cases.

Whether it may become necessary to resort to general rules, I do not know. It seems to me that whether or not that will become necessary depends largely upon the members of your profession.

I have often heard it said that accounting is not an exact science--that general rules and practices must be adapted to special cases, and that to attempt to force accounting principles and forms of statement into an unvariable course and form would retard progress and in many cases unfairly picture business results. It is not my purpose to deny that there are dangers such as those indicated, but no layman can examine the hundreds of statements which have been filed with the Commission without being impressed with the lack of general acceptance of uniform principles in respects where it would seem to him that fundamentals of accounting principle are involved. If an analogy may be drawn between accounting and engineering--it is as if engineers had no agreement on the required strength of foundations, structural steel requirements for skyscrapers, or efficient design for power plants.

I think that a governmental agency should frame rules to govern the exercise of professional functions only when the need for such rules has been shown to be of real public importance. Mere preference of the administrative agency for one method or form is not a sufficient reason for taking the formulation of principles and practices out of the hands of the members of a profession, and where the profession gives evidence of its capacity and willingness to develop and apply proper methods without evasion or undue delay, it should be encouraged to take on the responsibility. If the profession fails in its public duty to recognize and apply adequate standards, I believe the agency whose duty it is to administer laws such as the Securities Act must eventually move in.

It would be unfair not to acknowledge the influence which the accounting profession has had in the improvement of conditions within its scope, but it would be fatuous to assume that because the profession exists there is no occasion to be critical of results produced and no need of taking stock of what remains to be done.

It seems to me that we are coming to have a different conception of the functions and responsibilities of public accountants. Perhaps it would be better to say that our conception of the function of the public accountant is becoming clearer.

Only a small part of what should be the public accountant's responsibility has been performed when he reviews the accounts of a company for the purpose of assuring its management that it has accurate figures of financial results and status. By no means has the complete responsibility been met when reports, adequate for their purposes, are made to underwriters of securities who stand between the enterprise and those investors whose funds give it life.

In the light of our securities laws, the accountant has a responsibility for financial information which is important to the formation of an opinion as to whether a security should be bought or sold. The success of the application of the basic principle underlying the Securities Act, that complete and fair disclosure of all material facts should be made, is dependent on no one more than on the accountant.

Granted that many people are unable to read statements and certificates intelligently, it seems to me that the aim of the accounting profession should be to make those statements and certificates as clear and unambiguous as their technical nature permits. Financial statements which conform to convention and custom are not adequate if, in fact, they serve to conceal or fail to bring to light financial conditions or results which an intelligent investor needs to know in order to form a judgment. Certificates are not adequate if they evade expression of opinion regarding accounting practices which are not sound. I question how far an accountant may, in good conscience, resort to a multitude of notes attached to statements to explain unsound, questionable, or irregular practices where clarity of statement and of opinion would be better obtained by showing as a part of the statements themselves, the adjustments necessary to bring those statements into accord with sound practice.

Experience with statements which have been filed under the Securities Act clearly indicates to me that the profession has a long way to go to meet its full responsibility. In saying this I am not ignoring the many excellent statements and certificates which have been furnished, nor do I want to be understood as charging the profession generally with having failed, nor of failing to recognize that many of its members have conscientiously faced their duty in its broadest sense.

Nevertheless, I stand on the statement that the profession, by and large, has a long way to go. I think there are three or four principal reasons why this is so.

In the first place, the accounting profession is highly competitive. Competition exists not only within the ranks of those who have the status of certified accountants. There is a large body of practitioners as well who are not certified, which group shades down into a class who profess competency in accounting but whose qualifications make their use of any claim to be accountants altogether improper. Even under the Securities Act we have had experience with statements submitted on the authority of practicing accountants which showed on their face the utter incompetence of those who prepared them.

Accountancy has not yet reached the point which the legal and medical professions have attained, in which the practitioner must meet standards of professional knowledge before he may undertake to practice. For example, under the Securities Act, a public accountant has the same status as a certified public accountant.

If he is an accountant in public practice and is independent of the issuer, he may certify financial statements with all the authority of the best firm of certified accountants in the country. Apparently the only determinations which the Commission may make as to his qualifications are that he is independent, that he is in public practice, and that he is an accountant. Who is, in fact, an accountant is not always easy to determine. Probably the test would have to be sufficiently easy so that individuals lacking a great deal in true professional qualifications would come within the term.

What seems to me to be a second reason why accounting has not come closer to its goal is the fact that traditionally the services of American public accountants have been rendered to the management as distinguished from the investors. I do not mean that their work has not in a great many cases been of service to investors, but generally they have been the representatives of management rather than representatives of the investors, charged with the responsibility of reporting on what the management has accomplished. It may be very difficult to change this traditional relationship. Where large numbers of security holders are widely scattered, the proxy system of corporate government makes it questionable whether the selection of auditors by the stockholders would bring about their genuine independence of management. No single means of securing this independence seems available. Its gradual accomplishment is probably a matter of the stimulation of professional consciousness, of continual effort from within to raise the standards of the profession, and of pressure by public authority for the maintenance of high standards.

I have just indicated that the public accountant, though retained by management, has a responsibility to investors and to the public generally. I do not think that statement lays me open to the charge of being an idealist. It rests on a very sound business base. One of the most important assets of the public accountant, it seems to me, is his reputation for independence. There is a measure of public confidence that, although he is paid by the management, his first loyalty will be to the standards of his profession and to those who read the statements he prepares. Responsible accounting firms have worked consistently and unceasingly to build and protect this asset of reputation and public confidence. It seems clear that the public accountant who compromises his independence, whether by subservience to management or otherwise, not only injuress his own reputation but weakens public confidence in the independence of accounts as a class, and to that extent destroys one of the chief assets of the profession.

What seems to me to be a third reason why accountancy has not more nearly fulfilled its possibilities is the tendency to rely on precedent and authority rather than on the scientific method. The competitive nature of the profession and its traditional affiliation with management makes the acceptance of precedent dangerous. Perhaps when I come to a recital of a few of the specific problems which we have met, this danger will appear more clearly. Accounting authority also seems to me to be surprisingly lacking in critical analysis. As problems are presented to us, we usually make a study of the accounting authorities. Results have been disappointing, first, because there seems to be a complete lack of literature on many problems, and, second, because the authorities, even though often differing among themselves, seem too much inclined to state a rule without giving the reader the benefit of the reasoning on which the conclusion is based. The field for research in accounting seems to me to be a huge one. Practicing accountants should have a part in this research and colleges and universities should have a place in it comparable to that which they occupy in other fields.

The place which the Securities and Exchange Commission should take in this research program has so far not been clearly marked. Up to the present the Commission has developed its views largely by the case method. In a few instances resort has been had to stop orders to suspend the effectiveness of registration statements where accounting practices were clearly in violation of sound principles and erroneous in their portrayal of conditions and results. How far the Commission must take the lead in requiring the application of certain principles is a question about which there may be great differences of opinion. Much will depend upon what is accomplished in other ways, but unless the profession of accountancy moves forward consistently to develop principles and presentations with a view to meeting the investors' needs, the Commission may find it impossible to fulfil its responsibility in the program of securities sales regulation without going much further than it has in imposing requirements.

A business enterprise which asks the public to furnish it with capital or whose securities are widely held and actively traded surely owes an obligation to investors to furnish them with clear statements prepared in accordance with sound principles. The accountant who certifies the statements should have an obligation to tell investors clearly and unequivocally what his opinion is of the statements and of the accounting principles and practices which they represent. The instructions for registration forms which the Commission has prescribed provide that the accountant's certificate shall state his opinion of the results and of the principles upon which they are based. Yet one of the most difficult undertakings of the Commission in the field of accounting has been to secure certificates which stated such opinion clearly so that it could be understood by the investor.

Accountants have frequently told me that, when, in their certificates, they certify "subject to the foregoing comments", they mean to direct attention to the fact that the certificate would or might be misleading without the comments and should constitute notice to the reader that, to an extent, the statements reflect improepr or questionable practices.

Generally, however, they will not make a direct statement that the practices were improper or questionable. Sometimes they obviously do not mean that all of the matters commented on are subject to criticism. Frequently the comments will relate in part to practices which are questionable or improper and in part to procedures which are proper but need elucidation.

Such certificates do not clearly state the opinion of the accountant. Perhaps they would serve the purpose of the management or of the analyst, but if the reliance of the Securities Act upon presentation of pertinent facts to the public is to be justified, surely a clear statement of expert opinion is called for. Perhaps the explanation for the failure to meet the simple test of clarity and definiteness may be found partly in the lack of a general recognition of what are correct principles and partly in the historical development of the relation between the accountant and the management.

A fourth difficulty seems to me to arise from the fact that financial statements often contain figures for which the accountant is not willing to take responsibility and which he feels unable to criticize. An example is the provision for depreciation on a large and complicated property and the reserve for depreciation which appears in the balance sheet. Here the general practices seem to fall into three classes: First, a disclaimer of any responsibility for the figures; second, a modification of the first, which uses the phrase "subject to the adequacy of the provision for depreciation"; and, third, a statement of management's practice and whether or not it purports to represent a provision on a life and age basis.

It must be admitted that the accountant may not be in a position to certify to the adequacy or correctness of the depreciation accounting. There are a great many cases, however, where the provision has so patently been insufficient that it is questionable whether the accountant is not called on for the expression of an opinion. A difficulty here is that the practice in such cases of giving an opinion to the effect that proper standards have not been applied might lead to misunderstanding of the certificate in cases that are more nearly borderline, and where the determination is clearly beyond the province of the accountant.

This may well prove to be one of the classes of cases as to which the Commission should prescribe standards under Section 19 of the Securities Act.

It has been suggested that you would be interested in having me outline a few of the specific problems which have arisen in the administration of the Securities Act and indicate how they were handled. It will, of course, be impossible to present anything comprehensive within the limits of this paper and of your patience, but a review of a few cases may emphasize some of the respects in which it has seemed to us that accounting statements have failed, as originally submitted, to present a proper picture of the business. Some of the more flagrant cases have been discussed in stop order opinions but those which follow are cases where amendments have been worked out informally.

The first case that I will mention arose in connection with the registration of a bond issue of a large public utility.

CASE NO. 1

Prior to 1924, the registrant followed the practice of amortizing debt discount and expense by charges against income over the life of the respective issues. In 1924, it wrote up its fixed capital and investment accounts approximately $15,000,000, crediting about $7,000,000 to a retirement reserve and about $8,000,000 to capital surplus. During 1924 and 1925, it wrote off to capital surplus a total of approximately $8,000,000, which was substantially all of its then unamortized debt discount and expense. The effect of this write-off was to relieve the income account prior to August 31, 1934 (the date of the balance sheet included in the registration statement) of amortization charges aggregating approximately $5,000,000; the balance (approximately $3,000,000) would have been charged to income subsequent to that date. The accountants commented upon these facts in their certificate and in the final paragraph took exception to the procedure followed.

Objection was raised to the method followed by the company and considerable discussion both within the Commission and between the Commission and representatives of the registrant and the accountants was had. Without commenting upon the effect upon the property account and the increase in the reserve by additions made other than from earnings, the procedure followed raised the following principal objections:

(1) The earnings statements for the periods covered were overstated.

(2) The earned surplus account was overstated.

(3) Since the funded debt on which the discount was incurred was not yet due, the procedure would result in overstatements of earnings and earned surplus accounts in the future.

(4) The procedure failed to disclose that a deficit would have existed in the earned surplus account.

(5) It did not disclose the true interest burden of the company.

(6) It, in effect, capitalized discount.

(7) It understated the amount of the unamortized debt discount.

As finally amended, footnotes to the earnings statements, balance sheets and surplus schedules and more extensive comments in the certificate of the accountant fully revealed all of the facts involved. Any one reading the statement and taking into consideration the footnotes and comments of the accountant was put on notice of the fact that the company had followed incorrect accounting procedure and was given information necessary to determine the correct results that would have obtained had correct accounting procedures been followed. The company was not required to change its accounts or its accounting procedure.

The majority of the Commissioenrs thought the facts were sufficiently disclosed in the registration statement and prospectus as amended. Accordingly, the statement was permitted to become effective. Two of the Commissioners thought that adequate disclosure and treatment required that the balance sheets, the earnings statements, the earned surplus accounts and statements of dividends paid should be restated and should be accompanied by a description of the company's past accounting practices.

In considering the principles adopted in this case, it must be recognized that the Commission permitted this procedure to be followed only because it was possible to make, and the registrant had made, in the opinion of the majority of the Commission at that time, a disclosure that was sufficiently simple to make possible the reading of these statements without serious danger of misunderstanding.

CASE NO. 2

Shortly after that case, a holding company in the same system filed a registration statement. The financial data as originally presented by it included fifteen pages of notes pertaining to the balance sheet and profit and loss statement. The certificate of the accountants included numerous qualifications and exceptions. Because of this, it was practically impossible to determine with any degree of certainty either the company's financial condition or the results of its operations.

It appeared to the Commission that in this case adequate disclosure could not be made without some adjustment in the financial statements themselves. To overcome this condition, the various financial statements were amended to give effect to many of the adjustments referred to in the accountants' certificate and in the footnotes.

This was accomplished by showing on each such statement three columns, headed as follows:

	(1) Per Company's Books	(2) Footnote Adjustments	(3) Amounts if Adjusted as Explained in Footnotes
Items	________	________	________

Through the adjustments shown in Column (2) of the balance sheet, surplus was reduced from approximately $139,000,000 to a deficit of approximately $33,000,000 as at December 31, 1934. This reduction in surplus was offset on the balance sheet through the reduction of assets.

The final statements as drawn still had an extremely large number of footnotes and the accountants' certificate was long and complicated but we felt that it was considerably simpler and more understandable to the investor than it was before the statements were required to be changed.

The difference in treatment in these two cases was due largely to the fact that in the first case, the majority of the Commission felt that the information as presented was sufficiently revealing and the deviation from accepted principles of accounting was shown in a manner sufficiently easy to analyze that it was unnecessary to require further amendment of the statements; whereas, in the latter case, the information presented in supplementary notes and in the accountants' qualifications was so complicated that it was next to impossible to get any adequate understanding of the facts.

It is interesting to note that in a third case, that of the registration of an issue of another company in the same system, the entries which were the basis for criticism were reversed on the company's books after discussion with representatives of the

Commission, so that the statements as presented caused no difficulty.

CASE NO. 3

In 1930 a public utility company operating electric, gas and traction properties made a revaluation of its electric and gas properties, as a result of which their value on its books was increased approximately $8,200,000. This excess was carried to an account designated "Appraised Value in Excess of Book Value." The amount of this write-up was credited to "Capital Surplus--arising from revaluation of electric and gas properties."

During the years 1930 to 1935 inclusive, abandonments of traction property, amounting to something over $2,100,000, were written off against the capital surplus so created. The accountant's certificate made no reference to this and expressed no opinion concerning the propriety of the write-off of abandoned traction property against surplus created by the write-up of electric and gas property.

The Commission was of the opinion that this procedure was sufficiently questionable to necessitate a specific expression of opinion by the accountant with respect to the practice.

Accordingly objection was raised to the statement as it had been presented. Considerable discussion took place as to whether the company should be required to carry the amount of the abandonment to earned surplus and restore the appraisal surplus to its original amount.

The accountants in the case supported the claims of the registrant that the procedure followed was in accordance with accepted accounting practice and expressed a willingness to so state in their certificate.

The upshot of the matter was that amendments were finally made to the registration statement which, among other things, gave complete information on the appraisal, stated how and by whom it was made, described how the results were set up, described the abandonments of property and explained how they were handled. Also, the certificate was restated in such a manner that the accountants clearly expressed their opinion of the procedure in question. The amended certificate as it related to this item read as follows:

> "Losses on the complete abandonment of certain street railway operations have been charged against capital surplus arising from reappraisal of assets. Neither the practice of the company nor general accounting practice calls for provision for such losses out of income or out of reserves created out of income, and in our opinion they are properly chargeable against any capital surplus, including surplus arising from reappraisal of properties assuming the correctness of such reappraisal (which being

a question of valuation we, as accountants, cannot pass upon). In the absence of appraisal surplus, sound accounting practice would, in our opinion, have permitted the charge of the losses against a capital surplus created by reduction of capital or otherwise or, alternatively, they might have been charged against surplus earned prior to abandonment or over a period of years following abandonment; the extent to which the earned surplus on June 30, 1935 would have been reduced if the latter alternative had been followed cannot be stated. The earnings would not have been effected."

Here again, in my opinion, the procedure that was followed was in violation of good accounting practice. However, all the facts were clearly stated and the accountants expressed an opinion on the principle involved and seemed, at first reading, to do so with respect to the application of the principle in the particular case. Here again, full disclosure of the pertinent facts was the guiding principle in the settlement of the case. The accountants' disclaimer of responsibility as to the genuineness of the surplus, of course, raises a question of whether they had really expressed an opinion on the particular entries concerned.

The distinction between this case and the first one I cited is that in this case the accountants upheld the practice of the registrants as being in accordance with accepted accounting practice whereas in the other the accountants took exception to the method adopted. We felt that neither case followed good accounting practice, but, since all the facts in the case were presented in such a manner that the investor would not be misled and since the accountants had expressed their opinions with regard to the procedures, the majority of the Commission felt the statement might be permitted to become effective.

CASE NO. 4

An industrial concern acquired certain patents through the issuance of its own capital stock late in 1926. These patents were carried into its accounts at the stated value of the capital stock issued for them. The book value of the patents on this basis was approximately $1,200,000. From the date of their acquisition until June 30, 1933 a half million dollars of this cost was amortized. On that date the patents were appraised at $2,400,000 and surplus arising from appreciation was created in the amount of about $1,700,000.

During the period from the date of acquisition to September 30, 1936, the corporation was amortizing the appraised value of these patents. The amortization of cost was charged to income and the amortization of the appreciation was charged to surplus arising from their appreciation. By the close of September 1936, the operations of the company had resulted in a deficit in the earned surplus account so the stockholders approved a restatement of the capital stock from $10.00 a share to $1.00 a share, thereby creating approximately $1,800,000 of capital surplus. The company then not only wrote off the unamortized portion of the cost of the patents against this capital surplus but it also transferred from capital surplus to earned surplus an amount sufficient to restore to earned surplus all that had been charged off through the income account in the form of amortization of patents since the date of their acquisition. In this manner, a deficit of approximately $470,000 was changed to an earned surplus balance of nearly $400,000.

When this company filed a registration statement in December 1936, it included profit and loss statements for three years and nine months ended September 30, 1936, in which no deduction was made for the amortization of these patents. It also submitted a balance sheet as of September 30, 1936, in which earned surplus was shown at this written-up value of nearly $400,000. These statements were certified.

We considered it improper to show net income for the years in question without including deductions to provide for amortization attributable to those years. We are also in agreement with the generally accepted principle that capital surplus should not be used to relieve the income account of charges that would otherwise be made thereagainst. While there may be justification for using capital surplus to wipe out a deficit in the earned surplus account, we could hardly subscribe to its use to create earned surplus.

An asset should not, it seems to me, be written off to capital surplus when its consumption is part of the cost of operations and generally accepted accounting practice would amortize it by charges to income and particularly is this true when earned surplus exists. Statements drawn in conformity with such a procedure without extensive explanation and qualification would, in my opinion, be misleading. A company cannot honestly state that it has a surplus arising from earnings when expenses of doing business during prior periods have been charged to capital surplus in an amount so great that the earned surplus would have been completely wiped out had operations been properly charged. In saying this I recognize that there may be cases substantially amounting to reorganization where it will be proper to accumulate earned surplus from the date of such reorganization notwithstanding the fact that losses attributable to prior periods may have been wiped out against capital surplus.

Pursuant to our letter of deficiencies and after conferences with our staff, the registrant amended its statements. In the amended profit and loss statements, net income was shown before amortization of patents from which was deducted the amortization of patents, thereby arriving at a net income figure after amortization.

Possibly this treatment might be criticized on the ground that the amortization should have been included as part of the cost of goods but since the information was clearly set forth and a resulting net profit was arrived at after the deduction of amortization, we concluded that the facts in the case had been sufficiently revealed. In the balance sheet, the earned surplus was wiped out but a sufficient amount was transferred from capital surplus to leave no deficit in the earned surplus account. Full explanation of all the facts relating to the patent situation was contained in footnotes.

CASE NO. 5

In this case, there was included in the registrant's balance sheet approximately $302,000 for patents from which was deducted a reserve for amortization of about $296,000, leaving roughly $6,000. The following footnote appeared in the schedule relating to intangible assets:

> "There is included in the above reserve for amortization of patents $294,816.37 applicable to patents covering chain manufacture which were fully amortized prior to June 30, 1932."

It developed that a substantial part of these patents had expired and we questioned the propriety of showing them in the balance sheet, expressing the opinion that the expired patents should have been written off against the reserve. It seemed to us that the balance sheet should reflect only the unexpired patents and the reserve applicable to them. Inasmuch as the expired patents had no further value as patents at the date of the balance sheet, their inclusion seemed to be misleading.

The registrant objected to amending the financial statements, claiming that, although the patents had expired, there was still a substantial carryover of value to the company from having had them. This, they felt, entitled them to show what the patents had previously been worth. An amendment to the balance sheet was submitted to include a footnote reading as follows:

> "There is included in the above reserve for amortization of patents $294,816.37 applicable to patents covering chain manufacture which were fully amortized prior to June 30, 1932. However, a relatively small portion of this amount is applicable to patents which have not run the limitations of statute, and the segregation of this portion so applicable has never been made upon the books of the Company and would now be impracticable. Patents which have not been heretofore wholly amortized are being amortized over the life thereof. Patents are the only intangible asset shown on the books of the Company."

In view of the fact that the amount involved was relatively small, the net balance carried into the asset account was correct and the footnote clearly revealed the facts as to the expiration of the patents, we felt that the statement as amended was not materially misleading. Accordingly, further request for amendment was waived. However, it seems to me that when the patents have been fully amortized and have expired, they should be written off against the reserve so as to remove from the balance sheet both the asset and the reserve.

CASE NO. 6

Some years ago, a company acquired a subsidiary by purchasing its capital stock at a price considerably greater than its value as shown by the books of the subsidiary. The subsidiary owned very profitable patents carried on its books at a nominal amount.

In the balance sheet of the patent filed as part of a recent registration statement, the investment in the subsidiary was carried at about $10,000,000, which was about $6,000,000 more than its book value, at the date of purchase. No provision was made for amortizing any part of the investment. In the balance sheet consolidating the affairs of the parent and the subsidiary, the excess of $6,000,000 was carried under the heading "Patents, Patent Rights and Goodwill." No provision was made for writing off this excess to give effect to the expiration of the patents.

When the registration statement was examined, a deficiency was cited with respect to this procedure. In citing the deficiency, we were governed by the belief that the excess should not be designated as patents unless provision was made for its amortization to reflect the expiration of the patent rights. To us it seemed improper for the company to show in its consolidated balance sheet that it possessed patents without providing for their amortization in its consolidated profit and loss statement. We also felt that if a considerable portion of the value of the investment in the subsidiary was due to the value of the subsidiary's patents, as the registrant consistently maintained throughout its prospectus, such investment should be reduced in conformity with the expiration of the patents.

Had the value of the patents been reflected on the books of the subsidiary at the figures attributed to them in the acquisition of the subsidiary's stock, they would have been shown on the consolidated balance sheet in the same manner as they were in this case but would have been carried at an amortized figure and charges to income would have reflected the amortization in the consolidated profit and loss statement.

Representatives of the registrant contended that the value of the investment in the subsidiary was not actually decreasing and that, therefore, there should be no amortization of the excess cost. This continuation of excess earning power was due, they said, to several factors, among which were (1) improvements to the basic patents continued their usefulness indefinitely, and (2) contacts which the subsidiary had with certain large customers gave assurance of a continuingly profitable outlet for its products. They further stated that these factors were anticipated at the time the stock of the subsidiary was purchased and, accordingly, what had really been purchased for the excess was goodwill.

The responsibility for the truthfulness of the representations in the financial statements filed in connection with a registration of securities is that of the registrant and the accountant. We were in no position to determine whether this excess value was due to the expiring patents, as indicated by the caption of the account and reiterated elsewhere in the body of the statement, or whether it was due to goodwill, as was asserted in the course of the discussions relating to the deficiency memorandum. In our treatment of the deficiency, we did not undertake to determine whether the excess was paid for patents, for goodwill, or in part for both.

We did insist, however, that the treatment throughout should be consistent. We felt that if the position was taken that the excess was due in whole or in part to the value of the patents, it should be amortized and that this necessitated writing off the amount carried as patents in consolidation and writing down the investment as carried on the parent's books as the patents expired.

If, on the other hand, the excess had been paid for goodwill, it was not necessary that the excess be amortized. In such case, however, we felt the registrant should remove from its financial statements and prospectus all matter tending to indicate that this excess purchase price was paid because of the patents.

The registrant amended its financial statements and its prospectus by striking out the references to patents in support of the excess purchase price and labeled the item:

> "Goodwill, being the investment of ______________ Company in the capital stocks of subsidiaries consolidated in excess of the net assets exclusive of goodwill of such subsidiaries at dates of acquirement."

CASE NO. 7

During the years 1934 and 1935 a company engaged in the manufacture of aircraft was manufacturing three long-range multiple engine ships and, during each of those years, approximately a quarter of a million dollars of its expenses were deferred as representing experimental cost. It was anticipated that if the three ships were successful, the company would receive contracts for the manufacture of a substantial number of additional ships and the deferred experimental expense was to be written off as part of their costs.

In 1936, it was determined that no contracts for additional ships would be entered into. Accordingly, the company charged off the deferred expense against surplus. This procedure was, of course, in accordance with proper accounting practice. However, the registration statement which it filed in 1936 included profit and loss statements for the years 1933, 1934 and 1935 and for the seven months ended July 31, 1936. At the time of filing, the company was aware of the fact that its experimental expenses had been useful only in the construction of the three ships manufactured during 1934 and 1935 and had already made the charge to surplus. The facts relating to these expenses were given only in connection with the charge to surplus and no mention of it was made in connection with the profit and loss statements. It appeared to us, even though the charge was properly made to surplus, a retrospective statement of the actual results for 1934 and 1935, made after the loss had been ascertained, should clearly show what the results would have been if these losses had been charged to profit and loss at the time the expense was incurred.

When this thought was conveyed to the registrant, the profit and loss accounts for 1934 and 1935 were completely restated and the surplus charge of 1936 was eliminated from the schedule of surplus.

This procedure was, we believe, the most satisfactory method of presenting the facts in this particular case. While our deficiency letter did not advise the company to do more than reveal the pertinent facts in the profit and loss statements, our staff suggested the desirability of a complete restatement. The registrant and its accountants promptly accepted the suggestion and went the whole way in the amendment.

CASE NO. 8

One of the companies registered under the 1934 Act had charged to surplus and credited to income substantial amounts of dividends on its own preferred stock held in its treasury. In 1934, the fiscal year covered by statements examined, this amounted to nearly a quarter of a million dollars.

We thought that the policy of showing the dividends on treasury stock as income was highly improper. By this procedure, a company with a substantial amount of treasury stock could, on the basis of an earned surplus at the beginning of a series of years during which no profits whatever were made, show net income in the profit and loss statement and pay dividened therefrom during such years. To show net income under such circumstances appeared to us to be highly misleading.

Pursuant to a deficiency memorandum with respect to this item, the company amended its statement by reducing the dividends charged to surplus to the amount paid to outside holders and by removing from income the dividend on the treasury stock.

CASE NO. 9

As of May 31, 1934, a company by an amendment to its certificate of incorporation restated and reduced the stated value of its common stock. The total reduction amounted to slightly more than

$2,200,000, of which nearly $2,100,000 was carried to a reserve against investment in subsidiary companies and a little over $100,000 was credited to capital surplus.

This company owned a number of subsidiary companies that had suffered substantial losses since the date they had been acquired. As a result, the consolidated balance sheet at the date of the restatement of capital carried a substantial deficit in the surplus account although the parent company had nearly a half million dollars of earned surplus on its own books.

By the use of the reserve for investments created by the restatement of the capital stock, the company was able, in drafting a consolidated balance sheet, to eliminate these subsidiary deficits against the reserve created by the reduction of the capital stock of the parent. Accordingly, the earned surplus of the parent was carried out as consolidated earned surplus and the deficit disappeared in the consolidated balance sheet.

As a result of this procedure in 1934 the earned surplus account as shown in the consolidated balance sheet as of February, 1936, filed as part of a registration statement, was stated at half a million dollars more than it would otherwise have shown.

The consolidated balance sheet is intended to present the joint condition of a parent and its subsidiaries in the manner in which it would appear if only one corporation existed. There seems to be no good reason why a consolidated group should create earned surplus through a restatement of capital stock when an individual corporation could not do so. Accordingly, it seemed improper for this company, in its registration statement, to show an earned surplus of nearly $500,000 more than the consolidated net earnings after May 31, 1934, the date of the restatement; so we advised it that we considered the statements to be deficient in this respect.

As a result of this notice of deficiency, the parent company decided to adjust its accounts to take up the profits and losses of the subsidiaries from the date of their acquisition. The deficit which, on the revised basis, would have existed at the date of the restatement on May 31, 1934 was then wiped out by use of the reserve created by the restatement. The company then took up profits and losses of the subsidiaries from May 31, 1934 to the date of the balance sheet filed with the registration statement.

As a result of this procedure, the parent company now shows in its earned surplus account its own and its subsidiaries' profits and losses since the date of the restatement and its earned surplus account is dated to show that fact. The surplus on the consolidated balance sheet is, insofar as these factors are concerned, the same as on the balance sheet of the registrant itself.

What I have said may sound unduly critical of the work of the accounting profession. It would be most unfair to leave without acknowledging that a great deal of progress has been made and that a great deal of credit is due to members of the profession. I have the highest regard for the aims and standards of many accountants with whom I have come in contact. No profession is without its weaker members. Probably no profession has had to fight against greater odds to secure advancement of its standards. It seems to me that yours has a greater opportunity than ever and I must recognize improvement which is undeniably taking place. It would be pleasant to recount some of the evidence which we have seen of advancing standards. I have assumed, however, that you are more concerned with the other side of the picture. This paper has already reached such length that I am sure you will not object to my closing its presentation with merely a general acknowledgement of the progress which is being made and of our deep interest in having that progress continue.

#4 William O. Douglas

September 21, 1938

Capitalism and Trusteeship

Abstract

Douglas recognizes the dual role of managers: to make the company successful and to be trustees for the investors. He cautions, however, that when the area of finance starts to dominate, then the SEC must constitute:...various types of patrol of finance for the purpose of prevention of excessive practices.

In its aims and ideals the Securities and Exchange Commission has much in common with responsible and conservative business management. What we both seek, above all else, is a careful conservative stewardship of the interests of investors. Your responsibility, as corporate managers, is to your own stockholders and bondholders. Our duty, as public servants, is to American investors as a group.

Address at a dinner given by the Society for the Advancement of Management for the delegates of the International Management Congress.

The contact which the SEC has with management comes, as most of you know, from the financial aspects of business. Those of you who have brought out securities issues in recent years have come into contact with us through the Securities Act of 1933. This statute, probably the simplest we administer, requires that those who seek to sell their securities to the public must make a full and fair disclosure of their business history, their financial condition, the purposes for which the funds are to be used and the rights of the various classes of security holders. The theory of the Act is not to control the raising of capital through the sale of securities but simply that capital cannot be raised without full disclosure of all the facts when you are asking for other people's money. We do not pass on the merits of securities to be offered; that is left to the investor. All we ask for the investor is the facts. Those of you who have securities listed on stock exchanges have come to know us through the Securities Exchange Act of 1934. That law calls for a similar statement as to the company, its business and its financial condition for all so-called listed companies; it also calls for annual reports keeping that information up to date. In addition, the Securities Exchange Act operates to prevent pools and manipulations in the securities of your companies. It sets up standards for providing certain minimum information in the solicitation of proxies. Equally important, it recognizes that officers, directors and dominant stockholders are fiduciaries and should not trade on inside information; and accordingly it penalizes certain purchases and sales. Those of you who operate public utility companies, if your companies are members of holding company systems, may have done business with us through the Public Utility Holding Company Act of 1935 when you have issued securities, bought or sold securities or properties, solicited proxies, or made adjustments in your accounting methods of your financial structure. Under this law, we are required to give approval or disapproval to many holding company activities. Here there is an element of supervision over the acts of management which does not characterize the other laws e.g. a limitation by the Act of the geographical area embraced by any one holding company system; protection of investors against payment of dividends out of capital; limitations on the presence of bankers on the boards of directors; and the like. Finally, from now on, if any of you have the misfortune to go into bankruptcy for purpose of being reorganized, you will find the SEC serving in an advisory capacity to the courts and rendering them technical assistance in the analysis of plans of reorganization under Chapter X of the new Federal Bankruptcy Act.

These tasks of ours are varied. But whatever they are--whether they be insistence on disclosure of the truth, prosecution of manipulators, simplification of holding company structures--they constitute various types of patrol of finance for the purpose of prevention of excessive practices. They are in tune with the standards of conservative management for they reflect the simple fundamentals which should govern the relationship of a manager to an owner.

Responsible management has always recognized its position as the servant of the stockholders. Yet the blight of capitalism has been a specious brand of morality for corporations, a morality which draw a distinction between the allegiance which the management demanded of its staff and the allegiance which management owed to its stockholders. You know and I know that there can be no such distinction. You and I know that once capitalsim forsakes the standards of trusteeship, it bids fair to destroy itself. It is the job of the SEC to eradicate that specious brand of morality and to restore old fashioned standards which place business above suspicion or reproach for questionable financial practices.

The efforts of the SEC to buttress our corporate standards of trusteeship obviously serve the interest of all responsible management. For misrepresentation is unfair competition, whether it is used to attract capital or to solicit new business. But misrepresentation in bidding for capital, or in any dealings with security holders, is more than unfair competition. It is a direct undermining of that free economic system which is necessary for the preservation and perpetuation of capitalism under a democratic form of government. That is why, when a company enters the capital market for funds with which to carry on or expand its business, it is important that it has told the truth about its affairs as completely and truthfully as the high minded competitor who bid for capital last week. And when a company solicits proxies for its annual meeting of stockholders, or for some special project, it is important that investors feel that they have a solid basis of facts for an informed judgment. When your securities are listed on stock exchanges, it is important that no one make a football out of them. The country has learned that a manipulated security is a poor rather than a good advertisement for a company seeking additional capital as well as a curse to investors. Business at last knows that it does not pay to become a stooge for market traders since it knows that no conscientious management can divide its loyalty between its bankers and its stockholders. When finance becomes the master rather than the servant of business, a process of disintegration sets in.

There are those who would have it appear that the cost of living up to the requirements of our new securities regulation constitutes a restrictive burden on financing. That charge I feel perfectly confident in denying. We ourselves have been careful to guard against costs which might be burdensome or restrictive. I cannot at this time give you the details of our cost studies, but I do say that they satisfy the Commission that no real restrictive influences are present. Whatever costs there are, they represent only the pains which conscientious management has always taken in all of its activities. Obviously they are a restrictive influence on irresponsible management. For that, we may all well be grateful.

We know that at least conservative managements feel the same way about these things as we do. And we know that some other kinds of management do not. Fortunately, we do not have to try to please everybody. And we will never try to please those who want to forsake the path of genuine conservatism for the quick but costly profits of corner cutting.

Service to stockholders cannot be a passive thing. It is not something to be rendered wtih the lips. It calls for constant diligence and tireless devotion to the standards of fiduciary responsibility upon which our capitalistic system is based. It is not enough to make an honest and revealing annual report. Management must, in every act, inspire the confidence of investors whose funds are its life-blood. For, if the American public has a large stake in the country's corporate business, so American corporations have their stake in the public confidence. It is in that respect that this part of the President's program has its greatest significance to those who believe in capitalism and democracy.

#5 Robert E. Kline, Jr.

October 12, 1939

Accounting and the Commission's Enforcement Abstract Program

Abstract

The activities of the enforcement section of the General Council of the SEC are outlined in this address. Kline cites and describes the Kopald-Quinn, Whitney, Interstate Hosery, and McKesson & Robbins cases as examples of investigative cooperation between attorney and accountant.

When your chapter president, Mr. DeGrafft, asked me to speak to you this evening, I was delighted to have the opportunity of discussing with you some of the general questions which I believe to be common to both your fraternity and the Securities and Exchange Commission. I say this because I understand Delta Sigma Pi was founded for the purpose, among other things, "...to further a higher standard of

---

Address before the Chi Chapter of Delta Sigma Pi, Johns Hopkins University, Baltimore, Maryland.

commercial ethics and culture and the civic and commercial welfare of the community," while the Securities and Exchange Commission was established to effectuate the full and fair disclosure of information pertinent to securities sold in interstate commerce and through the mails, to regulate transactions on national securities exchanges and in the over-the-counter markets, to prevent inequitable and unfair practices, and to detect and prevent the consummation of frauds in the sale of securities.

All of us present can recall the days of active stock promotion in the middle twenties, with everyone from elevator boy to president, wildly speculating in a rising market. Stocks rose to nebulous heights, entirely out of proportion to any rpoper basis for their valuation. Huge paper profits were made. Anything was possible. The public was so credulous it was easy for a ruthless promoter to flood the market with worthless stock, beautifully embossed with a golden seal, with promises of fabulous returns for exceeding the rosiest dreams for the gullible investor. Get-rich schemes were commonplace. No investor was too small for him to contact; he exercised no conscientious or moral restraint in his activities. State laws could not hold him, state boundaries offered no resistance. He operated throughout the length and breadth of the land, relying on distance for his protection, using the mails, the telephone and telegraph to perpetrate his fraud across state lines, with no effective federal control to block his efforts. The investing public was swindled out of millions of dollars by these methods. Those who could ill afford it were induced to part with their life's savings.

With the market crash of 1929 and the financial crisis which ensued, many investors, even those comparatively well off, found themselves in greatly reduced circumstances, with the accumulation of years wiped away. Some lost everything. In desperation many made an effort to recoup their resources by investing their few remaining dollars in wildcat promotions, becoming the unwitting prey of these same unscrupulous promoters, who fleeced them again with promises of quick recovery.

These experiences could not be repeated. There came a public demand for effective federal regulation of these evils. Then followed the enactment of the Federal Securities laws, and the creation of a special agency devoted to their enforcement.

The first of these acts, known as the "truth in securities" act, was designed to provide a true and complete picture of new securities to be offered to the public by means of the registration process. The prospectus required to be furnished to each investor is designed to provide sufficient facts to enable him to determine for himself the advisability of the investment.

In addition, this act has a sweeping fraud provision, prohibiting in the sale of securities the use of the mails or the facilities of interstate commerce to devise fraudulent schemes, the obtaining of money by false or misleading representations, or the engaging in a course of business which would operate as a fraud or deceit upon the purchaser.

The 1934 Act effected similar provisions for securities registered on national securities exchanges. Requirements as to registration and reporting were adopted. Provisions were made against the artificial manipulation of securities prices; a fair and open market was sought to be maintained. In addition, over-the- counter brokers and dealers were required to be registered, if they used the mails or the facilities of interstate commerce to conduct their business.

The 1925 Act provided for the control and regulation of the vast public utility holding company systems, suggested reforms relative thereto, and placed upon the Commission certain responsibilities regarding their operation, coordination and ultimate simplification.

Thus we see generally the necessity for and the purpose of the three acts administered by the Commission. A brief word now on the mechanics of such administration.

The principal office of the Securities and Exchange Commission is located in Washington. In addition, the country has been divided into nine regions and a regional office set up in the principal financial center of each, under the supervision of a regional administrator, staffed with a force of attorneys, accountants, analysts, margin inspectors, mining and oil engineers, and so forth.

It is through the regional offices that a vast amount of the enforcement work of the Commission is conducted. The staff of each office is always available to any interested party desirous of discussing problems arising under the acts of seeking information. It is through the regional offices that investigations of possible violations of the acts are usually conducted.

In the usual course questions arising in the regional offices are referred to the appropriate Division of the Commission's Washington office, which has a general supervision over their work. These are the Public Utilities Division, Registration Division, Trading & Exchange Division, General Counsel's Office, and Office of the Chief Accountant.

The Public Utilities Division in general is charged with the duty of handling all questions relating to the registration of public utility holding companies; the Registration Division with questions involving the registration of securities issues; the Trading & Exchange Division with matters concerning the trading on national securities exchanges and in the over-the-counter markets; the General Counsel's Office with the interpretation and enforcement of the provisions of the several acts; and the Office of the Chief Accountant with questions involving accounting practices and procedures as they relate to all of the activities of the Commission.

The importance of questions of accounting practice and procedure in every phase of the work of the Commission cannot be over-emphasized. Every registration of a public utility holding company or of an issue of securities must be accompanied and supported by elaborate financial statements, profit and loss statements and balance sheets, certified to by an independent public accountant. Investigations into fraudulent securities transactions, manipulative or unfair practices on the exchange or in the open markets, all require and necessarily depend on the examination and conclusions of an expert accountant. We meet these questions in every phase of the Commission's enforcement program.

As my work with the Commission happens to be principally concerned with this enforcement program, I am naturally best qualified to speak on this phase of the Commission's activities. I thought it might interest you to have me go into some detail regarding the same and then to show how this program coincides with some of the principles which your accounting fraternity is seeking to establish.

To attempt to delimit the term "enforcement" by a precise definition would be impossible, for matters involving a problem of enforcement necessarily encompass questions relating to every phase of the work of the Commission. Broadly speaking, it might be said that the enforcement section of the General Counsel's Office is charged with the primary duty of insuring compliance with the laws administered by the Commission.

Most cases originate with a complaint. Some person, usually one who can ill afford to suffer a loss, writes in and complains about some investment he has made. Occasionally our information comes from some source other than a complaint--our own observance of a market trend, a "tip", a suggestion from a cooperating enforcement agency, some special study the Commission has made, and the like. But in each instance an investigation is instituted.

The direction that an investigation takes of course depends on the nature of the violation involved. Certain essential facts are fairly general, however, and sooner or later must be established before there can be any violation. Evidence of mailing, or of use of the instrumentalities of interstate commerce, such as the telephone or telegraph, or under the Exchange Act of the facilities of an exchange, must be developed. Similarly, under the Securities Act, it is essential to show there was a sale of a security involved, in contrast to the sale of something which could not be classified as a security within the statutory definition.

Let us take a typical case. A letter is received by the Commission from an investor who complains that at the solicitation of a salesman from a certain brokerage house he was induced to purchase 100 shares of preferred stock in a certain company for a total consideration of $1,000 and that he has failed to receive the promised dividend of 100. The letter from the investor and the material which he has attached reveals that the securities in question were delivered to him through the United States mails. The wheels of enforcement are immediately set in motion. A check with the Registration Division reveals that the securities of the particular corporation have never been registered, but the standard investment manuals tell us that that company was incorporated under the laws of Delaware in 1937, with an authorized capitalization of $500,000. The broker-dealer section informs us that the brokerage house whose salesman solicited the purchase has never filed a registration as a broker or dealer to conduct an interstate business in over-the-counter securities. Reference to the Securities Violation files in which are contained the names, personal histories and descriptions of some 30,000 known professional securities swindlers reveals that the president of the brokerage company has previously been enjoined and indicted in several states as a result of fraudulent securities practices. This information is assembled and correlated and forwarded to the proper regional office with the suggestion that an immediate investigation be made. The Regional Administrator upon receipt of the information assigns the case to an attorney and an accountant for investigation. A visit is made to the offices of the brokerage concern and a request made to examine its books and records. At this point the accountant must take the lead. A detailed examination and analysis is made of the books and records of the brokerage company. Probably it will be necessary for the accountant to trace the funds received from the sale of the securities through several accounts until their final disposition can be determined. The books may reveal domination and control of the brokerage company by still another company. Thus the field of inquiry broadens. Finally, a detailed analysis is prepared. Accounts are broken down, fictitious writeups exposed, diversion of funds brought to light. It is upon such facts, developed by the accountant, that the attorney must evolve his theory of a case. In addition, the attorney must completely rely upon the ability of the accountant to support his findings and conclusions--both as to facts and applied principles--should the case be subsequently brought to trial, and the accountant subjected to a gruelling cross-examination.

The importance of the accountant in the enforcement work of the Securities and Exchange Commission varies, of course, with each particular set of facts. But I feel I can safely say that there are accounting problems in practically every major investigation we have undertaken. The Kopald-Quinn, Whitney, Interstate Hosiery and McKesson & Robbins cases are examples of cases where everything depended upon the thoroughness, accuracy and proper handling of questions of accounting.

In the Kopald-Quinn case the investors were induced to buy securities on an installment basis, delivery not to be made until fully paid for, at outrageously advanced prices which had been achieved by clever manipulation of the market. When everyone had signed up, the plug was pulled; support was withdrawn from the market, which caused it to drop to practically nothing. Everyone's account was closed out, leaving all that had been paid in to be enjoyed by the perpetrators of the scheme. Ample jail sentences have taken care of the principal actors in this particular case, and their prosecution has had the desired result of frightening others from similar enterprises.

A case of wide public interest was the recent Whitney case in New York. Richard Whitney, former president of the New York Stock Exchange, and one of the leading financial figures in the country, was discovered to have hypothecated to his own account customers' securities going into the millions. An immediate and thorough investigation by the Commission and the New York State authorities resulted in his conviction for fraud larceny, and the Commission, in a detailed report following a public hearing, proposed certain additional rules to the stock exchanges, looking toward the more immediate detection of such malefactions.

In the Interstate Hosiery case, an accountant employed by an accounting firm which had been retained by the company to make its audits for a period of years created out of his own imagination and carried forward certain items of profit which had no basis in fact. His motive is still a mystery although he is now serving time in a New York prison for his machinations. The responsibility of the accounting firm employing him presented an interesting question.

More recently, the McKesson & Robbins case excited nation-wide interest. Donald Coster, or Musica, a former convict who had completely concealed his identity and had built up an enviable reputation as a leader in business and finance, was discovered to have falsified the assets of a whole department in his business. With the assistance of his brothers and others, he set up on the books of McKesson & Hobbins false assets in the Crude Drug department running into many millions when no such assets were in existence. The necessity of filing a registration with the New York Stock Exchange and this Commission under the 1934 Act enmeshed him in a violation of federal statute and resulted in a prompt indictment of the principals and Coster's suicide.

About a year ago the Commission was party to a most interesting case in this very city. William P. Lawson, then Police Commissioner of Baltimore, was registered with the Commission as an over-the-counter broker and dealer. The Commission had occasion to examine into Lawson's business which disclosed that he and his associates had sold to investors approximately a quarter of a million dollars worth of securities in non-existent companies, ranging from whiskey distilleries to oil companies. In addition, thousands of dollars worth of negotiably securities deposition by customers to be held in safekeeping had been unlawfully hypothecated. The Securities and Exchange Commission sought and obtained an injunction in the Federal District Court, perpetually enjoining him from carrying on the illegal practices complained of.

Action instituted by the state as a result of our investigation resulted in the imposition of a substantial prison sentence.

These cases, selected from a large number, illustrate the variety of problems encountered in our enforcement work. Even from these brief factual statements, I am sure you can appreciate the extent of the accounting investigations involved. Many months of the most difficult accounting checking and analysis were necessary before the true facts could be ascertained in any of these cases, on which could be predicated some sort of legal proceeding.

You would perhaps be interested in some statistics which will show more graphically than any other way I can think of the extent of the Commission's enforcement work and some of its tangible results. At the present time the Commission has approximately 600 active investigations in progress. During the five years the Commission has been in existence and up until June 30th last, the end of the fiscal year, the commission has obtained permanent injunctions in 258 cases, against 623 defendants. During this same period 257 defendants have been convicted in 75 criminal cases. This figure, of course, does not include a large number of other defendants who are presently under indictment for violation of our statutes, but who have not yet been brought to trial.

Much more far-reaching, however, has been the salutary effect these investigations, injunctions and convictions have had upon the securities underworld. Many who have not personally been looked into have been so frightened by the vigorous program the Commission has been conducting, they have literally, like the Arabs, folded their tents and stolen silently away into the night. Lessen our vigilance, of course, and we would soon be back to where we started. I cannot believe, however, that any Congress in any administration would sponsor such a return to the days of old-time stock racketeering.

But to return to my theme, which is the parallel between your aims as members of this great accounting fraternity, and the philosophy behind the securities laws which Congress has charged our Commission with administering, we are both striving for but one thing--truth--truth in securities selling; truth in audits upon which the investors rely. Half-truths are not enough. We can all agree that false statements have no place in our modern business concepts. But is not the half-truth--the statement which in itself is not false, but which fails to supply other facts, which, read together, would give the statement made an entirely different connotation--even more vicious? The securities acts have stamped this as fraud. Applied to accounting certifications, it should hold a real significance for you.

Accounting is no longer just bookkeeping. It has become a profession--and particularly certified public accountants, stamped with the approval of some state board, as having passed the exacting qualifications both as to education and experience to entitle them to be recognized as such, have assumed the full status of a professional class in the public eye, with all the resulting emoluments, and what is more important, responsibilities.

Compared to law and medicine, accounting is of course a new profession--it has grown up approximately within our lifetime. It arose because of the ever-increasing complexity of American business. Small businesses, privately owned, gave place to vast enterprises, the ownership of which was scattered throughout the length and breadth of the land. Increasing problems of state and federal taxation necessitated the employment of experts versed in the principles of accounting, to suggest systems of bookkeeping and prepare returns which would reduce the tax burden as much as possible. During the prosperous days of the early part of this century, accountants would simply certify financial reports as "correct", and that is all there was to it. Accounting firms were employed by the management; they worked for the management; they attempted to show the management how best to conduct its affairs. Even after the corporate structures became more complicated, and the ownership more far-flung, so that there were investors who had no intimate knowledge of corporate affairs, accounting firms were still prone to assume that the owners of the capital stock not connected with the management could imagine all the factors which had entered into their certifying financial statements as "correct." All went well until the tide of business turned. Then came a time, in the early thirties, when a shareholder would receive a solvent-looking balance sheet, and before he received another he would read of the company's receivership or bankruptcy.

He could believe it. Had not some accounting firm certified that the financial statements were correct? Couldn't he take that at face value?

Over the years accounting had made considerable progress in reporting to shareholders, and the debacle of 1929 served to give additional impetus to this movement. Then came the passage of the federal securities acts as a further impetus. Designed to furnish the invester additional and more accurate information, and bring within their province sooner or later the securities of all large and most medium-sized businesses, whether traded on the exchanges or in the over-the-counter markets, it was but natural that the Securities and Exchange Commission should concern itself, almost from the outset, with proper methods of accounting procedure and certification. It is now required in the certification to state the scope of the audit made, and the opinion of the accountant regarding the financial statements made, and the procedure and principles of accounting followed by the company in arriving at those statements; that they "fairly reflect the application of accepted accounting practices"; and that in the balance sheets and profit and loss statements "there is no omission to state a material fact required to be stated therein or necessary to make the statements therein not misleading." The standard of reasonable investigation and check is adopted as the basis for such a certification--such language is contained in the statute itself. And the standard of reasonableness is defined as "that required of a prudent man in the management of his own property."

More significant, however, is the additional requirement that the audit shall be <u>independent</u>. It seems to me axiomatic that the auditor shall be completely free from bias, and devoid of any affiliation with the company whose accounts he is checking. An officer, director, partner, or even employee of the company is clearly not so qualified. It can even go further--an accounting firm, nominally independent, if a particular company is its sole client, or the principal source of its revenue, can under particular circumstances lose its aura of independence.

Another thing upon which I feel the investor has a right to rely iss that the work has been done by an <u>expert</u>. This in effect is saying that accounting has become a profession, and that the public has come to look on it as such. I do not mean to say that <u>all</u> the work can actually be done by the accountant who affixes his, or his firm's name, to the certification. Division of work is often a necessity. But that does not eliminate the heavy responsibility, because of the public's regard for it, which is placed on the accountant who is responsible for the work, and actually does the certifying. Although he may of necessity delegate to those under him some of the detail work, he cannot escape the responsibility of carefully analyzing and planning the necessary work which is to be done--he must outline a program, and see that it is followed out. In delegating a part of the work, he must be sure that person is entirely qualified to do that particular part of the job. He must oversee the work, and carefully check it when it is completed. His review of the work should be more than a perfunctory examination of the audits which have been prepared; he should see that the original work papers are carefully integrated with the financial statements, and in addition, from his position as the supervising expert, he should pass upon the adequacy of the audit work, and the integrity and clarity of the financial statements themselves.

The next thing which the public has a right to expect, and upon which the certifying accountant should satisfy himself, is that an audit of the business has been made. He must be sure that the financial position and earnings of the company are fairly stated. He must have a reasonably accurate knowledge of the business under examination. He must understand its administrative organization and personnel, in addition to its financial records, in order to know how much reliance he can reasonably place upon its internal system of check and control. He should be able to reasonably establish the general authenticity of the transactions and the accuracy of the company's records as to such transactions. It is undoubtedly a physical impossibility in audits of any size to actually verify each item. A system of test checking of the results shown by the records should be resorted to; checking the records against each other, checking them against physical facts, checking them against the records of affiliates and subsidiaries, checking them against information from independent third persons with whom the company has done business. This test checking would of course vary, depending on how much the certifying accountant is justified in relying on routine systems already in effect in the regular course of the company's business. He should thoroughly inspect the systems, satisfy himself that they are sound and reliable, and operating as they were designed to operate--only then is he justified in relying upon them.

Before certifying, the last thing the independent auditor should be sure of is that the examination and its results are such as to enable him to express an informed, expert opinion, and then state that opinion as clearly and fairly as possible. There are some cases where no certification should be given. If there is no adequate basis for judgment, if the company's books are set up in a fraudulent manner, if the accounting principles and procedure followed by the company are such that the accountant would have to take so many exceptions as to make his certification meaningless--he certainly should not certify.

At the other extreme are cases where he can clearly certify, and make his certification mean just what it says.

In the middle group--where he can certify, but must qualify--come the difficult cases. In these cases, the precise nature of his exceptions should be clearly and unequivocally stated. Limitations as to the scope of the audit, exceptions to accounting principles and procedures, alternate preferable procedures and the differences that would result, unusual features of the audit--all these are significant and important to those who will rely on the audit--and all should be stated.

These, I believe, are a few of the things that an independent accountant and auditor is expected to furnish the public in these modern times. Some of them may seem too advanced, impractical, Utopian. But I urge you they are not. They conform to the ideal of truthfulness which underlies all our securities legislation. They should express, in practice, the high public purpose to which this fraternity is dedicated.

#6 William W. Werntz

June 7, 1940

Independence and Cooperation

Abstract

The Chief Accountant of the SEC discusses the Commission's role in establishing a minimum standard by providing workable forms and rules, and to monitor compliance with the standards. Issuers are responsible for accuracy and truthfulness in financial statements. He also enumerates the functions of a controller, and the Independent public accountant. However, he notes that "cooperation" between the controller and the auditor is essential, especially in the area of internal control. His emphasis is on the distribution of responsibility in such a "cooperative" effort.

Since Judge Healy in early 1935 appeared before your New York Control and sought to answer the questions you had prepared about the new Form 10 and the even newer Form A-2, much has happened. Statements have now been filed with us for six years. We have had to discuss with many of you a great many accounting problems. We have sought your advice in reexamining our requirements and in

---

Address before the Regional Conference of The Controllers Institute of America.

seeking to improve them. We have "cashed in" on your offer of assistance and cooperation. We have sought also to fulfill our offer to discuss frankly with you your individually vexing problems at any time--before or after filing.

So much has been written and said in the past few years, and especially in the past few months, about the duties of controllers and public accountant that it is difficult to add wholly new thoughts or novel departures to the discussion. I have therefore sought to summarize, from our point of view, the distribution of responsibility in the joint effort to secure comprehensive and dependable financial statements for investors.

In effect, the two statutes, the Securities Act and the Securities Exchange Act, approach this objective by setting up a Commission with power to prescribe forms and rules of accounting and to review material filed, and by requiring publicly owned companies, whose securities are listed or to be sold in interstate commerce, to file financial statements under appropriate sanctions. Such statements must be certified by independent public accountants. This three-point approach led me to the title of this paper--"Independence and Cooperation."

Independence is defined as "freedom from control by others"; cooperation as "operation together for a common object." Both of these are needed, if the objective is to be obtained: independence, to insure freedom from intentional or unconscious bias, to give due weight to different factors, and to gain a cross-checking of results; cooperation, to secure economy and harmony of effort.

The Commission

I shall take first the role of the Commission. It seems to me that our contribution lies in the field of providing workable forms and rules, establishing thereby a minimum standard. In drafting the basic rules and forms the experience and knowledge of management and public accountants has been sought and to a very large extent incorporated in the final drafts. Examination of the statements filed is the next step. If specific requirements or generally accepted standards of practice have not been observed, it is our obligation to take exception by appropriate action. Unless the deficiency is remedied, or an apparent deficiency explained away, it is our duty to apply the statutory sanctions of stop-order, delisting and, in appropriate cases, reference for original proceedings. A by-product of the duty to prescribe standards is naturally the duty to foster their improvement by research, consultation with registrants and accountants, and adoption of new rules and requirements--sometimes incorporating advances already won, sometimes resolving conflicts, sometimes initiating improvements which have substantial support but which are impeded by inertia or special interest.

The Issuer

In any discussion of the responsibility for accuracy and truthfulness in financial statements, it is easy to overlook the fundamental fact that in the usual case it is the corporation itself which is selling securities or furnishing information for others to rely upon. This fact is underscored in Section 11 of the Securities Act which, in specific language, denies to the issuer the defense of reasonable belief in the truth of the statements that is accorded those individuals who sign the statement or who as experts participate in their preparation. However, except for an issuer who is a natural person, and they have been exceedingly rare, it is the officers and directors, individually and collectively, who must see to it that the issuer's interests are protected and its obligations fulfilled by financial statements which are free from misstatements and misleading omissions. This obligation of the management and directors does not spring from these Acts but is fundamental in all corporate law. Realistically, however, the average director, as well as most of the officers, is not in a position to say that particular statements are in fact accurate and complete in their reflection of the business. Gross misstatements might be apparent to him from his general knowledge of the business, or by reason of inconsistency with previous statements he has seen. Or, familiarity with matters directly in his charge might uncover misstatements or omissions in a particular field. But here as elsewhere the greatest reliance is placed on the corporate machinery for the production of information about the business. This department is ordinarily the peculiar province of the controller.

It is not without reason, therefore, that the Securities Act requires the signature of the controller or principal accounting officer and that annual reports which must be signed by an authorized representative of the issuer, are more and more frequently signed by controllers. In practice as well as in theory the division of duties within the company throws upon the officer in charge of accounts and accounting the burden of writing an informative and accurate history of the business. As Judge Healy once said, "...it cannot be denied that the controller is the man who holds the key to sound corporate accounting. It is his system upon which adequate corporate reporting ultimately rests." I do not think that controllers have in any way sought to shift this burden. The atmosphere of nearly every conference I have had, including those which were highly argumentative, has been: "These are my accounts; I am proud of them; but if you have any doubts or question any of the principles, let's discuss them; I want to present the most informative and most accurate picture that I can."

In principle, this is the basis upon which Congress and the investing public have come to rely more and more on the controller's work. Such reliance, however, assumes the existence of certain conditions, and raises certain problems in practice. These I should like to discuss briefly.

What is a controller. Because of its newness the business and legal position of the controller is by no means settled. In one company, the controller is indeed the chief accounting officer; in another his functions may be narrow and his authority slight or ineffective. In defining what his position should be, opinions differ. Some ascribe to him a position wholly managerial in viewpoint, others would divorce him from actual management, so that he becomes a reporter and a critic of the way in which management has exercised its discretion. Some ascribe to him special duties and responsibilities to stockholders and creditors, others maintain that he has no such special duties and relations, that he is an employee of the corporation, which alone has duties and responsibilities to outsiders. While it is too soon to predict the outcome of these conflicting proposals, some of the essentials to any solution seem clear.

First, the controller or person charged with responsibility for the accounts should be an officer. His duties and powers should be so described in the by-laws that his position will not be subject to arbitrary modification or emasculating interpretation by his co-officers. He should be an elected officer, or one appointed, not by some other officer, but by the directors.

Second, his duties and his authority should be commensurate with his responsibility, in order that he may have at hand the tools with which to work.

Third, incompatible functions or duties should not be combined in his office. Inevitably a person who is directly charged with the administration of particular operations and is responsible for their profitable conduct is not in an unprejudiced position when he comes to record and report on the results of his department.

Fourth, he should be independent of other management officials in his determination of how the records should be kept, what checks and safeguards are necessary for reliable accounts, what accounting principles should be followed, and, perhaps most important of all, in his determination of what the actual results of operation are. To secure such independence, his general reports should be rendered to the board without change by other officials. To my mind this concept of his duties is not at all incompatible with requirements for rendering service to management by the preparation of special reports, nor with the obvious necessity of cooperation and consultation of mutual problems. What must be maintained, it seems to me, is the finality of his considered judgment on the matters mentioned, subject of course to the review of the board of directors.

Fifth, the controller's staff should be adequate. This is not of the same order as the first four points, but it is not less important. The very increase in the scope of the controller's duties carries with it a possibility of danger that only the controller himself may properly guard against. I have in mind the possibility that in discharging his manifold duties he may become personally so engrossed in the details of his numerous activities or be occupied with so many varied roles as to lose sight of the forest. As an executive officer one duty that cannot be minimized is that of integrating the various portions of his work so that the whole may be harmonious. In some recent cases we have found that this danger is only too real.

The Independent Public Accountant

The problem of distributing responsibility between the issuer and its controller on the one hand and the certifying accountant on the other is often summed up in the question: "Whose balance sheet is it?" This has been the subject of much discussion. Accountants who take the position that the balance sheet is that of the company have frequently pointed for support to the opinion of the Commission in the Interstate Hosiery Mills case where it was said:

> "The fundamental and primary responsibility for the accuracy of information filed with the Commission and disseminated among the investors rests upon management. Management does not discharge its obligations in this respect by the employment of independent public accountants however reputable. Accountants' certificates are required not as a substitute for management's accounting of its stewardship, but as a check upon that accounting."

Others have urged that the public accountant often draws up the statements, sometimes indeed supervises or carries out much of the detailed work of adjusting or even preparing the underlying records, and that as a result the statements are his. I think the problem cannot be intelligently discussed in terms of such a question, which is at best ambiguous, and which fails to state the real issues--who is responsible for misstatements and omissions and what is the extent of that responsibility. While it is obviously possible for an independent accountant to start from scratch and prepare statements which represent throughout his own judgment and his own appraisal of conditions, this is not frequent. Ordinarily, the company's internal accountants have drafted the statements or are responsible for the raw data that the independent accountant recasts in the form of statements. In these cases, the original decisions are those of the issuer and its internal accountants, not those of the certifying accountant who operates in a reviewing capacity but who, I am told, sometimes challenges those decisions. It is this usual case that I think is contemplated when the statute speaks of "certified financial statements", for then the principle of cross-check by separate and independent examination is in full operation.

Placing responsibility for the statements upon the issuer does not in any way lessen the obligations of the accountant. Other paragraphs in the Interstate opinion, not quite so frequently quoted by accountants, make this abundantly clear. The representations made by the accountant who permits his name to accompany financial statements included in reports to the Commission are to my mind these:

First, that he is a public accountant in good standing and entitled to practice as such in the place of his residence or principal place of business; that he has met those requirements of training and experience which are prescribed by law; and that he is therefore entitled to represent himself as one whose profession gives authority to a statement made by him.

Second, that he has made an audit which in scope and procedures followed would be recognized by members of his profession, generally, as an adequate basis upon which to rest a professional opinion as to the fairness with which the statements represent the business, and that except as specifically noted otherwise there has been no omission of any procedure which independent accountants would ordinarily employ for the purpose of presenting comprehensive and dependable financial statements.

Third, that he has expressed his professional opinion as frankly and fairly as he can.

There is one class of cases in which the significance of the cross-check by issuer and accountant becomes particularly plain. Occasionally, it will be found that statements have been prepared by the accountant and that the accountant has been charged by the company with the duty of supervising its accounting system and selecting and applying its accounting principles--in brief, the primary accounting duties of the management have been delegated for performance to an outside accountant. Perhaps the company's employees may perform some of the physical work of preparing the records, and in a general way the officials may review the final statements, but essentially the accountant is doing the work and making the decisions ordinarily attributed to the officers of a company. To my mind there is grave doubt whether statements accompanied by a certificate of the accountant involved would satisfy the statutory standard of certified financial statements. If the work be attributed to the accountant as an independent public accountant, then the obligations of the issuer have not been discharged; if the management be considered to have discharged its duties through delegation to a competent agent, the accountant, then the requirement of certification by an independent public accountant is not met, for the same accountant cannot be two men, nor can he play both roles. I do not think this issue has ever been as sharply raised as the hypothetical case cited; but in not a few instances the line of separation has been blurred. Nearly the same point is raised by the grosser cases involving lack of independence on the part of the certifying accountant. The purpose of the statutory requirement of independence is clear. As opposed to subservience, there is no question that it is essential, if any true cross-checking is to be obtained. In short, the greatest benefit for the issuer and for the persons who are asked to rely on the certified statements will not be obtained unless the auditor's approach is completely objective, free from bias, and devoid of any entangling affiliation.

Cooperation

I have sought to outline briefly the roles assigned to each of the participants in the joint quest of comprehensive and dependable financial statements--the issuer, the independent certifying accountant, and the Commission. I have alluded briefly to some of the ways in which the cooperation of issuers and accountants has been sought and found valuable by the Commission in the discharge of its duties. There remains the question of cooperation between the issuer, usually in the person of the controller, and the public accountant. As to this, I would like to point out a few specific problems in the solution of which effective cooperation would prove most helpful in reaching the joint objective.

Recent events have resulted in the glittering generality that investors should be educated as to the limitations inherent in certified statements. For a considerable number of years accountatns have sought to spread information as to the character of the work they do in the course of a normal audit, its advantages and its limitations. I have also seen attempts by companies to do this. Included in one annual report was a brief description of what the management had asked the accountants to do and a non-technical description of the nature of the work which the accountants did, both with a view to aiding the reader to understand the purpose of the annual audit and its significance. Since investor education is vital to a sound financial and investment community, cooperation to that end is essential and practicable.

Recent events have also resulted in a great deal of discussion on how to prevent gross irregularities, such as those that appeared in the McKesson, Interstate, Monroe Loan, and similar cases. The problem has been debated before professional societies of accountants, controllers, and others, in educational circles and in accounting forums. Many specific suggestions have been made of procedures designed to prevent the recurrence of such irregularities. Some of these have been incorporated in reports by professional accounting societies and the New York Stock Exchange. the Commission itself is engaged in preparing a general report based upon the McKesson case, which will likewise include specific recommendations.

Nowhere to my mind does the possibility of close cooperation between controller and public accountant appear more clearly than in designing an efficient method for recording and analyzing the transactions of a company in such a manner as to insure the dependability of the accounting records. To this problem the controller brings primarily, it seems to me, his intimate knowledge of the company's way of doing business, the personalities involved, and a thousand and one other details of the particular company. To this problem the independent accountant brings an objective outside point of view tempered by his experience with other clients and by his knowledge of what he needs in order to be able to give an informed opinion as to the financial condition and the results of operations. The decision as to what is necessary to insure reliable reporting in the particular case must rest ultimately with the controller. However, since the public accountant must in a large corporation rely extensively on the information produced by the accounting system, one of his first duties in making his examination of the company's affairs is to review anew the accounting system of the company and its methods of insuring the reliability of its records. This review, since it encompasses not only a study of the procedures designed but also the actual way in which those procedures have been carried out and the results which they have produced, should result in an intelligent appraisal of the company's methods. This in turn should serve as a basis for further cooperation between the controller and the independent accountant looking toward the strengthening of weak points that have developed, toward the introduction of new procedures to care for new conditions, and toward the general streamlining of the company's accounting methods.

In recent months this subject of internal check and control ahs received so much consideration that an historical digression may not be out of place. Present interest in the subject is so lively that the unitiated might believe that internal check and control is a new discovery. However, a volume published in 1892 reproduced an audit program of one David Chadwick, F.C.A., an accountant of fifty years' practical experience. One item in the list of twenty-two on this gentleman's program is perhaps of interest, since it advised the auditor to "ascertain and take note of the general system upon which the books are constructed, and the plan of checking the correctness of the accounts paid."

It is obvious that professional auditors in examining the accounts of modern industrial empires cannot practicably scrutinize all the numerous transactions. The question then is not whether independent public accountants may rely upon internal control, but what is internal control, how is it set up, how may it be strengthened, how can management periodically ascertain whether it is being faithfully carried out, and, most important in the preparation of certified statements, how can the auditor ascertain whether in a particular case there is justification for relying on it. Cooperation of the controller and the auditor in this field is perhaps more essential than in any other, for, if internal control fails, the financial statements and the opinion of the auditors are of doubtful value. Designing a system of internal control, checking that system to test its efficiency, and revising it to meet shifting conditions are peculiarly within your own province. Subjecting it to an impartial independent and expert analysis is peculiarly within the province of the independent accountant. His is the duty of determining by actual observation that the internal check and control is adequate. He must watch the system work and he must test the paper results it produced against the physical facts so far as he is capable, and so far as that is practicable.

Unless he has done this, he is not justified in accepting its product, and a good part of the value of his opinion is lost. Designing the system and maintaining it in good working order seems to me a joint undertaking of the internal accountant and the outside accountant to assure that under modern complex business conditions comprehensive and dependable financial statements may be obtained for investors and stockholders.

No discussion of the relation between controllers and public accountants would be adequate without some mention of cooperation in the planning of the audit. At the outset it seems to me that direct field-contact between the controller and the accounting partner in charge of the engagement should be much more extensive than has apparently been true in many cases. Frank discussion with the controller and direct observation should enable the experienced partner to appraise the particular controller and the system he controls. It should also aid in eliminating friction and misunderstanding. In short, the product should be an effective audit program fashioned to fit the particular case, utilizing internal reports and internally prepared schedules and anlyses to the full extent practicable and reasonable and substituting intelligent checking for expensive and laborious duplication of the work of the internal audit staff so far as may be consistent with the auditor's professional responsibilities. I need not discuss specific details--that has been well done elsewhere and in individual cases is a subject of some difference of opinion. But the principle is clear.

Nor should the atmosphere of cooperation be confined to the period of the audit. If the auditor is appointed or elected early in the year, as he by all means should be, there is a sound basis for continuous cooperation in the solution of difficult and unusual accounting problems faced by the company.

A final problem in the preparation of dependable financial statements and in the administration of the registration requirements under the Securities Exchange Act of 1934 is the determination of the most appropriate fiscal closing date. The concept of the natural business year is not new to members of your organization. Nevertheless the problem of concentration of fiscal closings at December 31 is so acute and so important both to controllers and public accountants that I feel justified in discussing it with you who should be in the best position to do something to improve the situation.

The most recent compilation of registrants with the Commission shows that of nearly 2500 annual reports filed with us, approximately eighty per cent report on the calendar year basis, about five per cent close their fiscal years at the end of June, and two and one-half per cent at the end of each of the months of January, March, September, and October. The heavy concentration at the end of December descends on the Commission in the last week of April and the first week in May and necessitates the employment of temporary clerks merely to record and file the reports. We do not employ extra examiners to review the reports as received but schedule the work over the entire year. As a result, the examining staff is constantly employed but some of your reports may be in our hands for many months before they are reached for review.

About ten per cent of the calendar year registrants ask for extensions of time in which to file their reports. Sometimes the reason given is that the firm's independent accountants have not had time to complete the audit on which their certificate is based and sometimes the reason offered is that we have just issued a deficiency notice regarding last year's statement which will require a revision in the statement then in preparation as well as in the offending report. We are sympathetic to such requests, in the latter circumstance especially, but we are powerless to improve the underlying difficulty without employing temporary help to clear the log jam or perhaps by making rules requiring certain industries to file reports on a natural business year basis. Neither of these methods appeals to me as a proper means of dealing with the problem.

Some of the public accountants who testified as expert witnesses in the McKesson & Robbins hearings indicated a reluctance on their part to urge adoption of the natural business year more vigorously than they have in the past because of a feeling that their motive appeared self-serving. All public accountants agree that the adoption of natural closing dates by business generally would improve conditions in the profession by spreading the work and thus relieving mental and physical strain now prevalent in the first quarter of the year and of still more importance it would provide continuity of employment for a better trained staff. I am convinced that improvement along these lines would be of lasting benefit to the client as well as to the accounting profession.

I sincerely believe that this is one of the most important problems to be faced in carrying out your avowed purpose of observing "the highest ethical standards in corporate accounting practice in the preparation of reports of financial and operating conditions of corporations to their directors, stockholders, and other parties at interest, in such manner that all concerned may know the actual conditions in so far as such reports may assist in the determination thereof." With your increasing authority in corporation affairs, the responsibility naturally falls to you to convince your companies' officers and directors that December 31 is not a mandatory closing date.

#7 Andrew J. Cavanaugh

June 7, 1941

Standards of Disclosure in Financial Statements

Abstract

Cavanaugh cites various and widely diverse practices as examples of why uniformity is needed in regard to reporting on major accounting questions. He also comments that accountancy tends to rely on precedent rather than on the scientific method. The Commission's approach to uniformity is advanced by the issuance of Regulation S-X in 1940. Prior to that, the opinions of the Chief Accountant, in the form of Accounting Series Releases, was an attempt to establish some uniformity. Specifically mentioned is ASR No. 4, in which it is stated that the lack of "substantial authoritative support" for a principle in the preparation of statements will, if material, lead to a presumption of the statements being misleading.

Being a fellow of the Virginia Society of Public Accountants I am happy to have the privilege of participating in this round table discussion of "Standards of Disclosure in Financial Statements." Your attendance at such meetings evidences a determination to explore the full extent of your responsibilities, and also indicates a desire to direct attention beyond the accounts

---

Address before the Middle Atlantic States Accounting Conference.

themselves in order to obtain a fuller realization of the implications of accounts in present day society.

It would be idle for us to pretend that corporate reports in the past have always been truthful and revealing. There are, of course, outstanding exceptions in this field, but too often accounting practices have been employed for the purpose of concealing rather than of revealing the true situation to the investing public. Then again, much of the concealment has been due to a certain secretiveness on the part of corporation executives, based upon the theory that only their competitors would benefit from such disclosure as might be made by informative financial statements. It is my understanding that in the past scarcely more than sixty percent of the companies listed on national securities exchanges revealed to their stockholders anything more about the operating results of their companies than some general figures with respect to their operating income. Although, of course, in some instances there may be validity in this claim for privacy, there can be no doubt that in the majority of cases the idea cannot be seriously entertained that to give a fair and full report of corporate assets and profits will give an unfair advantage to competitors. Certainly, except in unusual instances, where such a claim is insisted upon one may well doubt the desirability of encouraging public investment in the enterprise.

Without adequate corporate disclosures the basis of stable investment is, of course, lacking. If the figure given as earnings in an income statement represents other than true earnings or includes without disclosure a non-recurring profit, the uselessness of estimating market value in terms of a ratio to earnings is only too apparent. And market values, to reflect accurately corporate success rather than mere market activity, must bear some relationship to earnings.

The Securities Act of 1933 and the Securities Exchange Act of 1934 give the Commission a great opportunity to deal with this problem so as to evolve standards of corporate reporting that shall be both adequate and consistent. As you are aware, one of the main objectives of these two Acts is to make available to investors significant information about issuers of corporate securities. This is accomplished in part by requiring issuers of new securities and issuers of listed securities to file registration statements and periodic reports with the Commission and the exchanges. One of the most important parts of these filings is the financial information about the enterprise.

To insure that reasonably comparable principles be followed in statements filed under the Securities Act of 1933 and the Securities Exchange Act of 1934 these Acts give the Commission extensive control, not only over the form of financial statements but also over the principles to be followed in dealing with many types of financial facts. These Acts grant the Commission the power by rules and regulations "...to prescribe the form or forms in which required information shall be set forth, the items or details to be shown in the balance sheet and earning statement, and the methods to be followed in the preparation of accounts, in the appraisal or valuation of assets and liabilities, in the determination of depreciation and depletion, in the differentiation of recurring and non-recurring income, in the differentiation of investment and operating income, and in the preparation, where the Commission deems it necessary or desirable, of consolidated balance sheets or income accounts of any person directly or indirectly controlling or controlled by the issuer, or any person under direct or indirect common control with the issuer....."

At the time these Acts became law, accounting had developed to such a point that it was believed feasible to prescribe forms that in large part asked only for disclosure of some of the more significant principles upon which the statements were based, and for a disclosure of a certain amount of information believed to be of particular importance to investors. The form of presentation, the method of description, the inclusion of information beyond the minimum, and the fundamental responsibility for the quality of the statements were problems left on the shoulders of the issuers and their officers. In addition, it was required that independent accountants make a review of the accounting procedures followed by the registrant and its subsidiaries, and by appropriate measures satisfy themselves that such procedures were being followed, and state clearly their opinion in respect of the financial statements of and the accounting principles and procedures followed by the registrant and its subsidiaries.

The success of the application of the basic principle underlying the two Acts that complete and fair disclosure of material facts should be made, is dependent on no one more than on the accountant, and it would be unfair not to acknowledge the influence which the accounting profession has had in the improvement of conditions within its scope, but it would be fatuous to assume that because the profession exists there is no occasion to be critical of results produced and no need of taking stock of what remains to be done.

Granted that many people are unable to read statements and certificates intelligently, it seems to me that the aim of the accounting profession should be to make those statements and certificates as clear and unambiguous as their technical nature permits. Financial statements which conform to conventions and customs are not adequate if, in fact, they serve to conceal or fail to bring to light financial conditions or results which an intelligent investor needs to know in order to form a judgment. Certificates are not adequate if they evade expression of opinion regarding accounting practices which are not sound. I question how far an accountant may, in good conscience, resort to a multitude of notes attached to statements to explain unsound, questionable, or irregular practices where clarity of statement and of opinion would be better obtained by showing as a part of the statements themselves, the adjustments necessary to bring those statements into accord with sound practice.

However, experience with statements filed under these two Acts indicated that the profession had some way to go to meet its full responsibility. For example: The financial data of a registrant as originally presented by it included twenty-six pages of notes pertaining to the balance sheet and profit and loss statement. The certificate of the accountants included numerous qualifications and exceptions. The information presented in supplementary notes and in the accountants' qualifications was so complicated that it was next to impossible to get any adequate understanding of the facts. It appeared that in this case adequate disclosure could not be made without some adjustment in the financial statements themselves. To overcome this condition, the various financial statements were amended to give effect to many of the adjustments referred to in the accountants' certificate and in the footnotes. This was accomplished by reflecting in a columnar statement the figures as per the company's books, footnote adjustments, and amounts if adjusted as explained in footnotes. Through the footnote adjustments in columns 2 and 4 of the balance sheet, surplus was reduced from approximately $126,000,000 to a deficit of approximately $27,700,000 as at December 31, 1935. The final statements as drawn contained a large number of footnotes and the accountants' certificate was long and complicated, but it was felt that it was considerably simpler and more understandable to the investor than it was before the statements were required to be changed.

In one case a listed company reduced the net book value of its fixed assets as of a particular fiscal date from approximately $19,000,000 to a nominal amount of $1.00. Since that time it has been the policy of the company to maintain the fixed assets then in existence at a net book value of $1.00 and to charge all provisions for renewals and replacements to profit and loss. The company capitalizes the cost of new property other than replacements of the old property and accrues depreciation on the newly capitalized property at what appear to be reasonable rates. In footnotes appended to the financial statements it was disclosed that depreciation claimed for income tax purposes during the period from 1933 to 1937 exceeded by approximately $3,000,000 the amount charged to profit and loss over the same period for renewals and replacements of old property and depreciation of new property.

In another case a note was appended to the profit and loss statement of the registrant, indicating that in accordance with resolutions of the Board of Directors, losses on disposition of non-operating properties and investments for the year, aggregating $134,000, which in the absence of such resolutions would have been charged to Profit and Loss or Earned Surplus Accounts, were charged to Capital Surplus--Appropriated for Losses on Disposition of Capital Assets.

In still another case the following note was appended to the balance sheet of a registrant: (X) Company, (a subsidiary) also acquired 100,000 shares of the capital stock of (Y) Company (its parent) in exchange for 1,501,000 shares of its capital stock, which investment is carried at the par value of said 1,501,000 shares, $1,501,000, and is included in the item 'Investments in securities of affiliates'. The equity of (X) Company in the net assets of (Y) Company as shown by the books of the latter amounted to $111,065.16 at December 31st. The accountants did not comment in their certificate with respect to security valuation. I might add that (Y) Company carried the investment in (X) Company at $10,000.

I could cite a number of similar cases, but I shall not test your patience further because I am sure you will perceive from the above why the policy followed by the Commission at the outset was not entirely successful. A substantial number of the reports filed with the Commission revealed the application of a wide variety of accounting principles and practices, of more or less general acceptance but often highly contradictory, and the accompanying certificates showed that in many areas of accounting there exist nearly diametrically opposed theories.

It seems to me that one of the reasons why accountancy has not more nearly fulfilled its possibilities is the tendency to rely on precedent rather than on the scientific method. My observation of statements leads me to the conclusion that so-called standards in the field of accounting have been too frequently determined by what actually prevails in practice. Once a method has been followed there is a tendency to accept it without question or hesitancy. It becomes the proper thing to do because it has been done before or someone else is doing it. Too often it is accepted without inquiry as to the possible consequences. As a result it gradually develops into an accepted practice.

The need, therefore, for the development of uniform standards and practice in major accounting questions is clear. It is also clear that to be of service in the improvement of financial reporting, any statement of principle must avoid the pitfalls inherent in generalities.

As a result of the partial failure of its original policy the Commission found it necessary to take measures to implement the provisions of the statute dealing with the form and content of financial statements and with the accounting principles reflected therein. As a first step there was instituted a few years ago a series of accounting opinions of the Chief Accountant, which express a few standards as to principles which, it is believed, are accepted by a majority of accountants. The approach must, of course, be cautious, but I am convinced that accountants as a whole regret that standards are not more exactly defined. You are doubtless familiar with these opinions, some of which I shall refer to later. One issued in April 1938, I believe is worth repeating here since it suggests, in a broad way, the Commission's present approach to the problem of establishing uniform accounting procedure. It is Number 4 in the series of public releases announcing these opinions.

> "In cases where financial statements filed with this Commission pursuant to its rules and regulations under the Securities Act of 1933 or the Securities Exchange Act of 1934 are prepared in accordance with accounting principles for which there is no substantial authoritative support, such financial statements will be presumed to be misleading or inaccurate despite disclosures contained in the certificate of the accountant or in footnotes to the statements provided the matters involved are material. In cases where there is a difference of opinion between the Commission and the registrant as to the proper principles of accounting to be followed, disclosure will be accepted in lieu of correction of the financial statements themselves only if the points involved are such that there is substantial authoritative support for the practices followed by the registrant and the position of the Commission has not previously been expressed in rules, regulations or other official releases of the Commission, including the published opinions of its Chief Accountant."

While I believe it is recognized that the responsibility for furnishing fair and adequate information regarding a corporation is primarily the obligation of management, the independent accountant assumes the responsibility for reviewing the records and the reports of management for the purpose of expressing his professional opinion as to the fairness of the representations made in the financial statements.

It is apparent, therefore, that Release No. 4 is a prescription for curing some of the accounting ills. It is an effort to preserve and make effective those practices recognized as sound. It flows from the desire to improve and assist the profession in maintaining a high standard by adjusting where adjusting is required to reflect the application of sound practice, and disclosing where disclosing is required to reflect those pertinent facts and events essential to a clear understanding of the statements. Unless this is accomplished the aim of the profession will be defeated. For it is one of the primary purposes of disclosure to reveal such information regarding the condition and operations of a business as will enable a prospective investor to form intelligent conclusions regarding its affairs. Obviously it is the very availability of such information that distinguishes a good from a mediocre or poor report. The quality of the information which the average investor receives in forming his judgment of values becomes a matter of importance because it is intended to bring home to him better knowledge of what he is doing and to furnish him with better norms by which to estimate the character and quality of the security he is buying, holding or selling, a task which the accounting profession must work toward to accomplish its aims.

In considering when and where to make disclosure, care should be taken that the accountants' certificate contains a clear disclosure of the facts required therein, that the financial statements have been drawn to include such disclosure as is appropriate, that supplemental schedules which are submitted, when this method of disclosure is necessary to bring out the desired facts, are not too complex, that the required footnotes to the financial statements are not too vague and indefinite but do explain the point clearly, and that meaningless and unnecessary notes which tend to obscure rather than disclose are omitted. The inclusion of numerous comments concerning items of little or no importance, with only a few that are material, is confusing rather than enlightening and tends to bury those items that have real significance. Furthermore, no amount of contradiction in footnotes can avoid the effect of improperly applied principles in the preparation of the statements themselves. Footnotes should contain explanatory material, but not qualifications and exceptions which of course belong in the certificate itself.

As you are aware, considerable effort has been made in the past to stimulate the recognition and adoption of some basic standards of disclosure in financial statements. Accounting texts and publications by the American Institute of Accountants and other groups have advocated, recommended, and suggested certain disclosures which should be made, but the adoption of these suggestions was left to the voluntary action of the practitioners and their clients, which, in the absence of definite requirements, naturally resulted in the lack of uniformity in disclosing pertinent financial information. These efforts, however, were important contributions to the development of standards and paved the way for subsequent advances.

Standards of disclosure may be said to be concepts which are not finished concepts, but are still evolving. When the Commission promulgated its rules governing the financial statements required to be filed under the two Acts, a forward step was taken in establishing certain standards as requirements. As a part of its program of seeking simplification of its accounting requirements, after a comprehensive study the Commission, in February of last year, made certain changes in, and combined under one pamphlet, the rules and regulations applicable to various registration statement and annual report forms, and designated it as "Regulation S-X", which sets up standards of disclosure in financial statements required by such forms.

While most of you are probably familiar with these standards, for the benefit of those who may not have had occasion to refer to Regulation S-X, I shall make a general review, particularly of those standards which are most frequently omitted in financial statements, and of others which I believe it is important to repeat to impress upon members of the profession the fact that they are recognized as actual standards. First, I shall review the disclosure requirements with respect to certain of the items required to be reflected in the balance sheets of commercial and industrial companies. Rule 5-02 under the indicated sub-paragraphs provides that, among other things there shall be disclosed:

(2) The basis of determining the amount at which marketable securities are carried, and parenthetically or otherwise, the aggregate cost and aggregate amount on the basis of current market quotations.

(6) The major classes of inventory, the basis of determining the amount, and, to the extent practicable, a general indication of the method of determining the "cost" or "market": e.g., "average cost" or "first-in, first-out".

(11) The basis of determining the amount of "Other Security Investments" and parenthetically or otherwise, if available, the aggregate amount on the basis of market quotations.

(19) The method used in amortizing debt discount and expense and;

(20) What provisions have been made for writing off "Commissions and Expense on Capital Shares."

(30) Whether "Other Long-Term Debt" is secured and the total amount by years of the respective maturities for the succeeding five years.

(33) For each class of "Capital Shares" the title of issue, the number authorized and outstanding, the capital share liability thereof, the dollar amount subscribed but unissued and subscriptions receivable thereon, and, unless required to be shown as a deduction from surplus, the amount reacquired.

(34) As to surplus, the rule requires that it be segregated into the usual categories of earned, paid-in, other capital surplus, and also surplus arising from revaluation of assets. This is subject to the exception that if in the accounts separate balances for these classes of surplus are not maintained the unsegregated items may be stated in one amount, in which case the account titles used shall be such as will indicate the general type of surplus included therein. Furthermore, if undistributed earnings of subsidiaries are included, the amount shall be disclosed.

To supplement certain of the major items reflected in the balance sheet, Rule 5-04 requires that schedules be furnished to disclose the additions and deductions during the period, and in some cases, other pertinent information.

Turning to the profit and loss statement--The disclosure requirements are in general similar to those recommended by the American Institute. Rule 5-03 requires disclosure of the usual major items--Sales, Cost of Sales, Other Operating Expenses, Selling, General and Administrative Expenses, and, in reasonable detail, the financial and miscellaneous items of income and expense. In addition, it requires disclosure in the statement, or in a note therein referred to, of the amounts and the basis of determining such amounts, of inventories used in computing cost of goods sold and, where profits or losses on securities are reflected, a statement of the principles followed in determining the cost of securities sold, e.g., average cost or first-in and first-out.

The details of such items as depreciation, taxes, maintenance and repairs, rents and royalties, and the amount of dividends received from subsidiaries, together with the equity in earnings in such subsidiaries, are required to be disclosed in the two schedules prescribed by Rules 12-16 and 12-17.

Next, I should like to cite some of the further disclosures which are required to give a clearer understanding of the accounting policies pursued and of those significant items of financial information which are not usually indicated in the face of the statements. Perhaps I should mention, before proceeding further, that the Commission, realizing that simplification, where feasible, contributes to a clarification, particularly in those cases where notes bulk large, adopted Rule 3-08 which suggests but does not require that footnotes be collected in an integrated statement of accounting policies to which appropriate cross reference from the pertinent captions may easily be made. Continuing, there is Rule 3-18 which provides that, if present in the accounts, there shall be disclosed in the balance sheet or in notes thereto:

(a) The amounts of assets mortgaged, pledged, or otherwise subject to a lien, and the obligations secured. However, this requirement need not be followed with respect to assets (other than current assets and securities) given as security for funded debt.

(b) If practicable, the amount of any significant intercompany profits or losses included in inventory.

(c) The facts and amounts with respect to any default in principal, interest, sinking fund, or redemption provisions of any issue of securities.

(d) (1) If preferred shares are callable, the date or dates and the amount per share and in total at which such shares are callable.

(2) The arrears in cumulative dividends per share and in total for each class of shares.

(3) The preferences on involuntary liquidation, if other than par or stated value, and when the excess is significant.

(i) the difference between the aggregate preference on involuntary liquidation and the aggregate par or stated value;

(ii) a statement that this difference, plus any arrears in dividends, exceeds the sum of the par or stated value of the junior capital shares and the surplus, if such is the case;

(iii) a statement as to the existence, or absence, of any restrictions upon surplus growing out of the fact that upon involuntary liquidation the preference of the preferred shares exceeds its par or stated value;

and lastly,

(e) A brief statement as to significant contingent liabilities.

Turning again to the profit and loss statement, there is Rule 3-19 which provides that, if present in the accounts, there shall be disclosed in the profit and loss statement or in notes thereto:

(a) The basis of taking profits on instalment sales into income;

(b) The amount, if practicable, of any significant inter-company profits or losses included in the statement; and

(c) The policy followed during the period with respect to--(1) and (2). The provision for depreciation, depletion and obsolescence of physical properties and/or intangibles, or reserves created in lieu thereof, including the method and, if practicable, the rates used;

(3) The accounting treatment for maintenance, repairs, renewals, and betterments, and

(4) The adjustment of the accumulated reserves for depreciation, depletion and obsolescence, amortization, or reserves in lieu thereof, at the time properties are retired or otherwise disposed of.

A further disclosure is required by Rule 3-07 which provides that a statement shall be given in a note to the appropriate statement of any change in accounting principle or practice, or any significant retroactive adjustment of the accounts of prior years made at the beginning of or during any period covered by the profit and loss statement, and, if the change or adjustment substantially affects proper comparison with the preceding fiscal period, the necessary explanation.

Then there are the rules governing disclosure in connection with consolidated or combined statements. For instances, Rule 4-04 requires that the principle adopted in determining the inclusion and exclusion of subsidiaries in each consolidated and combined balance sheet, and whether there have been included or excluded any persons (naming them) not similarly treated in the corresponding statements for the preceding year, shall be stated in a note to the respective balance sheet.

Similarly, Rule 4-05 (a) calls for a statement, in a note to each consolidated balance sheet, of any difference between the investment in subsidiaries consolidated, as shown by the parent's books, and the parent's equity in the net assets of such subsidiaries, as shown by the books of the latter, and the disposition made of such difference in preparing the consolidated statements, naming the balance sheet captions and stating the amounts included in each.

Not wishing to tire you with too much detail, I shall pass over a number of the rules and refer at this point to a few of the additional disclosures called for in several of the Accounting Series releases.

In Release No. 15, dealing with the quasi-reorganizations, the opinion is expressed that in addition to designating the point of time from which earned surplus dates, any statement or showing of earned surplus should, in order to provide additional disclosure of the occurrence and the significance of the quasi-reorganization, indicate for at least three years the total amount of the deficit and any charges that were made to capital surplus in the course of such reorganization which would otherwise have been required to be made against income or earned surplus.

In connection with quasi-reorganizations the question will occasionally arise as to what disclosure is necessary for the investor when a legally permissible course of action is not in accord with sound accounting. I have reference to the case where, under a company's charter and the applicable state of law, it is permissible to effect this type of reorganization without approval of stockholders. Accounting Series Release No. 16 deals with this problem and concludes with the opinion that it is necessary to make a complete disclosure of all of the attendant facts and circumstances and their effect on the company's financial position in each balance sheet and surplus statement filed thereafter. For a description of the details required to be reflected in the balance sheet I refer you to this release.

Moving on the accountants' certificate, I believe I can safely state that one of the functions of the public accountant (to suggest to an impartial mind the accounting practices and policies of issuers) has often been lost sight of by his failure to furnish that protection to investors which might be afforded by disclosure in the accountants' certificate. Too often the accountant has been inclined to follow the easy course by stating the facts in general terms, leaving the reader to his own interpretation, and contenting himself with the use of the phrase, "subject to the foregoing" or some other equivocal phrase. It is this course which must be resisted if advancement is to be made. Effective resistance must take the form of constantly re-appraising and testing the soundness and propriety of those conventions which tradition and practice have fashioned, but which experience and the protection of investors frequently prove to be not only inadequate, but meaningless. As a consequence, the revised rule regarding accountants' certificates, known as Rule 2-02, was issued on February 5, 1941, effective as of March 1, 1941. This rule sets up the standards of disclosure for accountants' certificates accompanying financial statements filed with the Commission. I shall refrain from reciting the details required by this rule, because it has been clearly explained in the releases announcing its adoption, as well as in Bulletins Nos. 5 and 6--"Statements on Auditing Procedure"--issued by the Committee on Auditing Procedure of the American Institute of Accountants. Believing, however, that you will be interested in the type of certificate now being submitted under this rule, I shall read excerpts from one recently received, which includes the opinion of the accountants with respect to changes in accounting principles or practices or adjustments of accounts, required to be set forth by Rule 3-07.

"In connection with the examination of such financial statements and supplemental schedules, we reviewed the system of internal control and the accounting procedures of the Companies, and examined or tested accounting records and other supporting evidence by methods and to the extent which we deemed appropriate, but we did not make a detailed audit of the operations or cash transactions for the period. Our examination was made in accordance with generally accepted auditing standards applicable in the circumstances, and included all procedures which we considered necessary.

****

"During the year, the company reduced from 22-1/2% to 7-1/2% the portion of the net finance charge on discounts receivable which is taken into income in the month of acquisition as an offset to acquisition costs; in our opinion, this was a change from one acceptable practice to an equally acceptable one. The change has the effect of postponing the taking up of income; it was impracticable to determine its effect on the net income for the year.

"During the year an amount of $55,816.17 was transferred from the loss reserve to income to adjust the reserve on October 31, 1940 to 2.25% of discount receivables on that date; and $78,116.47 was charged to income in adjustment of the cost of insurance placed with ______________ Insurance Company during the six months ended November 30, 1940. In our opinion, such adjustments were proper except that, since the original provisions for the loss reserve and the insurance cost were made from gross finance charges, and since a portion of such gross finance charges remained as deferred income on November 30, 1940, the adjustments should preferably have been prorated between income and deferred income; however, such prorations would have involved so many computations as to render them impracticable, and since the adjustments tend to offset one another, the omission of the proration had no material effect upon income.

"In our opinion, the accompanying statements and schedules with the notes appended thereto, fairly present, in accordance with accepted principles maintained consistently by the Companies during the year (except as noted in the immediately preceding paragraphs), the financial condition of the Companies on November 30, 1940 and the results of their operations for the year ended that date."

I need not go into the details of the reasons which underlie these requirements, first, because every rule of substantial importance evolves from observation, research, and consultation with outside experts, and second, because I am sure you will agree that investors are entitled to have all the facts necessary to make an intelligent appraisal of the information given in the financial reports. Moreover, it must be realized that standards of disclosure cannot be molded into a fixed formula but must remain flexible to take care of events that occur under varying circumstances. For this reason and to retain this flexibility, there is Rule 3-06 which states:

> "The information required with respect to any statement shall be furnished as a minimum requirement to which shall be added such further material information as is necessary to make the required statements, in the light of the circumstances under which they are made, not misleading. This rule shall be applicable to all statements required to be filed, including copies of statements required to be filed in the first instance with other governmental agencies."

In many cases there may be no ready standard of measurement for gauging the materiality of information to determine whether it should be disclosed. In such cases, if any doubt exists that its omission would leave a gap in the information needed for a clear understanding of the report or would lead to an incorrect interpretation of the data furnished, it is my opinion that disclosure should be made in the statements. In order to shed further light on this subject I think it worth while to cite from a few of the Commission's decisions some of the opinions expressed therein with respect to certain disclosures in financial statements. For example, in the case of Mining and Development Corporation the Commission held that where property was set up as an asset, with disclosure that it secured a debt but without disclosure that default on the debt had taken place, it was misleading despite the fact that at the hearing creditors asserted that they had no present intention of foreclosing if the registrant could float sufficient securities to repay the loan.[1]

Then in the case of Bankers Union Life Company the Commission said:

> "The balance sheet is misleading in other respects. Claimed as an asset is the item $666,073.41, representing 'deferred payment--12-year endowment bonds'. This sum represents the total amount payable on subscriptions to bonds and five times as many shares of capital stock, in accordance with the subscription agreement already referred to. This asset item does not represent obligations legally enforceable against subscribers, for

[1] 1 S.E.C. 786.

they may, at any time, in accordance with the subscription agreement, discontinue payments and surrender their endowment bonds without subjecting themselves to any further liability to the registrant. It is misleading to claim this amount as an asset without indicating by a footnote or otherwise that the amount may be reduced at the election of a subscriber who fails to make payments."[2]

In the same case the Commission also stated:

"It is clearly misleading to represent as a general asset of the company bonds which have been pledged for the benefit of special classes of purchasers of endowment bonds. To fail to indicate that certain of the assets stated in the balance sheet were thus not available to the class of investor to whom the balance sheet is addressed is deceptive."[3]

In the matter of Canusa Gold Mines, Ltd. the Commission took the position that where an underwriter had sold and distributed stock in apparent violation of the Securities Act of 1933, and where minutes of the board of directors showed that the corporation had

---

[2] 2S.E.C. 68 and 69.

[3] 2S.E.C. 69.

full knowledge of such distribution by an underwriter, and where no exemption under Section 3 of the Securities Act appeared applicable, that while the Commission would not adjudicate the question of civil liability provisions of Sections 11 and 12 of the Securities Act of 1933, a possible contingent liability existed and that a failure to disclose such contingent liability on a balance sheet and a statement that there were "no known contingent liabilities" rendered the financial statements untrue.[4]

Also in the Canusa opinion the Commission said:

> "The registrant has clearly shown under both the assets and the liabilities on the face of the balance sheet, as well as in the footnotes thereto and in a supporting schedule, that 'mining properties' includes the six claims held on option and that the amount of $115,000 is yet to be paid thereunder. Nevertheless, it seems to us that the failure to follow proper accounting practice makes the balance sheet materially deficient in this respect.
>
> "At no place in the financial statements or in the footnote related thereto is there any indication of the amount of other assets that would be lost to the

---

[4] 2 S.E.C. 549.

registrant if the remaining payments provided for under the option should not be made. This we also deem to be a material deficiency."[5]

While in the matter of Metropolitan Personal Loan Company the Commission held that the failure to disclose the lack of a necessary reserve for repossessed cars, in the light of registrant's previous losses on such cars, constituted an omission of a material fact.[6] In that case the Commission also took the position that inclusion in notes and accounts receivable of items, substantial amounts of which were known to be uncollectible or doubtful, without disclosing that an adequate reserve had not been provided, was grossly misleading.[7]

In the Queensboro Gold Mines decision the Commission enunciated the principle that the face of the balance sheet containing untrue and misleading statements through overvaluation was not cured by a footnote disclosing the stated value to have been arbitrarily fixed by the buyer's board of directors controlled by seller.[8] This case

---

[5] 2 S.E.C. 556.

[6] 2 S.E.C. 803.

[7] 2 S.E.C. 804.

[8] 2 S.E.C. 860.

should be particularly noted for the points set out in that portion of the Commission's opinion which I now quote:

"The balance sheet submitted, moreover, is itself deficient. While custom permits an enterprise to set up its property in its balance sheet at cost, we have repeatedly held that the arbitrary valuation of assets at the par value of stock issued in their purchase is not such a cost and is misleading when, as appears here, the actual value of the stock at the time of the acquisition was substantially less than par. (In the matter of Unity Gold Corp., 1 S.E.C. 25, 33 (1934); in the matter of Canusa Gold Mines, Limited, 2 S.E.C., 548 (1937).) Nor is the mischief fully cured by an explanatory note revealing that the figure is 'purely arbitrary' and that teh vendor who purchased the property 'at a nominal cost' to himself, 'controlled the board who valued' the property. (In the matter of Mining and Development corp., 1 S.E.C. 786, 799 (1936).) Such disclosure, while helpful, is not sufficient. If, as asserted in the explanatory note the 'actual value is now known,' the investor is at least entitled to know the cost, in this case, the actual value of the stock issued, as measured by all available standards, and this both the balance sheet and the explanatory note fail to show."[9]

[9] 2 S.E.C. 862.

In the Potrero Sugar Company decision the Commission characterized as misleading a note explaining an asset described in a balance sheet because of inclusion of optimistic statements therein without disclosure of other factors having an adverse effect.[10] And in the Oklahoma Hotel Building Company proceeding the Commisison pointed out that failure of a registrant to make the required monthly deposits under a sinking fund arrangement must be disclosed in the balance sheet or by way of a note thereto.[11]

Finally, there is the important problem of determining what disclosure should be made of events occurring between the date of the balance sheet and the date of the accountants' certificate. However, since this problem is an unsettled one, I shall dwell upon it only long enough to state that it is obvious that there is no need for the accountant to comment upon events subsequent to the date of the balance sheet if the effect is not significant. On the other hand, there is no question in my mind but that the accountant should disclose known happenings after the date of teh balance sheet if disclosure will serve the interest of the investor and, at the same time, preserve the qualities of impartiality and reliability required of the independent accountant.

---

[10] 5 S.E.C. 983.

[11] 4 S.E.C. 580.

In this connection the language of the Commission in the Oklahoma Hotel Building Company case is significant. I quote:

> "It is true that although a large interest payment was due the next day it was not necessary to indicate the pendency of this obligation on the face of a balance sheet dated November 30, 1938.
>
> "However, the accountant was charged with the duty of disclosing in the balance sheet or by way of a note thereto any material defaults in interest payments occurring before the date of the certificate. This duty rests both on accepted accounting standards (See Proceedings of American Institute of Accountants [Fiftieth Anniversary Celebration, 1937], 317.) and on the requirements of full disclosure under the Securities Act. Such a default did occur. It was admitted by counsel for the registrant that the interest due December 1 on the second mortgage bonds was not met between that date and January 10, the date of the certificate. The failure of the accountant to disclose this fact was a material omission."[12]

It is hoped that this paper will stimulate increased interest in the subject and lead to its further development. In facing the

[12] 4 S.E.C. 583-584.

work that is yet to be done, let us hope that in the troublesome days which lie ahead, the profession, responsive to experience and sensitive to the insistent demands of public interest, will set even higher standards of disclosure in financial statements than those now enduring.

#8 James J. Caffrey

November 5, 1947

Plain Talk in Accounting

Abstract

In the complex welter of conflicting legal and economic interests, the accountant is expected to produce a single adequate, truthful, and understandable statement. Thus, the accountant has ascended into a position of power, with the accompanying burden of responsibilities. Caffrey indicates what he and laymen expect from accountants in applying "their art" as truth in the accounts and complete disclosure of material facts. Further, he stresses the importance of efforts between the Commission and accountants in establishing professional standards.

Mr. Chairman, Gentlemen:

I bring you greetings on behalf of the entire Commission and of myself. We wish you a pleasant and fruitful meeting. We would all like to be with you, but since that is impossible I have accepted

---

Address before the American Institute of Accountants.

your invitation as an ambassador to a group with which we have worked closely, amicably, and effectively for a long time.

This is my first address to a professional group of accountants; and, I understand, this is the first time a Chairman of the Securities and Exchange Commission has addressed the Institute. It is a perfect occasion for high-sounding phrases. But I would rather use it to do some plain talking. I do that because plain talk is the substance of my message to you.

I cannot afford the luxury of either a personal or professional bias on accounting problems. Although I am a lawyer I do not view accounting with the squint-eyed hostility of some lawyers. Although I like to speculate about technical accounting I have no technical axe to grind. My position requires me to bear in mind the needs of investors, to think in practical terms of the effect of regulation on company managements and on those who render professional services to companies, to make decisions based on legal considerations and to reach judgments based on accountants' presentations. I discovered early that there were two important things I had to do; think straight and talk plain. Out of the welter of complicated legal, accounting, analytical, and other elements that enter into our deliberations the challenge is to find the issue reduced to its simplest form and to state the conclusion in the plainest way possible.

To my mind the accountants' job is very similar. Out of the welter of raw elements that go into the making of a financial statement he must find the simplest and most sensible rules of order and he must state his conclusions in the most understandable form possible. The single, most important challenge which faces the profession is, to my mind, the challenge to talk plain.

I do not by any means underestimate the extent of that challenge.

Perhaps the most striking thing about your profession is the enormous change that has taken place in the position of the accountant. From the simple scrivener tabulating receipts and disbursements, with limited functions and limited responsibilities, he has become the processing plant through which the raw data of finance must pass before it can be compiled in the vast financial encyclopedia of our time. To the terminology of receipts and disbursements he has had to add a language to describe newer concepts; within the framework of the balance sheet and income statement he has had to find a place for items of multiple, complex, and ambiguous character. To the simple dimension of income and outgo there have been added new dimensions in which to reflect spending not yet done and receipts not yet in hand.

Further, the accountant for the large enterprise is often called on to account for the operations of an "entity" only in the bare legal sense. Within a single corporate framework there may be divisions, each one of which represents an enterprise almost independent in its organization and operation. The holding company system, as, on the other hand required the development of techniques of combination and consolidation to account for a diversity of corporate entities in reality joined in a common economic enterprise.

To these difficulties have been added many others. Not only is the imagination staggered by the growing size and complexity of what the accountant must account for, but it is not always clear even for whom accountants account. The single enterprise is no longer the personal concern of one owner or a small group of owners. Its ownership is likely to be spread among vast numbers of security holders, aggregating into a welter of conflicting legal and economic interests in the single business unit. In any given situation the exercise of an accountant's judgment may vitally affect the ownership interests of one competing group of security holders as against another.

History seems to have an endless storehouse of burdens for the accountant. His presentation must also satisfy the regulatory agencies interested in the operations of the economic enterprises for which he accounts. One group in government is charged with protection of the revenue, another with the protection of security holders, another with the protection of rate payers, another with the protection of employees, and so on. Each of these bodies may approach the balance sheet or the income statement with a different emphasis, and may read it for a different message. Nevertheless, the accountant is expected to produce one single adequate, truthful and understandable statement.

History has thus thrust the accountant into a crucial role. Management, labor, conflicting groups of investors, potential investors, and governmental interests make vital decisions based on the story told by the accountant. Yet the accountant is no mere reporter who sits by the sidelines giving a play by play description of the business. Save in the simplest kinds of business he has been given a task which embraces interpretation as well as mere recording; judgment as well as mere tabulating; art as well as science.

What does this add up to? Perhaps the simplest way of putting it is to say that the accountant's position has become a position of power. In this regard history has an even hand, with power she doles out responsibility. The full measure of that responsibility is a full bible of accounting. I have neither the time nor the ability to cover that much ground. I would like to touch briefly on some problems that, with the layman in mind, strike me as basic and perpetual.

An accountant necessarily deals with terms of art. But those terms have popular meanings to the non-professionals who read and rely on accountants' statements. While I might be ill at ease in technical arguments about the full implications of such words as "profit", "income", "surplus" and "depreciation", when I read an accountant's statement I have a very well-defined reaction to these words. I assume that their character and quality of these accounts are the same for different statements of the same or different businesses. I assume that the accountant has told me how much the business made or lost during the year and how much it can pay out without impairing the investment. I expect the statement to be complete; if it covers income and outgo I feel entitled to believe that charges and credits have not been tucked away or placed anywhere else. If there are necessary qualifications to what I read in the figures I assume that these will be flagged for me where they are most pertinent and will be stated in such a way as to permit me to appraise the statement intelligently.

These are the things a layman expects. In my opinion these expectations are the core of accounting. They are the common ground upon which the public and the profession communicate; they are the only source of vitality for accounting concepts; they define ideals--vague and difficult as they may be--toward which the philosophy and language of accounting must move to be vigorous and meaningful. When accounting terminology loses touch with common meanings it becomes at best a verbal exercise and at worst a polite method of lieing. As necessary as it may be for the accountant to choose between alternative theories or alternative applications of theory in the course of making his statement; as multiple and as complex as may be the elements that go into the achievement of the net result, it must mean pretty much what the layman thinks it means or it has no public meaning at all.

Thus, there are necessary limitations to the art of accounting. It cannot e permitted to take the accountant so far afield that his language loses its essential touch with reality. The common man's understandings of accountants' words are heavy anchors against drift in representation of financial facts. They must form, in all statements, for all companies, and wherever used, the essential content of accounting terminology.

Every generation brings with it those who strive for certainty, and it brings also those who insist that certainty is a will-o'-the-wisp. Of course, absolute certainty in accounting is not now, and may never be, an achieved fact. But it is nonsensical and dangerous to deny its validity as an ideal. Your profession has in the past decade made many improvements in that direction. They are palpable evidence that we can go still further.

There is a vast premium in continuing efforts to achieve certainty, comparability, and rigid independence in accounting. We must remember that an accountant's presentation is, to most people who read it, like a mariner's compass in the fog. It is all they have to go by. If the guide fails they are lost. They cannot trace back the method of arriving at the statement. They do not have the skill to temper their reading with sophisticated judgments about diversities in accounting treatments. They have no choice but to assume that the accountant's presentation means what it says and that it tells the whole truth, on the basis of an independent and thorough survey of the facts.

Full respect for the stewardship inherent in the position of the accountant requires more than conscientious performance by individual practitioners. Who is to blame if the balance sheets and income statements of the X and Y companies certified by different firms, are found to use the same language, within the scope of accepted or acceptable accounting principles, to describe different things? There may be excellent arguments to justify both presentations and both may have been conscientiously certified. However, if they use the same words to describe different things even an experienced investor who makes a comparison between them has been seriously misled by a dangerous though honest falsehood. Each statement, telling the truth in its own way, is justifiable. Put together they distort each other.

It is here that the Institute has done much in the past and can do more in the future. Individual practitioners, working alone cannot reduce their concepts to generally applicable formulas. Comparability, which is one of the vital elements of meaningful accounting, presupposes broadly applicable standards, so concise and well-defined that variability is eliminated or reduced to an insignificant minimum.

How can we do this job best? First I think it obvious that we must preserve and improve the close cooperation of the past between the

S.E.C. and the Institute. Accounting standards cannot be improvised or manufactured in a vacuum. The Commission needs the benefit of the close touch with facts and practice which the profession gives us in talking our rules over with us. Only in that way can we be sure of vital and meaningful standards. On the other hand accountants need our continuous support. What is inevitably a part-time effort of busy members of the Institute and its committees is a full-time effort of the Commission. What, in the end, the Institute can only suggest to the profession we can require.

I cannot stress too strongly the importance of keeping and improving our cooperative relations of the past.

The American Institute of Accountants and the Securities and Exchange Commission have been partners in a common endeavor. We at the Commission who have worked with you know how much the public owes to accountants who have devoted so much of their time and effort to bring about improvement in accounting standards and accounting techniques. You have shown your deeply felt responsibility in many ways; you have given unstintingly of your time and skill in reducing ideals to workable formulas; you have been an important vehicle in transmitting the benefit of new developments to the accounting profession in general, to the businesses for which you account, and to the public which depends so vitally upon your efforts. Because of this, you are much more than an association of professional practitioners devoted to your own interests--you are a means of safe-guarding and transmitting the heritage of your art and science.

We at the Commission know, too, how important the Institute has been as a standard bearer in its field. So-called "Regulation" of accounting by the Commission has not meant policing a best. Because of the high ethical sense of the profession it has involved, most pertinently, a <u>legislative</u> job; it has meant mutual effort in the development of a rational code. Once you and we have agreed on the general acceptability of an accounting principle or practice, whether it is promulgated by you or by us, we feel reasonably sure that the profession will obey it. What in some other fields is done largely through coercion and discipline is done in the accounting field largely through voluntary adoption of, and voluntary adherence to, professional standards. We have through this valuable partnership built an enviable record of progress. We do not dare do less and the public looks to us to do more.

Lastly I wish to stress the importance of <u>scope</u> in any program to improve the adequacy and comparability of financial statements. Among those whose interest is served by such improvement the investors stand prime. They are, in the classical sense, the owners and creditors for whom accountants account. At the very least any program of improvement should embrace all companies in which public investors have an interest. The Commission had this in mind, among other things, when it recommended to the Congress that the Securities Exchange Act of 1934 be amended to make it applicable to some 1,000 companies--each having at least $3,000,000 in assets and 300 security holders--not now required to file financial statements with the Commission because they do not happen to have securities listed on a national securities exchange.

To the members of your group--those who know best what sound accounting means for investors and the public generally we shall look for help in framing workable and intelligent legislation. We have no unalterable, pre-conceived ideas about how the law should read, or about what the extent of its coverage should be. You gentlemen would have much to do with translating such a law into action. Your voice should be heard in the councils of deliberation.

Our direct interest in these matters is limited to businesses in whose securities there is a public interest. But you have no such limitations. Financial history seems to indicate that any business may be a candidate for development into a corporation with a wide public interest. The transition accountingwise would have been eased in many cases which have come to our attention if the guiding hand of truly independent accountants working with sound principles and procedures had been applied earlier in the life of the business. Most of you, I suspect, literally have grown up with many of your principal clients. This process will continue. Failure on your part to maintain a progressive and constructive attack on accounting problems on a broad front can only lead to a usurpation of the field by others. With proper foresight and a cooperative attack upon new problems of accounting as they arise in the future conflicting procedures will be avoided and your profession will retain the confidence of clients and investors alike.

Thank you.

#9 Harry A. McDonald

September 21, 1950

The Investor Looks at Accounting

Abstract

McDonald cautions that investors are not interested in technical accounting disputes; they look at the accounts through the statements and are likely to turn to the income statement to see the end result. They are not aware of the judgment used in determining the figures reported nor the impact of using different principles. He stresses the need for objectivity and uniformity in accounting principles and practices and cites examples where non-operating profits were credited directly to earned surplus. This leads to a discussion of the "all inclusive" concept and the SEC's insistence on the use of that concept.

I have called this talk "The Investor Looks at Accounting." But it would be more practical, at least, to say "The Investor Does Not Look at Accounting." The average investor, and even most securities professionals who give investment advice are not interested in the technique of accounting. They are not interested in its technical disputes. The investor, either directly or

Address before the Annual Reports Forum, University of Michigan.

through his advisers, looks not at accounting as such, but--when he looks at all--looks at accounts. And the stockholders' report is one of the direct ways of getting the accounts to the investors.

Sometimes the stockholders' report contains little more than the financial statements. Sometimes it is more elaborate. American business is beginning to realize that the stockholder welcomes a discussion of the progress and problems of management. I am whole-heartedly in favor of full reports. The wisecrackers may remark about the "gorgeous technicolor" of some of these "travelogues." But while some reports do seem unnecessarily elaborate that is error in the right direction. Management's efforts to make the stockholders' report interesting and readable are to be commended. And I particularly congratulate the university and business groups that have combined to stimulate management to improve these reports. In making the stockholders' report more readable and interesting we are recognizing one of the essential obligations to the stockholder--the obligation to account for the stewardship of his money.

Through stockholders' reports millions of Americans are finding out about the businesses they have helped to finance; they are being helped to a more enlightened participation in the enterprises of which they are, ultimately, the owners. The stockholders' report is bridging the gap between management and investor. The interest and knowledge that results from good reports will be extremely important in keeping open the channels between savings and enterprise.

But it does not matter how elaborate a report is; it does not matter whether the report makes good or bad bedtime reading. The investor is likely to do what many detective story readers do--turn to the income statement to see how it all came out.

It is impossible, therefore, to talk meaningfully about the stockholders' report without talking about the role that the accountant plays in preparing the financial statements. And it is impossible to appraise some of the vital issues which the accounting profession faces without considering the investor and the investor's approach to a financial statement.

Certified by a public accountant, precise down to pennies, financial statements carry with them an atmosphere of definiteness and certainty. The ordinary investor does not realize how much judgment lies behind the making of a typical statement. He does not realize how great can be the effect of applying different principles to the same set of facts. He does not know how fundamental are some of the disputes over principle which rage in the accounting profession.

In his quick glance a stockholder may not notice whether a non-recurring item has been run direct through the surplus account rather than income. He is not likely to observe whether depreciation is taken on a replacement or historical cost basis. I doubt if 999 out of 1,000 stockholders who read reports can tell you whether their companies carry inventory on a last-in first-out basis, or other basis. Even if the stockholder did notice these items he would not be likely to grasp their meaning. In short, the stockholder reads the financial statement as a book of revelation. Technical disputes about accounting are to him like the disputes of scholastics over theological mysteries.

It is easy to say what an investor should get out of accounting--he should get a simple statement of the truth about his company. In fact, the accounting profession can share with corporate management and with the S.E.C. (whose statutory aim is to get truthful statements) great credit for the strides industry has made in this direction. We tend to take good reporting by many of our large enterprises as a matter of course. But not too long ago there were some managements who tended to regard the accounts as an internal secret to be kept from stockholders. Even as late as the 1920's accounting was sometimes called an art of "impublicity."

We have come a long way since then. To keep up with the growing demand for publicity, to provide the means for presenting, in an objective and understandable way, our increasingly complex business structures, accounting has left simple bookkeeping far behind. It has built up an impressive body of skills and concepts. In fact it has even built up organizations that can handle a project like a big audit which is in itself a big business.

Nevertheless, many accountants will tell you that accounting is far from perfect. They will tell you that, on some issues, "truth" in accounting is an elusive thing, even when the facts are handled honestly and skillfully. Don't expect all accountants to agree on what these issues are. Accountants are likely to have pet peeves against certain existing conventions and practices while they find no fault with others. And, as you might expect, disputes about accounting principles are prone to change with changes in business conditions. When profits are low some managements may tend to hunt for accounting devices that will improve the showing of profits. When profits are high the tendency may be naturally to the contrary. Profits or losses, in the language of Shakespeare, are the stuff that accounting disputes are made of.

The science of accounting is a science of measurement. Adequate and objective accounting principles, uniformly applied, should give us a consistent story of the development of any one enterprise and a basis of comparing that enterprise with others. A management may wish to preserve, despite changing business levels, a normal income level in its financial reports. But a science of accounting that permits it is not a science at all. It is worth no more than a thermometer that always stands at 75 degrees.

We, at the Securities and Exchange Commission, have a vital interest in the development of objective and uniform accounting. We do not regulate the accounting profession. Our direct concern with accounting principles and practice is limited to financial statements officially filed with us under the statutes we administer. We do not generally pass on stockholders' reports; they are not even filed with us except in connection with proxy solicitations by companies whose securities are listed on an exchange. But companies that propose to make public offerings of securities are required to register those securities with us and to file financial data. Companies which have registered large issues and companies which have securities listed on exchanges are required to file annual reports with us.

The statutes administered by the Commission authorize it to prescribe the form or forms in which required information shall be set forth. The Congress, recognizing that financial information would be the most significant information, made specific provisions with regard to accounting. You will find some of them in Section 19 of the Securities Act of 1933, Section 13 of the Securities Exchange Act of 1934, Sections 14 and 20 of the Public Utility Holding Company Act of 1935, Sections 30, 31 and 32 and 38 of the Investment Company Act of 1940. Let me read to you some of the provisions of Section 19(a) of the Securities Act--the statute that provides for the registration of public offerings of securities. Under that section the Commission has:

> "...authority from time to time to make, amend, and rescind such rules and regulations as may be necessary to carry out the provisions of this title, including rules

> and regulations governing registration statements and prospectuses for various classes of securities and issuers, and defining accounting, technical, and trade terms used in this title. Among other things, the Commission shall have authority, for the purposes of this title, to prescribe the form or forms in which required information shall be set forth, the items or details to be shown in the balance sheet and earning statement, and the methods to be followed in the preparation of accounts, in the appraisal or valuation of assets and liabilities, in the determination of depreciation and depletion, in the differentiation of recurring and nonrecurring income, in the differentiation of investment and operating income, and in the preparation, where the Commission deems it necessary or desirable, of consolidated balance sheets or income accounts of any person directly or indirectly controlling or controlled by the issuer, or any person under direct or indirect common control with the issuer;"

Similar powers are granted under the Securities Exchange Act of 1934 in relation to annual filings of financial information with the S.E.C.

Both the Commission and the accounting profession have worked side by side in the evolution of accounting practices. We, at the S.E.C., do not want to create a tight little island of accounting under these laws remote from the mainland of accounting generally. Nor does the accounting profession want to see that happen. For that reason both we and the profession have put a high premium on constant and intimate contact with each other in the development of accounting practice.

The Commission has, of necessity, always defended objective and uniform accounting practices. The statutes we administer require information to be given to the investor. Financial statements are presented to us by thousands of companies who file official information that must be reviewed. Each of these statements, in some form or other, directly or indirectly, is destined for use by investors. These statements are guide lines and, unless they are objective and uniform, much of their usefulness is destroyed. We must, therefore, constantly be on guard to prevent the confusion that may result from a loss of objectiveness and uniformity.

It is not my intention to dispute or redispute accounting principles. My aim is to illustrate the importance of keeping accounting objective and uniform. I am going to cite some examples. Let me make it clear that I do not cite these to put into issue the principles involved. I cite them because they illustrate the hazards of sacrificing objectivity and uniformity.

One of my examples involves a large textile company that has many stockholders and whose stock is actively traded on one of our large exchanges. Recently the company made public an interim earnings report which indicated that a net profit of over $500,000 arising from the sale of certain non-manufacturing properties had been credited direct to earned surplus. In a similar period for the previous year it had credited direct to earned surplus a similar net profit of over $1,200,000. In neither year did the income account show these profits.

Both the New York Times and the Herald Tribune, on the same day, September 13, carried summaries of the company's report. One newspaper commented on the direct credits to surplus. The other did not. In 1949 the item not shown in the income statement amounted to fifteen cents a share. For 1948 the similar item amounted to over thirty cents a share.

Which newspaper did you read? Depending on the accident of your reading taste, it so happens that if you subscribed to one of these newspapers you would have been able to make a more adequate appraisal of the earnings then if you subscribed to the other. The fault was not, however, that of a financial report. He cannot be expected to do a full scale analytical job to find items neatly tucked away in the balance sheet that he would expect to find reflected in the income statement.

The company's official filings with us for the year 1949 showed that an aggregate of almost $3,000,000 of such profits had by-passed the income statement and been charged direct to surplus.

Of course our staff has taken exception to the treatment of these items.

Those of you who are familiar with this type of problem recognize that the filing I am discussing raised the issue of the so-called "all-inclusive income statement." Whatever your views may be about that issue I think you will agree that neither an analyst, nor an investor, nor a reporter would have had any difficulty in locating an item of that character if it were carried in the income statement with other revenues and expenses.

There has been some criticism of the practice of the S.E.C. to insist on including all such items in the income statement. One of the reasons frequently given for the criticism is that the inclusion of unusual, non-recurrent items in the profit and loss statement may distort that statement. However, this criticism overlooks the fact that the Commission accepts, and even encourages, a segregation of such items in the profit and loss statement so that their unusual character is made amply clear in an appraisal of the statement of net income.

Let me give you another example. Again I want to make amply clear that I am not citing this example in order to defend one side or another in a dispute over accounting principle. I cite it because it illustrates some of the problems that an agency like the S.E.C. can face in dealing with an attempt to depart from objective and uniform practice.

In my view, one of the most competent and dramatic presentations of the economic problems faced by management in a rising price cycle was made several years ago by United States Steel Corporation. U.S. Steel added an item of over $26 million as additional "depreciation" for estimated replacement costs. The effect of that change was of course to cut down correspondingly the statement of net income for the year. Steel's argument was simple. It said in effect: "Costs have gone so high that when a machine now in use wears out, it will cost more to replace it than when it was installed. If, by the time the machine wore out we were to lay away only the historical cost, we would not be able to replace the machine. Therefore we must take added depreciation as an expense and show less profits."

The Commission decided that it could not accept Steel's income statement presented in that form. That presentation was not in accordance with the conventional concept that the aim of depreciation accounting is to amortize cost and not to provide for replacement.

But the critic of the conventional concept argues that the conventional concept does not show the real facts about profits. He points out that a statement of net income according to traditional accounting is far from being a statement of economic profit if some of that income must be retained to keep the business tooled up. The defenders of the conventional view recognize that for practical purposes the businessman and the analyst must look beyond the accountant's presentation to find significant economic realities. But that, they say, is no more regrettable than the fact that a good thermometer records temperature but doesn't diagnose sickness.

When we decide issues like those presented by United States Steel we know that practical businessmen and financial analysts cannot read the whole story in the financial statement without looking further into broader economic realities. But consider for a moment the other problems presented to the Commission as an agency having responsibility for corporate disclosure. If depreciation is not to be based on cost, why should assets be carried at cost? Shouldn't the plant account be reviewed with every change in the price level? And if so, whose revaluation will be accepted, and how often? What, if not cost, should be the basis of depreciation: --today's replacement price? or what? Should an index be used? Whose index, taken how often, and how many indices should there be for different types of equipment? Should this be allowed on a permissive basis, or should all companies be required to change their method of accounting? Suppose the new equipment is more productive than the old? And so on almost endlessly.

I repeat that only an objective and uniform system can avoid such problems.

The happy marriage between economic reality and accounting convention may never be achieved. Economic reality is perhaps no more "real" than accounting convention. Economic ideas are often as ambiguous as any others. What is income? There are as many answers as there are reasons for asking the question. But the accountant is expected to produce one single reliable statement of income.

Uniformity and objectivity in accounting are values that can sometimes be realized only at the cost of other ideals. Business life is dynamic--it surges through year-ends and other fixed periods; business values change in ways that are not comprehended in the accountant's idea of "realization"; and sometimes those changes cannot be expressed with certainty or adequacy in terms of a nominal dollar.

It is not surprising therefore that criticism of accounting conventions should be dramatized by rapid changes in business cycles. If you look back at earlier literature you will see that many of our accounting principles represent victories over internal manipulation of accounts. Early experience tended to show that if you let everyone tell the truth in his own way too many people were going to tell you something other than the truth.

But the fear of manipulation is not my reason for defending uniformity and objectivity in accounting. More important is the fact that even honest differences of approach in an accounting presentation will result in statements that may tell the truth in their own way, but will distort each other. Perhaps refined and detailed analysis can make any honest statement comparable with any other honest statement. But it is hopeless to expect the ordinary investor to make such an analysis. He looks at the end results and they are to him "like the mariner's compass in a fog."

The evolution of sound principles of accounting has represented what might be called a "tooling-up" development of the profession. It is only part of the profession's enviable history of achievement. A more fundamental development has taken place in the stature of the profession and in its ideals of service and independence.

Let me stress that word--independence. The management of a company may hire and fire accounting firms. But the accounting firm's obligation runs far beyond management. It runs to the public. The accountant needs to be independent in order to fulfill that obligation. The Commission, under the law, requires certification by independent accountants. But, in addition, the very existence of the Commission is an aid in maintaining independence. It is a great comfort to a truly independent firm to be able to tell an occasional management that tries to depart from sound accounting that the S.E.C. has the ultimate authority to accept or question an official filing, and that the management cannot change an accounting principle by changing accounting firms.

The Commission has, since its creation, encouraged the profession itself to evolve accounting practice out of the actual, bread and butter problems with which the profession deals. The commission continues to seek the cooperation of the profession because that cooperation has been so fruitful in the past.

Of course, differences of opinion develop. Our staff and we should be patient and willing to listen to justifications for unconventional ways of doing things. Sometimes we are persuaded. Often a middle ground can be worked out. But whether the arguments persuade us or not, the participants generally are convinced that we don't exercise our ultimate statutory authority for the mere sake of having the last word. We can't help but carry out our statutory job of umpiring the disputes. When we do umpire them we must bear the needs of the investor in mind. And those needs include objectivity and uniformity.

Often an accountant will concede to the point of volunteering to present in a footnote the facts according to conventional accounting if we permit him to make an unconventional presentation in the body of the statement. Our policy is to reject that procedure. The policy has been criticized; but the critics tend to forget that the law imposes upon us the responsibility for determining the presentation in financial statements officially filed. They must not forget that investors, dealers and newspaper reporters are not likely to be footnote readers. As my previous example showed, there is no assurance that what gets tucked away in a financial statement will ever see the investor's light of day.

At first blush it might seem that I have wandered from the main subject of this forum--the stockholders' report. In fact I have not wandered at all. As I indicated, in my view the financial statements are the heart of the stockholders' report. No fine words can cover up a surplus deficit. A net loss will show through the most gorgeously colored photographs. In the end the level of usefulness of the stockholders' report cannot rise above or fall below the level of accounting skill, independence and conscientiousness that goes into the preparation of the financial statement.

Many streams make the river of history; many factors have shaped and will shape the history of accounting. If I can play once more on the words of the title of these remarks, let me say that one fact will always be dominant in shaping the course of accounting--and it is the fact that whether directly or through his advisers, whether alone or through the medium of an agency like the S.E.C., the investor cannot help but look <u>to</u> the accountant. That fact is both the setting of the accountant's responsibility and the measure of the accountant's performance. It is what has changed accounting from a routine to a profession and, I think, a profession with great fulfillment and great promise.

#10 Donald C. Cook

October 3, 1950

The Concept of Independence in Accounting

Abstract

Cook's address is an extensive discussion of accountants' independence, supported by specific cases and hypothetical situations. He feels independence is a state of mind that combines the impartiality of a judge and the responsibility of a fiduciary. The "Ultramares Case" established the legal concepts of independence and liability, and the ethical rules of the AIA exceeded that limited concept of legal liability. Conditions that would make an accountant not independent in fact are mentioned. However, it is conceded that actual abdication of independent judgment is difficult to establish.

Mr. Chairman, Gentlemen:

The last time a member of the Commission addressed the annual meeting of this institute was in 1947. To have been invited again so soon may be interpreted as evidence either of your fortitude or of the number of common problems we have which it is mutually

Address before the American Institute of Accountants

advantageous for us to discuss. I should like to assume that it is our common interests which motivated your decision to invite me today.

In 1947 Mr. Caffrey, then Chairman of the Commission, discussed with you the relationship between rigid independence in accounting and the presentation of the facts of business life. Today I should like to elaborate upon a portion of that theme and discuss the basic concept of independence.

During the early years of accountancy, around the turn of the century, the business world had not yet come to recognize the need for this concept. Generally, an accountant's duties consisted of opening and closing books, detecting frauds upon the owners of the enterprise, and straightening accounts which had become charmingly mixed up by amateur bookkeepers. As one writer expressed it, the general notion seemed to prevail that an accountant was "merely a man of figures, a rapid and unerring calculator who could add up two or three columns of figures at a time, could tell you immediately the square or cube root of any given number, or say off-hand, for example, what one dollar put out at six per cent compound interest per annum at the time Columbus discovered America would amount to today."[1]

---

[1] Anyon, James T., Recollections of the Early Days of American Accountancy, p. 41.

Perhaps the greatest impetus to the new profession was given by the passage of the Sixteenth Amendment in 1913 and the War Revenue Act of 1917. Commercial banking institutions and mercantile creditors were quick to avail themselves of the services of the new profession, and it grew. These creditors required audits and verified financial statements. I believe full maturity was reached upon passage of the Securities Act of 1933, which for the first time imposed the legal requirement that statements be certified by independent accountants.

You will remember that General Carter, who testified on behalf of the accounting profession at the hearings upon that bill, experienced some difficulty in persuading the Senate Committee that there were professionally qualified persons who could and would audit accounts of registrants and express an independent opinion upon their correctness, uninfluenced by the fee they received. Senator Barkley was frankly skeptical about such a procedure and suggested that if an independent audit were really necessary it might better be obtained by the use of accountants employed by the government.

General Carter then observed, in a statement that I am sure was not justified by some of the incomes enjoyed by public accountants in the early thirties, that the government could not afford to employ the necessary number of qualified accountants. The Committee did not then pursue Senator Barkley's suggestion.

At another point in the hearings Senator Barkley asked whether there was any relationship between the corporate comptrollers, who had testified that they were responsible for the accuracy of the financial statements, and the public accountants. General Carter answered: "None at all. We audit the controllers." Senator Barkley then asked, "Who audits you?" to which General Carter quickly replied, "Our conscience." It is your conscience which is my subject today.

General Carter's reply sums up a substantial part of the concept of independence. It is not tangible, nor even in most instances clearly demonstrable. It represents a state of mind. In the entire field of human relationships it is difficult to find an exact analogy. The independent accountant must combine the impartiality of a judge with the high sense of reponsibility of a fiduciary. In addition, he must possess a full knowledge of the tools and methods of his profession. Though hired and fired by management, he must divorce his mental processes from any bias in their direction when making accounting judgments. Such a standard of professional conduct must be maintained if the auditor's certificate is to be more than a snare and a delusion and the public obligation of the accountant satisfied.

Of course, we are all fully aware of the difficulties inherent in enforcing such standards. The influences which may affect accounting judgment are extremely subtle and tenuous. In their most dangerous form it is possible that the accountant himself does not recognize their effect. Under such circumstances an accountant may be lacking in independence despite the highest professional qualifications and the most complete integrity. It is our duty--both the Institute's and the Commission's--to guard the public against such unconscious bias.

That is by far the most important purpose of our rules and interpretive opinions governing the qualification of accountants. No serious administrative problem arises in the obvious case where an accountant is plainly derelict, where he certifies to statements he knows to be misleading, or where he consciously and deliberately falsifies the facts.[2]

Even the common law, with its cultural lag, holds the accountant responsible if he should supply a certification when he knows or should know of its inaccuracies. I am sure you are all familiar with the case of Ultramares v. Touche, decided almost 20 years ago by the New York Court of Appeals. In that case Justice Cardozo, then Chief Judge of that court, made clear that every accountant who certifies a financial statement owes a duty to the public. If he should be grossly negligent in the discharge of that duty, he may be compelled to pay damages to any person who relied upon that statement. That was the first complete articulation of the legal

---

[2]See, e.g., American Terminals and Transit Co., 1 S.E.C. 701 (1936).

concept of independence, which has now been generally accepted by all the courts which have considered the matter.

The legal liability which flows from this concept was extended and enlarged somewhat by the Securities Act. Section 11 of that Act imposes upon the accountant the duty to make a reasonable investigation into the truth and completeness of the statements he certifies. This necessarily implies that the audit should be thorough and that the system of internal controls carefully checked. Such matters as depreciation and obsolescence allowances, legal requirements inhibiting dividend payments, and all similar items requiring the assistance of experts should be carefully scrutinized. The accountant is held to the same standard of care as that required of a prudent man in the management of his own property.

Negligence in this respect is strong evidence of lack of independence. Or, if an accountant, either directly or through an affiliate, enters into an agreement which attempts to immunize the accountant from liability for his negligent acts, I believe he thereby forfeits his independence.

The self-regulation undertaken by the profession has, of course, outstripped the limited concept of legal liability. Five rules of the Institute relate to this concept. They are: Rule 5, which prohibits false or misleading statements; Rule 9, which prohibits, except in limited circumstances, the use of contingent fees to pay for accounting services; Rule 13, which direct accountants to refrain from expressing any opinion upon the statements of any enterprise in which he may have a financial interest; Rule 3, which prohibits the payment of any portion of an accountant's fee to non-accountants or the acceptance of any portion of the fees or profits received by non-accountants from work turned over to them by accountants as an incident of their services to a client; and Rule 4, which discusses occupations incompatible with public accounting.

The Commission has attempted to adapt the concept of independence to the needs of investors. When a registration statement or annual report is filed with the Commission it is designed for use by the public. In lieu of government examination of each financial statement the certificate of an independent accountant is required. I believe that the duties inherent in furnishing such a certificate impress upon the auditor a fiduciary obligation toward the public as well as toward the client if full confidence in the publicly held securities is to be maintained. The Investment Company Act expressly recognizes this obligation by providing that the accountant's certificate "shall be addressed both to the board of directors...and to the security holders." If investors are to be fully protected, the accountant-fiduciary must be free of all the entangling alliances which might be engendered by relational or contractual connections with the registrant. He must be free to approach his task with complete objectivity, intent upon a critical examination of all the practices and procedures of the registrants. We have expressed this view in a rule as follows:

"The Commission will not recognize any certified public accountant or public accountant as independent who is not in fact independent. For example, an accountant will not be considered independent with respect to any person in whom he has any substantial interest, direct, or indirect, or with whom he is, or was during the period of report, connected as a promoter, underwriter, voting trustee, director, officer, or employee.

"In determining whether an accountant is in fact independent with respect to a particular registrant, the Commission will give appropriate consideration to all relevant circumstances including evidence bearing on all relationships between the accountant and that registrant, and will not confine itself to the relationships existing in connection with the filing of reports with the Commission."[3]

---

[3]On July 12, 1950, the Commission promulgated for comment a proposal that the rule be amended to read:

> The Commission will not recognize any certified public accountant or public accountant as independent who is not in fact independent. For example, an accountant will not be considered independent with respect to any person, or any affiliate thereof, in whom he has any financial interest, direct or indirect, or with whom he is, or was during the period of report, connected as a promoter,

To me that rule means two things. First, it states that independence is a question of fact, and if it can be shown as a matter of fact, regardless of the absence of any business or personal relationship, that an accountant's decisions are controlled or influenced by someone else, that accountant is not independent. Secondly, and this is perhaps of more significance, it points to certain relationships which indicate a lack of independence and provides that when these or similar relationships which might influence an accountant's judgment exist, the accountant cannot be considered independent regardless of the amount of proof available that his judgment was, in fact, uninfluenced.

---

[3](continued).

> underwriter, voting trustee, director, officer or employee.
>
> In determining whether an accountant is in fact independent with respect to a particular registrant, the Commission will give appropriate consideration to all relevant circumstances including evidence bearing on all relationships between the accountant and that registrant or any affiliate thereof, and will not confine itself to the relationships existing in connection with the filing of reports with the Commission.

This was intended as a codification of the Commission rulings upon independence and not as a change in view.

Proof of the actual abdication of judgment to another is nearly always difficult. The coincidence of the result of a decision with the wishes of another can, in many instances, be explained as the result of independent logical reasoning. It is in the selection of the applicable accounting convention, about which there are sometimes great differences of opinion among the authorities, that judgment must be exercised. Even when the decision cannot be logically justified, who can say whether the error was an honest one? It is in this context that independence is particularly important.

Usually, it is only when the accountant has been foolish enough to venture his personal judgment and it can be shown that this is different from that reflected in the financial statements that absolute proof of lack of independence can be shown.[4] Even when misleading or fraudulent statements are certified there can be only strong presumption of lack of independence, which must be coupled with other factors if there is to be clear evidence of actual subservience to management influence.

---

[4]See Metropolitan Personal Loan Co., 2 S.E.C. 803 (1937); A. Hollander & Sons, Inc., 8 S.E.C. 586 (1941); Associated Gas and Electric Co., 11 S.E.C. 975 (1942).

In the only three cases thus far decided involving lack of independence in which the Commission has taken disciplinary action against accountants the mental state of the accountants could be proved. In the first[5] the accountants gave management a private audit report materially different from that furnished the public. The public report failed to disclose, among other things, that the client was carrying a trading account in the name of the accountant. Although the accountant protested, he did not take effective steps to stop the practice for two years.

The second case[6], a year later, was very much like the first. It differed only in the fact that the accountant knew of the trading account and acted as an accomplice of management in the stock market enterprise. The client and the accountant did not even profit financially from the trading. They suffered substantial losses despite market advice by the president, the secretary-treasurer, and a director of the company. I suppose this proves both the biblical precept that the wicked shall reap no profit from their wickedness and the Wall Street axiom that market speculation should be left only to the professionals.

---

[5] Puder & Puder, Securities Exchange Act Release No. 3073 (1941).

[6] Kenneth v. Logan, 10 S.E.C. 982 (1942).

The third disciplinary action[7] was not until seven years later, when an accountant blandly certified accounts which carried a leasehold at $100,000, which was ninety percent of stated assets of the enterprise, although he knew only $15,000 had been paid for the property the year before and it was assessed at only about $5,000. Since it was also shown that the accountant assisted in the promotion of the venture, the proof of lack of independence seemed conclusive. Three other disciplinary actions against accountants[8] raised questions of independence because of the technical incompetence of the accountants there involved, but the Commission's decisions were based principally upon the omission of specific auditing procedures prescribed by Commission rule. The certificates in those cases represented little more than the loan of the accountant's name. Therefore, insofar as they pretended to be an objective and critical analysis, they were false and misleading.[9]

---

[7]Accounting Series Release No. 68.

[8]Accounting Series Release No. 48 (1944); Accounting Series Release No. 59 (1947); Accounting Series Release No. 67 (1949).

[9]For other examples of such examinations see National Boston Mines Corp., 2 S.E.C. 226 (1937); Red Bank Oil Co., Securities Exchange Act Releases Nos. 3110, 3770 (1946).

The paucity of disciplinary actions and the nature of the offense charged in those cases indicate how reluctant we are to institute such actions. However, I do not believe the profession may assume that appropriate action will not be taken unless there is evidence of corrupt and venal conduct. I believe every accountant is chargeable with the knowledge of the mechanics and the ethics of his profession. They are the rules of the game and their observance is essential if we are both to fulfill our high public trust.

Most of these rules, like those which govern any fiduciary, are prophylactic in nature. They are designed to prevent any conflict from arising between the accountant's duty to the public and his personal interests. Thus, just as a trustee of an estate in reorganization under the Bankruptcy Act may not ally himself with any creditor or stockholder interest in the estate, trade in securities of the estate, or purchase trust property, the accountant may not have any financial interest in a client's enterprise, even if it can be shown that the personal financial stake of the trustee or the accountant will have no effect upon his judgment. As a matter of fact, persons sensitive to their obligations may lean over backwards and act in opposition to their personal interests.

Nevertheless, I believe it is a salutary principle which arbitrarily denies to fiduciaries or people in a quasi-fiduciary position such as accountants the right to risk their independence.

Not all people are strong enough to resist temptation, particularly when it may easily be hidden behind a convincing rationalization. Even if there is no conscious attempt to favor a personal interest, unconscious pressures may cause a shift in the normal judgment exercised by the accountant. For both these reasons, and because the public will have greater confidence in certifications when they know there is no conflict between personal desires and professional opinions, the accountant must carefully scrutinize his relationships with his clients.

I recognize the impracticality of restricting or denying all intercourse between accountants and their clients. Nor do I believe this is either necessary or desirable. The accountant cannot be an ivory tower examiner, inaccessible to his client and remote from the market place. The nature of his business demands constant communication with management and recognition of all creditor and stockholder interests. In our opinions and interpretations at the Commission we have tried to stake out the safe and unsafe areas which the accountant who wishes to protect his independence should observe.

I assume that all of you are familiar with Accounting Series Releases 22 and 47, in which there are summarized Commission decisions and informal rulings upon the question of independence. Since 1944, when Release 47 was published, five Commission decisions and some one hundred staff opinions have dealt with this problem. Apparently there is still some need for clarification and delineation.

The problems fall, roughly, into three groups. First, there are those instances in which the accountant has a managerial or financial interest in his client such as when he is an officer, director or partner, or when he owns stock in the enterprise. Secondly, there are those instances in which there is a family relationship between the accountant and the client; and thirdly, there are those instances in which the accountant also acts for the client in some capacity other than as an accountant. Many problems, of course, involve more than one of these relationships, and within each classification a single factor may not disqualify an accountant but it may raise sufficient doubt so that if any other similarly inconclusive factor is present the accountant should be disqualified. I believe we may best discuss these problems by referring to our rulings under each of these classifications.

The question most frequently asked us is what constitutes a financial interest. Seven of the twenty illustrative cases which appear in Release 47 deal with this problem. Until recently we have analyzed that interest and if it was substantial we have decided the accountant could not be independent. An interest which exceeded one per cent of the personal fortune of the accountant was considered substantial. Experience has demonstrated, however, that even less than a one per cent financial interest may result in a conflict of interest. For instance, the percentage of net worth might be less than one percent although the proportion of income represented by the holdings might be substantial; persons may be affected differently by losses or gains or comparatively small sums; often exact values cannot be calculated. Accordingly, we take the view that any financial interest in a client, no matter how small, will disqualify the accountant and it is proposed that Rule 2-01 be revised to reflect this viewpoint. This financial interest may be in the form of a contingent fee contract, or a contract which is expressed in terms of a fixed fee plus a percentage of sales, or an investment in an underwriter, a promoter, an affiliate, a parent or a subsidiary of the client, for the definition of financial interest should be broad enough to insure the complete objectivity of the audit. In this connection I believe it would be wise to adhere strictly to Polonius' injunction, "neither borrower nor lender be" to any client, even if the borrowing or lending is only of office space.[10]

Nor can a firm of accountants be insulated from the holdings or acts of any partner, even if that partner should separate himself from any connection with the audit. Thus, an accounting firm was held to be lacking in independence where the partner who held stock in the client did not participate in the audit and the certificate

---

[10] See Southeastern Industrial Loan Co., 10 S.E.C. 617 (1941).

was signed jointly by the partner who had performed the audit and the firm.[11] Nor would the situation be remedied by the sale of these shares subsequent to the audit.

This disqualification will extend even to the audit for years prior to the date when the stock was acquired when a registration statement is filed which includes financial statements for those years, for a certification speaks also as of the date the registration statement becomes effective. Consequently, a financial interest at that time would interfere with the complete objectivity of the entire audit.

Similar problems are presented when an accountant or a partner in an accounting firm serves as a promoter, underwriter, voting trustee, director, or officer of a client, or administrator or executor of an estate with an interest in a client. It seems to me obvious that an accountant should not certify accounts which cover the period of time when he held office. I am continually amazed at the number of requests for an opinion in these circumstances.

In one instance a member of a firm of certifying accountants, although not an officer, consulted with management on accounting matters and exercised some supervisory powers with respect to the

[11] See Richard Ramare Gold Mines, Ltd., 2 S.E.C. 377 (1937).

corporation's accounting procedures. We held that despite the lack of a formal title, the accountant acted in the capacity of controller and he and his firm were therefore disqualified from certifying the financial statements.

A more difficult problem is presented after the accountant disposes of the financial interest which has disqualified him and resigns his office with the company. It has been urged that since he has cured his disability he should be henceforth fully qualified to exercise an impartial judgment. I believe that if he participated in the formation of significant accounting policies which persisted beyond the year in which he resigned or gave up his financial interest, he should not be permitted to place himself in a position to audit those decisions. A variation of this question is presented where another firm audits the accounts for the years when he was connected with the company and he attempts to rely upon this audit in submitting a certificate covering those, as well as subsequent years, when he had no connection with the client. The Commission has held, properly, that such a certification will not be accepted. The accountant may not rely on others, for part of his certification unless he would be fully qualified to perform that audit himself and did, in fact, supervise it.

This does not mean, however, that these earlier years may not be covered by a separate certification by others.

The second category of cases dealing with the independence of accountants on which we are frequently asked to express an opinion deals with family relationships. The typical case is one in which the accountant is the father, son, husband, brother, cousin or uncle of an officer, director, or bookkeeper of a registrant.[12] In accordance with well recognized legal documents governing fiduciaries, we have taken the position that such a relationship disqualifies the accountant. Obviously, if the persons involved live under the same roof and are part of the same economic unit, the accountant has a direct interest in the finances of his client. To the extent that the client pays the officer, it contributes directly to the support of the accountant's household. Even if the relative is not part of the same household it would be very unrealistic not to recognize the strong influence exerted upon the accountant by virtue of a close relationship.

Disqualification because of family relationship extends also to instances in which the relative has a financial interest in the client's enterprise. Thus, we ruled that where the wife of an accountant had a 47-1/2 per cent interest in one of three principal underwriters of a proposed issue, the accountant could not be considered independent.

---

[12] See Examiner's report adopted by the Commission in American Metal Mining Co., Securities Exchange Act Release No. 3537 (1944), where the wife of the accountant was bookkeeper for the registrant.

The third category of rulings we have rendered dealing with independence involves non-financial relationships. It is clear, I believe, that membership in the same civic, fraternal or social organizations as a client does not disqualify an accountant. I fully realize that many young men must get their start by enlarging their circle of acquaintances, and memberhsip in organizations is a well-accepted method of accomplishing this. Even when it was shown that an accountant and his client became joint obligors, together with others, upon a mortgage to secure a clubhouse, and that this accountant prepared personal income tax returns and audited the personal books of the principal stockholders of a registrant, it was not considered controlling by the Commission.[13] The possibility of improper influence arises when the relationship becomes more closely connected with either the finances of the accountant or his duties as an auditor.

In one case the stocks and bonds of a registrant, an investment company, were kept in a safety deposit box in a bank, and the members of the accounting firm were given exclusive custody of the key to the box. We ruled that the custodian of portfolio securities could not be considered independent for the purpose of certifying the financial statements. In another instance, it was found that a registrant who proposed to issue preferred stock was

[13] A. Hollander & Sons, Inc., 8 S.E.C. 586, 616 (1941).

indebted to a bank in a substantial sum and the member of the bank's examining committee which reviewed loans requiring special attention was a partner in the accounting firm which proposed to certify the financial statements. I believe the Commission properly ruled that the accountants could not be considered independent.

Finally, included in this category are those cases in which the accountant engages in an occupation incompatible with the concept of independence. Thus, he may not serve as a securities salesman and audit the accounts of brokerage houses or serve as a partner in a law firm engaged by one of his accounting clients to pass upon the legality of securities being registered.

These are the general problems with which we are presented upon the question of independence. They admit of many ramifications, permutations and combinations. Not all are easy of solution.

All of the factors which might possibly influence the accountant's judgment are considered. Often it is clear that any one factor would be insufficient to affect the honest discharge of an accountant's duties, but that, when taken in combination with others, it would be ground for disqualification. In such circumstances I cannot offer you the certainty of a rule of thumb. I can only suggest several of these to you as pitfalls to be avoided.

Among the most troublesome cases are those dealing with employees of an accounting firm as distinguished from partners. Adequate review procedures should be maintained to guard against employee inefficiency or deliberate falsification.[14] For a lapse in this regard I believe the firm is responsible. Either it has been negligent or it does not have the minimum knowledge of auditing procedures required of independent accountants. However, when the employee is both efficient and honest but it appears he has some disqualifying interest in the client, a more difficult problem is presented. If he should participate in the audit, it would, of course, invalidate that audit. Assuming, however, that he does not participate in the audit, what should be the effect of his interest? The employee is not in a policy-making position. Presumably, therefore, he has no influence over the accounting judgments exercised. On the other hand, the firm should not be placed in the position where it audits the actions of one of its employees. Certainly the firm may not loan an employee to a client to do bookkeeping, and then be permitted to audit that work. Even when the bookkeeping consisted simply of posting general ledger entries and making closing entries covering a month's work, we have refused to consider the firm employing that accountant independent. The same considerations are applicable where the employee has

---

[14]See Inter-state Hosiery Mills, 4 S.E.C. 706 (1939), where the employee forged checks, falsified the statement of assets and made unverified summaries instead of applying generally accepted auditing procedures.

served as a director or officer of the client. If the accounting firm must audit his decisions, it cannot be independent.

In these cases the employee's interest is considered as one factor and all the surrounding circumstances are examined to determine whether there is any possibility that the accounting judgments might have been swayed. For instance, if another employee was a second cousin of an officer of the client the two factors together might invalidate the audit although neither, alone, might be sufficient. Similarly, if it is shown that the wives of partners in an accounting firm engaged in speculative transactions in a registrant's stock prior to the audit, that fact would adversely affect, if not destory, the firm's independence. Certainly, if there were also other borderline factors present the firm could not be considered independent.

I know that you in the accounting profession agree with our concept of independence. In fact, credit for the inclusion of that concept in our laws belongs largely to the profession. Nevertheless, some of my friends in the profession have said:

> "Oh yes, we believe wholeheartedly in this ideal of independence but it is sometimes impractical. If a client refuses to permit us to verify inventories or if an inactive partner happens to own a few shares of a client's stock do we have to give up the account? Why can't we simply make full disclosure of the limited

nature of the audit or the financial interest in our certificate? The public can then assess those factors for themselves in analyzing the accounts."

To me, that represents a completely erroneous viewpoint of the nature and purpose of the concept of independence. I am reminded of a poem I once learned which ran something like this:

There was a little dachshund once,
So long, he had no notion
How long it took to notify
His tail of his emotion.

And thus it was that while his eyes
Were filled with tears and sadness,
His little tail kept wagging on
Because of previous gladness.

If a qualified certificate were permitted we might very well have a certificate filled with tears and sadness while the financial statements express only the previous gladness. Moreover, it seems to me that such a certification would be no better than no certification at all, for there would be no independent audit such as the Acts and rules of the Commission require. I remember one case in which the certificate had so many exceptions that all but

$35,000 of total stated assets of $9,000,000 were excluded from the purview of the certificate.[15]

On all these matters which I have discussed the Commission has proceeded slowly, with an eye to the needs of the investing public and a full realization of the effects of its rulings upon the accounting profession. We are thankful for the full measure of support and cooperation you have given us. Without it, I believe our task would be well nigh impossible. We could easily have a system in which accounting was the handmaiden rather than the measure of management. That we do not have such a system is a great credit to a young profession. I will hazard the guess that even Vice President Barkley, who as a Senator was skeptical of the practicality of using an accountant's conscience as his guide, has been convinced by the uniformly impressive achievements of the past seventeen years.

---

[15]Resources Corporation International, 7 S.E.C. 689, 739 (1940).

#11 Ralph H. Demmler

March 22, 1954

Providing Funds for Our Enterprises by the Issue of Securities

Abstract

If the modern corporation is looked to for the gathering and administering of large amounts of capital investors should be kept fully informed; financial information should be reasonably complete and in accordance with generally accepted accounting principles; and, securities markets should be free from manipulation. Demmler's approach represents a departure from the philosophy of prior commissioners. He sides with the CPAs view namely that while uniformity is a worthwhile goal it should not be pursued to the exclusion of other benefits. His analogy is that "It is not possible to forever clothe a growing boy in the same set of clothes."

The subject of my remarks was announced, I believe, as "Providing Funds for Our Enterprises by the Issue of Securities." I didn't think up those ringing words. That was obviously the work of a

Presented to the Eastern Springs Conference of the Controllers Institute of America.

mind which controls a tongue more eloquent than mine. I can't think of a topic, however, which gives me a wider freedom of choice and, hence, I shall use the title which was handed to me.

The economic history of this nation is a history of response to forces of incalculable magnitude--growth of large aggregations of economic power, the availability, indeed the rush, of surplus wealth for investment, the struggle of the great powers, the responsibility of world power, the development of weapons of mass destruction. Let us try to classify, if we may, the techniques by which such forces are handled. At the risk of over-simplification we can say that two methods have been employed--sometimes alternatively, sometimes concurrently--the development of counter forces or the imposition of legal controls.

Let me illustrate what I mean. Take the development of large aggregations of economic power represented in our giant corporations. Counter forces operating to control that power are competition of rival businesses and the collective bargaining power of labor unions. The legal controls operating to control the power are the anti-trust laws, the labor management relation laws, and the securities laws. Sometimes there have been attempts at voluntary self-imposed controls such as the cartels of Europe or the old NRA codes under the short-lived and unconstitutional National Industrial Recovery Act.

Take another example--the struggle of the great powers. On the one hand, we set up counter forces, rearmament, EDC, the winning of the atom race. On the other hand, we attempt controls, the League of Nations, the Naval Disarmament Treaty of 1922, the United Nations.

The wisdom with which we select a method or combination of methods of responding to these great challenges of our time determines the strength of our nation and may determine our survival.

Let me illustrate again. In some European nations private business has met the pressure of competition by a system of privately imposed controls--cartels with price fixing, allocation of markets, resistance to efficient methods of production, low wages, feeble attempts to develop mass markets. The result? A dangerous lack of popular support for private enterprise.

Now let me get a little closer to the announced subject of my remarks. This country has generated surplus wealth--savings if you will--available for investment. Corporations have been developed as a legal vehicle to bring together the savings of millions. There are some 7,000,000 stockholders in this country. One corporation has over a million stockholders. If you consider the indirect investment represented by ownership of insurance policies and interest in pension funds, the savings of many more millions are invested in the American industrial economy. The result of this is a peculiarly American and Canadian phenomenon, a literal pressure of money saved by the general public to find a place for investment in business and industry.

What do we do with these forces? The corporations call for capital. The members of the public press forward to invest their savings. We might depend entirely on an automatic system of self-adjustment. Investors could learn by bitter experience; the buyer could beware; businesses which forfeited public confidence would fail; the strong would survive; there would be no restriction in gathering capital into enterprise. Any such concept involves an inexcusably naive confidence that good will always triumph over evil.

It is inherent in the nature of things that there must be some legal controls imposed on one man who gathers together and administers capital furnished by others. That is true of trust funds. It is true of bank deposits and in its own way it must be true of corporate capital. Corporations are artificial entities, creatures of the state. They are empowered to do only what the law says they may do. Their directors have duties both as to good faith and prudence. Their property must be handled with due regard to the rights of creditors and stockholders. These general concepts are incontrovertible, but an effective system of legal controls involves the development of detailed rules and effective techniques to insure compliance.

When we look at the function of the modern corporation in gathering and administering capital, what ends do we desire? What abuses do we seek to prevent?

(1) We want to encourage investment--money in the mattress, jewelry in a vault are static wealth.

(2) We want no foolish, meaningless obstacles to the accumulation of capital.

(3) We want opportunity for initiative and imagination to develop the full economic potential of an enterprise.

I don't need to tell you that there are a number of other things that we want also:

(1) The investor should know what he is getting into when he buys securities.

(2) The public owners of an enterprise are entitled to current information.

(3) Financial information should be presented to investors with reasonable completeness and in accordance with generally accepted accounting principles.

(4) The investor should have a remedy against someone who deceived him by misrepresentation or concealment.

(5) A public stockholder should have a chance to vote intelligently at corporate meetings--not blindly.

(6) The markets for securities should be free of manipulation.

(7) People with inside information should not be allowed to make use of such inside information to the disadvantage of their fellow security holders, and transactions between such persons and the corporation should be subjected to careful scrutiny.

(8) People engaged in businesses involving recommendation of investments, sale of securities, handling of other people's money and securities, should be registered and should be required to file publicly available information about themselves.

(9) Trustees for corporate bond and debenture issues should be sufficiently independent to assure conscientious performance of the duties of such a trustee and the trustee should be required to perform its obligations with prudence.

(10) In cases of reorganization of corporations in which there is a large interest of public creditors or public investors, there should be some assurance of administration by an independent trustee, a vigorous inquiry into the true financial status, and a sound, feasible, fair and equitable reorganization plan.

I am not going to go into detail as to how the several Acts administered by the Securities and Exchange Commission in the aggregate contribute to the attainment of these general objectives. This audience is acquainted with the statutory pattern of disclosure and regulation.

The effectiveness of both the disclosure provisions and the regulatory provisions of the statutes administered by the Securities and Exchange Commission is based in great measure on the reliability of financial information and the presentation of that information in accordance with sound accounting principles.

Generally speaking, the information most determinative of the value of a security and the progress of its issuer is the financial condition of a business and the financial results of its operations.

Many of you remember the comment made in 1926 in William Z. Ripley's book "Main Street and Wall Street":

"The advocacy of really informative publicity as a corrective for certain of our present corporate ills must be placed in its proper relation to the whole matter of democratization of control. A prime argument which raises its head at the outset of all discussion of shareholders' participation in direction is that the shareholder--the owner, in other words--is hopelessly indifferent to the whole business. His inertia as respects the exercise of voting power, and almost everything else, is an acknowledged fact. But no one expects it to be otherwise. No one believes that a great enterprise can be operated by town meeting. It never has been done successfully; nor will it ever be. The ordinary run of folks are too busy, even were they competent enough. Nor is it true that the primary purpose of publicity, the sharing of full information with owners, is to enable these shareholders to obtrude themselves obsequiously upon their own managements. But such information, if rendered, will at all events serve as fair warning in case of impending danger. And this danger will be revealed, not because each shareholder, male or female, old or young, will bother to remove the wrapping from the annual report in the post, but because specialists, analysts, bankers, and others will promptly disseminate the information, translating it into terms intelligible to all.

"...This, then, is the ultimate defense of publicity. It is not as an adjunct to democratization through exercise of voting power, but as a contribution to the making of a true market price. This is a point but half appreciated at its real worth."

Not only is the information concerning its financial affairs important to the present and prospective investor as a means of evaluating the security which he owns or considers buying, but it is obviously the most significant source of information for the Commission and the courts in carrying out the regulatory provisions of the statutes which Congress has enacted in the public interest and for the protection of investors. In other words, accurate accounts are a tool for performing most of the jobs required to attain the general objectives which I listed a few minutes ago.

For this reason each of the various Acts administered by the Commission vest in the Commission extensive powers with respect to accounting matters.

I will not enumerate these powers beyond saying that the statutory language in each case is broad enough to give the Commission power to prescribe principles of accounting and classification of accounts.

The Commission nevertheless has not generally speaking adopted rules which prescribe principles of accounting except in the case of public utility holding companies and service companies.

Rather, the Commission looks to the standard of general acceptability of the accounting principles followed in a particular report or registration statement in determining whether or not such report or statement should be accepted without comment. The basic concept is stated in Accounting Series Release No. 4, April 25, 1938:

> "In cases where financial statements filed with this Commission pursuant to its rules and regulations under the Securities Act of 1933 or the Securities Exchange Act of 1934 are prepared in accordance with accounting principles for which there is no substantial authoritative support, such financial statements will be presumed to be misleading or inaccurate despite disclosures contained in the certificate of the accountant or in footnotes to the statements provided the matters involved are material. In cases where there is a difference of opinion between the Commission and the registrant as to the proper principles of accounting to be followed, disclosure will be accepted in lieu of correction of the financial statements themselves only if the points involved are such that there is substantial authoritative support for the practices followed by the

> registrant and the position of the Commission has not previously been expressed in rules, regulations or other official releases of the Commission, including the published opinions of its Chief Accountant."

If a registrant makes a filing stating accounts on principles for which it claims there is substantial authoritative support, there can readily arise arguments as to whether the claim for support is well founded.

You cannot write rules to answer questions like that. The discussions will go on through the years because accounting is not a branch of mathematics like arithmetic or geometry.

I would like to associate myself with a thought expressed in the introduction to the Restatement and Revision of Accounting Research Bulletins, published in 1953 by the American Institute of Accountants:

> "Changes of emphasis and objective as well as changes in conditions under which business operates have led, and doubtless will continue to lead, to the adoption of new accounting procedures. Consequently diversity of practice may continue as new practices are adopted before old ones are completely discarded."

It is not possible forever to clothe a growing boy in the same suit of clothes. If it is not practicable to have accounting principles formulated for SEC purposes, the occasional arguments and disagreements must go on. We must reconcile ourselves to suffering together from accountancy's growing pains.

The ideas which survive are those which become accepted because their application produces sound results in the multiplicity of particular situations which arise in a practical world.

From my own field, the law, I call to your mind Justice Holmes' remark: "The life of the law is not logic but experience."

Recognizing the fluid character of the stuff we work with, the Commission tries to keep itself informed not only through careful discussions in passing on specific problems, but also by conferences with representatives of the accounting profession, both with controllers and with independent accountants. We have been taught the importance of moving but not moving too fast. We are inclined to heed the injunction of the eighteenth century poet who said:

> "Be not the first by whom the new is tried,
> Nor yet the last to lay the old aside."

We have had discussions on accounting for stock options and the accounting problems raised by accelerated amortization. On the former we have adopted a rule permitting disclosure treatment. On the matter of amortization of emergency facilities, we have been pulled both ways by registrants, by the June, 1953 Bulletin of the Controllers Institute and by Bulletin 42 of the American Institute of Accountants. We are accepting in respect of 1953 reports statements of accounts which amortize the portion of the cost of properties covered by certificates of necessity over the five year period as well as statements of accounts which depreciate the cost of such facilities over the probable useful life of the facilities but give recognition to the resulting reduction in income tax benefit after the close of the amortization period. The transitional stage of the thinking on this subject exemplifies the process of getting an accounting principle generally accepted. The registrants in filing statements on either basis have been making adequate disclosures as to the method followed and the effect which would have been produced if the alternative method had been followed.

We have been importuned to greater liberality in balance sheet treatment of assets acquired as a result of a fortunate purchase, but we shall continue to be practically deaf to the persuasion of appraisals.

We have had several discussions--some practical and some academic--on departures from cost in the handling of depreciation. We find that that last mentioned subject stimulates equally passionate argument on the part of both proponents and opponents.

I will not breathe a thought on that subject this morning. We have had discussions as to the responsibility of the independent accountant to insist upon employing adequate auditing procedures.

We have had several problems in respect of foreign issuers. Nice questions are frequently posed by the arithmetical impossibility of converting the result achieved by the application of another. An overall policy question is presented to us in the matter of accounts and other disclosures by foreign issuers. The national interest in encouraging American investment abroad would naturally suggest removal of purely artificial barriers to the access of foreign issuers to American capital markets. On the other hand, if foreign standards of disclosure and accounting are not up to our standards, it might well be that lowering our standards for foreign issuers would result in a general lowering which would not be in the public interest. It is hard to conceive of an aggressive, two-fisted, American corporate executive not insisting upon "most favored nation" treatment from an American regulatory commission.

The fact that these problems exist does not indicate a turmoil of controversy. When one considers the vast complex presented by the accounting problems of American industry, it is almost a miracle that the areas of controversy are so small.

Private organizations like the Controllers Institute and like the American Institute of Accountants have had a great deal to do with the achievement of the high standard of American accounting. The

Securities and Exchange Commission and the Acts administered by it have contributed to the development of better and more informative corporate accounting and reporting.

The discipline of legal liability has been imposed upon issuers, officers, directors, controlling stockholders, underwriters and experts. At the time the Securities Act was adopted there was strong protest to the effect that the imposition of such liability would deter capital formation. While the liability provisions have been restrained exuberance in the presentation of material, they have not materially slowed down the process of capital formation nor have they resulted in a wave of law suits. As controllers your name goes on a registration statement under the Securities Act. the Form S-1, as you know, calls for the signature of the issuer's controller or principal accounting officer. The liabilities of Section 11 of the Securities Act are imposed upon every person who signs the registration statement. On matters of accounting, therefore, the controller cannot avoid being "it." It would be hard to argue that this liability has not contributed to improved accounting standards and procedures.

The Commission has loaned both moral and legal support to those who have helped to develop better and more informative corporate accounting practices. It has goaded a good many stragglers into falling in line. I cannot see, in view of the categorical language of the statutes which it administers, how the Commission can do otherwise.

#12 Byron D. Woodside

November 20-22, 1957

Particular S.E.C. Merger Considerations

Abstract

This address relates to the very technical provisions of the Securities Acts governing mergers, consolidations and reorganizations. A major concern is that a majority of such activity has been accomplished outside the Acts. Woodside discusses section (4)1 of the Securities Act and section 14(a) of the Securities Exchange Act both of which would require greater compliance with the securities laws for proxy statements. He also points out the differences between a "purchase" and a "pooling of interest."

An analysis of the impingement of the Federal statues administered by the Securities and Exchange Commission upon plans to acquire or dispose of a business by merger or otherwise begins with a determination of who is involved and how the proposed action,

---

Presented at Finance Orientation Seminar #121-91, American Management Association.

including perhaps some of its collateral aspects, is to be accomplished. Who you are and how you propose to handle the transaction can affect significantly your obligations under the Federal Securities Laws and the interest of the Commission in your affairs.

The two statutes with which we are primarily concerned are the Securities Act of 1933 and the Securities Exchange Act of 1934. I doubt whether it is necessary to consider the Public Utility Holding Company Act or the Investment Company Act for purposes of this meeting.

Reduced to its simplest terms, I believe the proposition can be stated that if in the process of effecting an acquisition or disposition of a business, securities are publicly offered and sold, the registration and prospectus provisions of the Securities Act must be complied with absent some exemption; and if in the process a company having a voting security listed on a stock exchange solicits the holders of those securities for their proxies, consents or some person or group solicits their opposition with respect to the transaction, the persons soliciting must comply with the proxy regulations of the Commission under Section 14(a) of the Exchange Act.

Having stated the proposition so briefly and clearly, I hasten to caution you not to be deceived by its seeming simplicity. The interpretation and application of the statutes and the Commission's rules to corporate reorganizations, of which I regard acquisitions of various types to be an aspect, continue after many years to present puzzling questions at times both for industry and the Commission. Some of these questions I propose to discuss with you today.

Viewed in relation to the law and the Commission's rules, the most striking feature of the vast volume of security transactions arising out of statutory mergers, consolidations, acquisitions and recapitalizations which we know have occurred is that they have been achieved without the necessity of complying with the registration provisions of the Securities Act at all. In the main, the only cases involving transactions of this character which are affected by the registration provisions and disclosure requirements of this Act are those for voluntary exchange offers made by one person or corporation to the public security holders of another company and those where securities are sold to the public for cash and the proceeds are to be employed to acquire another business or significant assets. These cases have not represented any substantial volume of financing in terms of the total offerings registered under the Securities Act in any year. They certainly have been insignificant in relation to the tremendous number of corporate acquisitions and mergers reported in various publications dealing with the subject.

The annual report of the Federal Trade Commission for 1956, in referring to merger investigations, states: "An information sheet containing such information as is readily available from press reports and recognized reference manuals is prepared for each merger. In fiscal 1956 more than 1,000 of these information sheets on reported mergers were prepared."[1]

Our own annual report for 1956 shows that of total securities registered under the 1933 Act during the year aggregating $13,000,000,000, less than $500,000,000 was for exchange for other securities.[2]

The Federal Trade Commission in its report on corporate mergers and acquisitions states: "During the period 1948-54, 1,610 formerly independent manufacturing and mining concerns were reported in the financial manuals to have disappeared as a result of mergers and acquisitions. To this may be added 74 whole subsidiaries and 89 whole divisions, bringing the number of disappearances up to 1,773."[3]

---

[1]Annual Report of Federal Trade Commission, 1956, page 21.

[2]Annual Report of SEC, 1956, Appendix Table 2, page 231.

[3]FTC Report on Corporate Mergers and Acquisitions, May 1955, page 20.

I have no figure for the period which would provide any accurate measure of the registered security offerings which might have been primarily for the purpose of aiding in a major acquisition of another company directly or indirectly. My impression is that they have been relatively few. We know that in virtually all instances where the transactions take the form of a statutory merger or acquisition of assets pursuant to a vote of security holders, no registration occurs.

The avoidance of the Securities Act in these merger transactions the aggregate volume of which in the last ten years has been commented upon as one of the significant economic developments of the post-war years has come about not by virtue of any express statutory exemption but as a consequence of a rule[4] of the Commission adopted in the first instance in 1935, and of reliance by many people on constructions of the provisions of Section 4(1) of the Act.[5]

I will comment further upon these provisions in a moment.

At this point I merely wish to observe as a generalization that the principal problem of businessmen and their counsel Security Act-wise in connection with corporate mergers and acquisitions has

---

[4]Rule 133, General Rules and Regulations under Securities Act-SEC.

[5]Section 4(1) of the Securities Act of 1933.

beem to understand the procedures for availing themselves of an exemption from the registration provisions rather than to encounter and deal with the disclosure problems which might arise were the security issues involved to be registered.

Two companies might be mentioned as an illustration of the growth of public shareholder investment over a period of time without Securities Act disclosures.

The Federal Trade Commission report on mergers, in referring to corporate acquisitions in the 1948-1954 period, states: "The most active acquiring firm during this period was Foremost Dairies, which made 48 acquisitions, as reported in the financial manuals."[6]

This company, as a Delaware corporation, filed its first registration statement under the Securities Act in 1935. At that time it had a capitalization of 52,000 shares of 6% preferred stock and 20,000 shares of 20 cents par value common stock. In 1949, the Delaware company merged into Maxson Food Systems, a New York corporation, the latter changing its name to Foremost Dairies. Since that time the company has filed four registration statements under the '33 Act, one of which was for the sale of common stock for the account of a selling stockholder.

---

[6] FTC Report on Corporate Mergers and Acquisitions, May 1955, page 3.

The company became subject to the '34 Act in 1955. It has not filed any proxy statements with the Commission relating to mergers or acquisitions. Information on file indicates that apparently 2,000,000 shares of common stock and 270,000 shares of preferred stock were issued in connection with the acquisition of 43 companies between 1952 and 1956 in transactions for which exemptions from registration under the Securities Act were claimed. The company now has in excess of 37,000 shareholders.

Penn-Texas Corporation (formerly Pennsylvania Coal & Coke Corporation) has never filed a registration statement under the Securities Act. It registered under the Exchange Act in 1935, at which time it had slightly less than 1,000 stockholders owning 165,000 shares of common stock. The company has filed proxy statements on nine occasions with reference to mergers, acquisitions or authorizations of additional stock. The company now has about 30,000 stockholders, and, as you know, it has become a large, diversified manufacturing enterprise.

The Securities Act, of course, may apply to any company making a public offering of a security regardless of its size, age, financial history or condition.

The problem under the Exchange Act is quite different. Only those companies having voting securities listed on an exchange who may solicit proxies of the holders of these securities are required to comply with the Commission's disclosure requirements as set forth in the proxy rules in connection with mergers and acquisitions.

During the 1956 fiscal year, about 2,000 solicitations were made under the Commission's proxy rules by the managements of 1,700 companies. Of these, approximately seven per cent related to mergers, consolidations, acquisitions of businesses, purchases and sales of properties and dissolutions of companies.[7] The corresponding figures for fiscal 1957 and fiscal 1952 were six per cent and two per cent, respectively.

Should the Fulbright bill become law in its present form, an additional 650 companies might become subject to the Commission's proxy rules. At the present time there are 2,015 issuers having voting securities listed on exchanges, of which about 75 per cent solicit proxies for annual meetings.

Under the Exchange Act, your SEC problems, if any, depend on whether you are listed and whether the acquisition is one which must be put to a vote of security holders or may be accomplished in the discretion of management without seeking stockholder approval or ratification.

---

[7]Annual Report of SEC, 1956, page 102.

These requirements of the Exchange Act give rise to some peculiar situations. If two or more companies propose a merger or other acquisition requiring the vote of security holders, one may be required to comply with the proxy rules--because the securities are listed--and the other parties to the proposal not having listed securities are free to solicit without Federal supervision of the solicitation. If the acquiring company has sufficient authorized stock to permit an acquisition without securing specific authority of its security holders and the acquired company is not a listed company, it is possible that the acquisition could occur without being subject to any of the Commission's disclosure requirements other than a report after the event.

I am not here, however, to advertise exemptions from or means of avoidance of our product and services. Those who may encounter the problem of meeting some business deadline in company with the Commission's requirements are interested in the practical operation of the rules. That is one of our prime interests, too.

The statutory basis for the Commission's proxy rules is stated in general terms in Section 14(a) of the Exchange Act. Penalties for willful violations are prescribed by Section 32(a) of the Act. Maximum penalties upon a conviction may be a ten-thousand dollar fine or two years' imprisonment or both for "any person who willfully violates any provision of this title, or any rule or regulation thereunder...or any person who willfully and knowingly makes, or causes to be made, any statement in any application, report, or document required to be filed under this title or any rule or regulation thereunder...which statement was false or misleading with respect to any material fact..."[8]

Civil liability provisions are found in Section 18(a) which provide that "any person who shall make or cause to be made any statement in any application, report or document filed purusant to this title or any rule or regulation thereunder...which statement was at the time and in the light of the circumstances under which it was made false or misleading with respect to any material fact, shall be liable to any person (not knowing such statement was false or misleading) who in reliance upon such statement shall have purchased or sold a security at a price which was affected by such statement, for damages caused by such reliance unless the person sued shall prove that he acted in good faith and had no knowledge that such statement was false or misleading.[9]

As I understand the law, it is doubtful whether a person could recover damages under this section from a person soliciting proxies for a misleading statement in proxy material, in reliance upon which the security holder executed a proxy, absent circumstances which would give rise to the conclusion that the giving of the

---

[8] Securities Exchange Act--Section 32(a).

[9] Securities Exchange Act--Section 18(a).

proxy itself involved a purchase or sale of a security, or absent some other transaction involving a purchase or sale of a security. In any event, I know of no court decisions under Section 18(a) arising out of a proxy transaction. It is possible, however, that a person who executes a proxy in reliance upon proxy material which violates the rules and is damaged thereby might recover as a matter of general law.

If a company is subject to the rules, they apply whether in the acquisition transaction the issuer is the acquiring company or the company being acquired. Items 14, 15 and 16 of Schedule 14A of Regulation X-14 outline the information to be included in a proxy statement with respect to Mergers, Consolidations, Acquisitions and Similar Matters. Item 14 applies in five situations:

(a) The merger or consolidation of the issuer into or with any other person or of any other person into or with the issuer;

(b) The acquisition by the issuer or any of its security holders of securities of another issuer;

(c) The acquisition by the issuer of any other going business or of the assets thereof;

(d) The sale or other transfer of all or any substantial part of the assets of the issuer;

(e) The liquidation or dissolution of the issuer.

The material features of the plan, the reasons therefor and the general effect thereof upon the rights of existing security holders of the issuer must be stated. In addition, certain basic data must be included concerning the other party or parties to the transaction. These latter requirements are stated in general terms designed to indicate the nature and scope of the information desired rather than to specify in detail particular items of information.

The market history of the shares of each company for at least two years is required.

Certified financial statements of the issuer and its subsidiaries (usually consolidated financial statements are required) must be included in the proxy statement. These, as indicated by Item 15, include a balance sheet as of the close of the last fiscal year and profit and loss and surplus data for the three full fiscal years then ending. Schedules other than those pertaining to supplementary profit and loss information may be omitted.

Since the soliciting issuer is one having securities listed on an exchange, it already will have financial statements certified by an independent public or certified accountant and presumably any major accounting problem with respect to its financial statements for prior periods will have been resolved in the course of filing the customary periodic reports required to be filed with the Exchange and the Commission pursuant to Section 13 of the Exchange Act.

In addition, however, equivalent financial statements for the other party or parties to the proposed transaction likewise must be included in the proxy statement, with the proviso, however, that such financial statements need not be certified.

Item 16 inquires into consideration and factors bearing on fairness of consideration.

These provisions for disclosures by an issuer in its proxy statement of information concerning another issuer or issuers give rise to difficulties in certain cases, depending upon the relations between the parties and the reasons underlying the action of the parties. Furthermore, a question frequently is raised on the part of an issuer and its officials concerning the responsibility of the issuer to its security holders for information concerning another company over which the issuer has no control, and with respect to which it may or may not have access to the latter's books and records. In general, our position has been that an issuer under these circumstances may state the sources of the information concerning another issuer contained in its proxy statement--assuming an arm's length relationship--but efforts to include disclaimers of responsibility for such information are objected to. Assuming good faith, there could be no criminal liability. Section 18(a) provides that in a civil suit a person sued may escape liability if he can prove good faith and that he had no knowledge of the falsity or misleading character of the information, the truth of which is challenged. Whether an official of the other company giving the issuer false information which the issuer innocently includes in its proxy statement might be held liable under Section 18(a) is a question which to my knowledge has not arisen and I don't know the answer.

A proxy statement filed with the Commission for an acquisition or disposition of a business becomes for us another problem of security analysis and disclosure, within the framework of the rules and the general standards of materiality applicable to all financial reporting under the Exchange Act.

It will do not harm to repeat here the fundamental theses of the Securities Act and the Exchange Act and the Commission's administration of them--that we do not pass on the merits of an acquisition or other corporate action nor approve or disapprove terms and conditions of the transaction or, indeed, the disclosures made concerning them. It seems that no matter how frequently or emphatically we make this assertion, many people have the notion that we have some power to prevent a transaction because some feature, objective or anticipated result of a proposed acquisition or disposition is offensive to some person or interest. Petitions that we prevent, delay or attempt to change the terms of a proposed transaction come with particular frequency and insistence in those situations in which opposition groups organize to solicit proxies to oppose the consummation of transactions for the approval of which proxies are solicited by the issuer and its management.

It is not our job to pass judgments concerning these business transactions in terms of their social or economic desirability, their possible effect upon labor or some community in which plants may be located, concentration of economic power or conflicts with the antitrust laws.

Our purpose is to attempt to secure a fair and truthful disclosure of certain basic material business and financial facts in accordance with the established standards in order to assist security holders and the market place to come to a reasonably informed judgment of the proposal.

Since our basis interest is analysis and disclosure, such problems as are encountered--other than procedural and mechanical matters--tend to approximate those which arise in the review of registration statements and prospectuses filed under the Securities Act. I say "approximate" because the disclosures required in proxy statements and in registration statements are not governed by precisely the same rules.

The proxy rules are grounded on the Exchange Act, and the disclosures specified in Sections 12 and 13 of that Act for purposes of financial and other reports are somewhat less comprehensive than the corresponding provisions of Schedule A of the Securities Act. Furthermore, the proxy rules as they relate to mergers and acquisitions are less specific than the registration forms and related rules and instructions under the Securities Act.

It is fair to say, I think, that there may be a little more administrative improvisation in our handling of proxy statements than in the case of the Securities Act cases, in part because of the less specific character of the governing regulations. On the other hand, it is much more difficult to be specific in writing rules and disclosure requirements directed particularly to the variety of transactions which are encountered in the field of corporate reorganizations.

In the ordinary Securities Act filing we are concerned with disclosures relating to a single business and one or more issues of equity or debt securities of a single issuer. In the field of mergers and acquisitions under the proxy rules, the issuer and the commission must deal with disclosures as they relate to at least two issuers on an historical basis and the various classes of securities which may be present and a third set of data which represents a pro-forma presentation showing the effect of the proposal in terms of financial position, operating records and the rights of security holders. Various measures of corporate values and earnings will be employed which may not appear in the conventional Securities Act prospectus. Textual matter is more likely to include material which falls in the category of argument and persuasion rather than the mere factual recitations found in prospectuses.

It goes without saying that the financial statements of the parties to the transaction are the data most important and essential to any presentation in a proxy statement with respect to meregers and similar transactions. The financial statements required for both companies are those which would be filed in an application for registration of securities under the Exchange Act. Accordingly, balance sheets, profit and loss and surplus schedules must be submitted in the content and scope required by Form 10 and must be prepared in accordance with Regulation S-X.

If both companies are listed companies, the preparation and presentation of appropriate financial information should be a relatively simple task. In addition to the required financial statements of both companies, you will probably be requested to supply a tabular summary of earnings for a period of five years or more for each company and, depending on the circumstances, a pro-forma summary giving effect to a combination of the operations of the two companies on the basis of certain stated assumptions with such adjustments and explanations or qualifications as may be necessary and a pro-forma balance sheet.

Extraordinary transactions which may have affected the operating or balance sheet figures during the period will require explanation or in some circumstances, elimination from or special treatment in the summary or pro-forma figures.

Problems arise as to the proposed basis upon which fixed assets and other accounts will be stated for balance sheet purposes upon consummation of the merger transaction.

Frequently these matters become the subject of prefiling conferences with our staff--a practice we welcome. In clear-cut cases these discussions may cover questions of presentation of financial data rather than of principle. Usually the parties involved know when they have a marginal case and arrange a discussion before printing rather than risk a conflict in views which might require reprinting to reflect, for example, "acquisition accounting" rather than a "pooling of interests" solution. Such a result may arise in a situation when factors favoring a "pooling of interests" solution have been deemed by the registrant to justify this procedure, whereas the staff, on the basis of the evidence initially at least, may have been more impressed with factors which would seem to lead to a contrary result.

The concept of "pooling of interests" accounting (which avoids the booking of goodwill as would be required in many "purchase" transactions and permits the combining of earned surplus of the constituent companies rather than "acquisition accounting") has been recognized by the Commission for about fifteen years. At first this accounting was deemed appropriate when the corporations to be combined were of about equal size and were engaged in similar or complementary businesses. This latter test is now outmoded with the emphasis on diversification in corporate mergers.

In 1945 the Commission considered a merger proposal in which all facotrs other than size clearly supported a pooling of interests solution. The result was that goodwill was not recorded and the earned surplus of both companies was carried forward. In this case the assets and common stock equity of the smaller company were less than one-fifth and one-third respectively of the larger. From this point on, relative size was considered to be less important than other factors in considering whether a business combination was a pooling of interests or not.

The significant next step in the case-by-case consideration of the problem by the Commission was raised in a proposed merger involving the possibility that a minority interest would remain after an exchange offer and the smaller company would continue as a subsidiary. It was concluded that in these circumstances it would be inappropriate to treat the transaction as a "pooling of interests" and therefore the earned surplus of the acquired company could not be combined with that of the registrant. On a purchase basis goodwill would have been negligible.

Adhering to this interpretation that pooling of interests accounting was inapplicable when parties to a merger continued in a subsidiary relationship led to a reconsideration of Section C of Chapter 7 of Bulletin No. 43 of the American Institute of Accountants, which succeeded Bulletin 40 with only minor changes. Bulletin No. 48,[10] published in January of this year, omits the requirement of similar or complementary business and permits a pooling of interests when <u>substantially all</u> of the ownership interests in the constituent corporations continue and permits a subsidiary relationship to survive "if no significant minority interest remains outstanding, and if there are important tax, legal, or economic reasons for maintaining the subsidiary relationship, such as the preservation of tax advantages, the preservation of franchises or other rights, the preservation of the position of outstanding debt securities, or the difficulty or costliness of transferring contracts, leases, or licenses." The revision retains the tests of continuity of ownership and of management or power to control the management and introduces a specific test of relative size. Although relative size may not necessarily be determinative, the bulletin says that "where one of the constituent corporations is clearly dominant (for example, where the stockholders of one of the constituent corporations obtain 90 percent to 95 per cent or more of the voting interest in the combined enterprise), there is a presumption that the transaction is a purchase rather than a pooling of interests."

---

[10] Issued by the Committee on Accounting Procedure of the American Institute of Accountants.

As you would suspect, the first questions raised under Bulletin 48 were with regard to the size test and minority interests. The first cases involved combinations in which the smaller company fell in the range of five per cent to ten per cent of the combined equity. No objection was raised to pooling of interests accounting in these cases when it appeared that a strong case had been made under the other tests. As a general proposition we have objected to pooling of interests when the equity of the smaller company would be less than five per cent. However, in some situations pooling of interests accounting has been accepted when the acquiring company's interest has exceeded 95 per cent, when, for example, the other factors involved were persuasive and the size and position of the companies were such that any other view would, for all practical purposes, have the effect of excluding certain industry leaders from the pooling of interests doctrine entirely.

If any extended period of time has elapsed since the date of the certified financial statements for the latest fiscal period, you may be asked to include interim earnings data in the summary for one or both companies together with later balance sheets. These frequently are supplied voluntarily but if not, you need not be surprised if a request is made. In any event, you probably will be asked to supply--either for our own information or for inclusion in the proxy statement--information concerning the trend of sales, orders and costs since the date of the financial statements. The commission and its staff have been extremely sensitive with respect to this problem after several cases in which failure to secure responses to specific questions on this subject led to later difficulties.

The financial statements and earnings summary provide the basis for comparisons and explanations which should be included in every proxy statement in order that the reader may grasp the essential features, purpose, and effect of the plan. It should be remembered that the purpose of the proxy statement is to explain and reveal to the stockholder. Our experience too frequently has been that they seem designed to obscure and distort various aspects of a proposal.

I asked our examining staff to give me some illustrations of problems encountered in recent experience with merger proxy statements. Their responses are illuminating:

(a) necessity for calling for data which will illustrate graphically by the use of well-known statistical and financial analytical presentations the values passing and being received as a result of the merger;

(b) the use of appraisals or projections of earnings to explain or support exchange ratios;

(c) securing adequate disclosures of the relative rights and values of various classes of securities of the constituent companies as they will be affected by the transaction;

(d) adequate disclosure of the effect of income tax carry-forwards.

Other comments not directly related to financial and statistical data include the following:

(a) adequacy of the description of the businesses of the constituent companies;

(b) reasons for the transaction are not given adequately in many cases. In this connection, one of our analysts stated: "Often there are reasons for a merger not presented in the proxy statement nor evident from the facts which may be readily obtainable. Conversations with counsel or other persons sometimes reveal important motivating factors;

(c) disclosures of interests of officers and directors in the business of the constituent companies and the survivor;

(d) in multi-line businesses, information as to the relative importance of major business lines;

(e) dependence upon large customers or limited sources of supply;

(f) effect of the plan upon compensation and option arrangements;

(g) failure to respond to Items 6 and 7 of the proxy rules when the merger agreement in effect involves an election of directors--these items requiring information as to the identity and interest of directors and nominees and remuneration and other transactions with management and associates.

(h) failure to explain reasons for increase in authorized stock substantially in excess of requirements for the capitalization of the surviving company;

(i) description or explanation of changes in the articles and bylaws which may affect materially the rights of security holders such as quorum requirements, cumulative voting or a classified board of directors, preemptive rights, indemnification of officers and directors and limitations upon dividends;

(j) disclosure of any antitrust problems;

(k) disclosure of status of surviving corporation as listed company--if one of constituent companies is a listed company and the survivor will not have its stock listed, a statement to this effect and its significance will be required;

(l) adequate disclosure of dissenters' rights and the procedure to be followed to perfect such rights.

I do not wish to suggest that the foregoing recital indicates proxy statements generally are defective in these many respects. They are not; in fact, many of them when filed reflect careful consideration of the many factors as to which discussion in the proxy statement is essential or appropriate. When problems do arise, however, they are quite likely to fall within one of the categories I have mentioned.

Obviously a proxy statement must be a short summary of the vast amount of thinking and paper work which precede the formal presentation of a merger proposal. There can be many reasons for a firm conviction that a particular way of describing or handling a transaction is the most desirable from the point of view of the proponent. On the other hand, we know, too, that frequently a proxy statement for a merger transaction like a Securities Act prospectus takes the form it does because it is modeled on a published proxy statement or prospectus employed by some other company and ignores or fails to emphasize facts or circumstances which give meaning to the particular transaction being considered.

Two or three of the subjects mentioned above deserve a word of explanation. Some of our most difficult problems as adminitrators of disclosure statutes have arisen in connection with attempts to employ appraisals and projections of earnings in prospectuses and proxy statements.

It is probably impossible to give you any brief, generalized statement of Commission policy or practice with respect to the use of appraisals. It is obvious, of course, that the proposed basis of exchange of the securities of two or more merging companies in an arm's length transaction is the result of a valuation process by the parties. Frequently this value judgment relates to an extremely complex and wide array of business and financial factors which are not necessarily given equal weight by the various parties concerned.

The management should, in response to the rules, set forth in the proxy material a reasonable explanation of the pertinent factors which they considered in arriving at their price judgment. When an appraisal report is mentioned as one of these factors, we, of necessity, must be concerned with the nature of the appraisal or valuation report and the circumstances of its use.

Certainly there can be no objection to management securing expert advice to aid it in coming to a conclusion which it is willing to submit for shareholder action. Usually we inquire as to the nature and scope of the report and its conclusions, and request that a copy be submitted for inspection. We find that they represent all types of expressions ranging from property valuations to letter opinions which contain no indication of how or why the opinion was reached. Further, they range from comprehensive engineering reports by well-known appriasal concerns to various types of economic opinions by business consultants.

If the opinion or conclusion of a consulting or engineering firm is included in the proxy material, the nature of the opinion should be clearly explained, the expert identified and such explanation or qualification given as may be necessary to indicate the scope of his review and the factors considered by him. Further, the general nature of the reliance by management upon the outside opinion should be indicated.

It is our general practice to object to the use of reproduction cost appraisals of physical assets for the obvious reason that they are almost invariably employed to indicate an upward reach of values which have little or no significance in the usual merger problem. It is also our general practice to object to the inclusion in proxy material of projections of estimates of specific future net income to support an enterprise valuation. We frequently are asked to explain our reasons for this position, particularly in view of the fact--our critics remind us--that in Chapter X cases the Commission itself indulges in the practice.

In the first place the problem is not the same and, further, the Chapter X case in all its aspects is before a court where all the contentions of contesting interests are subjected to scrutiny and argument for the purpose of permitting the court to reach a decision in equity.

A merger is a bargain arrived at without supervision and it may or may not be a good bargain in terms of apparent equities, although it may represent a good business solution to certain problems.

Securities, in fact all sorts of property, have been sold since commerce began on the basis of promises of future values and future income. We cannot project the Commission's administration of the disclosure provisions of the statutes into every conversation or communication in which this device may be employed. The Commission has always stood firm, however, on the proposition that literature filed with it in response to statutory provisions designed to lay basic material business facts before the public may not properly include predictions of future net income. For the Commission to lend its procedures to this device would involve it in an impossible and indefensible task. We are not prepared to accept someone's opinion as to future profits of an enterprise as a material fact for purposes of the statutory standards.

In all cases involving business acquisitions, it is necessary that we keep in mind that the transaction may be of interest to the Antitrust Division of the Department of Justice and the Federal

Trade Commission, both of which have the responsibility for enforcing Section 7 of the Clayton Act.

We have worked out over the years a fairly simple procedure of being sure the Antitrust Division and the FTC know about the transaction. Any prospectus or proxy statement involving a proposed merger, consolidation, or other form of acquisition of a business where the transaction is in excess of $3,000,000 and not subject to specific authorization by another Federal agency, such as the Interstate Commerce Commission, Federal Power Commission, etc., is brought to the attention of these two agencies.

The actions taken by the Department of Justice through its Antitrust Division fall into four main categories insofar as our problems of disclosure in prospectuses and proxy statements are concerned:

(1) The Department takes no action at all.

(2) The "no action" letter. If requested by the parties to the transaction, the Department of Justice will issue an official letter, signed by at least an Assistant Attorney General, to the effect that the Department "does not presently intend to take action with respect to the proposed acquisition."

(3) The "we will see you in court" letter.

(4) Without any notice to the parties, the Department of Justice will move directly into court in an attempt to block the proposed transaction by a restraining order and an injunction. Failing that move, the Department will file a civil antitrust complaint in the court when the transaction is consummated.

By far the largest number of cases fall under the first category of "silence." The next largest number fall under Category (2), the "no action" letter.

Because of the time limits under which we operate in Securities Act and proxy matters, it is essential that we complete our examination and other processing procedures in a relatively short period of time after the date of the filing. Since it may take weeks, or even months in the case of Category (3) and (4) cases for the Antitrust Division to complete its work to the point of "clearing" with the Attorney General's Office, it is obvious that we cannot very well coordinate our examining procedure at the Commission with that of the Department of Justice in every case.

Accordingly, in the vast majority of these acquisition cases, we go ahead and complete our examination, prepare our letter of comments, and if by that time we have not heard from the Antitrust Division, we send out our letter.

There is of course no real problem of disclosure if the Department of Justice has taken "official" action under Categories (2), (3), or (4). The same is true if either the Department or the Federal Trade Commission has sent out to the parties a questionnaire or letter of inquiry. We consider that a brief factual statement of the situation is all that is necessary to be made in the prospectus or proxy statement. Of course, the statement may be followed by a further statement that counsel are of the opinion that the proposed transaction, if consummated, will not violate the antitrust laws.

Our real disclosure problems arise when we have completed our examination and are about to send out our letter of comments on a preliminary proxy statement, or we are about ready to "clear" a registration statement and we are advised that the staff of the Antitrust Division is about to recommend, or has already recommended, to the Attorney General's Office the sending of their Category (3) "see you in court letter", or, where the staff of the Antitrust Division are prepared to recommend to the Attorney General's Office that court action be commenced to block the transaction.

About all we can do, and have done, in these situations if we know the parties have received a questionnaire from the Department of Justice or a letter of inquiry from the Federal Trade Commission, or if it is otherwise no secret that the transaction is being investigated by these agencies, is to request the parties, in addition to including in the prospectus or proxy statement information about the receipt of the questionnaire or letter of inquiry, to let us know by letter what they intend to do if the Department's Category (3) "we will see you in court letter" is received before the exchange offer or proxy solicitation commences.

Earlier, I mentioned the fact that in most merger transactions the securities being issued have not been registered under the Securities Act.

The question of the applicability of the registration provisions of the Securities Act to a statutory merger or consolidation was one of the first major policy decisions to be faced by the new SEC shortly after it succeeded the FTC in the administration of the Securities Act in 1934.

Initially, it was determined administratively that no objection would be raised by the Commission if a statutory merger under the laws of New York and New Jersey were consummated without registration. Later--in 1935--a rule was adopted, as a note to the reorganization registration form, which provided in effect that no sale to security holders was involved when a plan of consolidation or merger was submitted to a vote of security holders pursuant to the provisions of State law where the affirmative vote of the required majority bound the minority holders.

In 1951, an amendment to the general rules and regulations under the Securities Act was adopted--Rule 133, which provided that for purposes of Section 5 of the Act only, no sale or offer for sale shall be deemed to be involved so far as the stockholders of a corporation are concerned when, pursuant to statutory provisions in the State of incorporation or provisions contained in certificates of incorporation, there is submitted to a vote of stockholders a plan or agreement for a statutory merger or consolidation or reclassification of securities or a proposal for the transfer of assets of such corporation to another person in consideration of the issuance of securities under such circumstances that the vote of a required favorable majority will operate to authorize the proposed transaction so far as concerns the corporation whose stockholders are voting and will bind all stockholders except as to dissenters' rights.

The significant change in the rule at that time was the specification that the rule applied for purposes of Section 5; i.e., registration, only, the clear implication being that the Commission considered that the rule should not operate to remove a security transaction, in an acquisition of the character specified, from the operation of Section 12--which creates civil liabilities in connection with the sale of securities--and Section 17(a), which makes certain activities unlawful in the sale of securities.

The theory of the rule briefly is that the transaction occurs as a corporate act rather than as a consequence of the volition of individual shareholders in a contractual sense.

I don't want to discuss the rightness or wrongness of the rule or its underlying premises. The rule is on the books and as long as that is so, it may continue to be relied upon.

I think it is important to point out, however, that the Commission in recent years has tended in the direction of narrowing the application of the rule to the merger transaction itself and to the view that the issuance of securities in a Rule 133 transaction did not create "free stock" for all purposes. In other words, Rule 133 does not provide a "security exemption--, at most it may be relied upon as a "transaction exemption"--and the Commission has ruled in various situations that public distributions of securities subsequent to the merger transaction must find their own and some other exemption if registration is to be avoided.

The safest course to follow in planning procedures in a projected merger or other acquisition by stockholder vote is to consult with the Commission's staff if it appears likely that the merger transaction is but a step in a process which involves a public distribution, to others than the voting stockholders, following the merger transaction.

About a year ago, the Commission announced in a published release a proposal to repeal Rule 133. After receiving many objections from inudstry and the bar and after a public hearing on the proposal, the Commission on March 15 of this year announced deferral of any action and that further study would be given the problems involved before making any further proposals.

The other type of transaction which I mentioned earlier, in which registration under the Securities Act is considered unnecessary, is the so-called "private sale." In these cases the issuers rely upon Section 4(1), which provides that the registration provisions do not apply to transactions by an issuer not involving any public offering. The usual pattern of these cases is the acquisition of stock or assets of another company from a limited group of stockholders or owners (a group small enough not to be considered as "the public"), payment being made in stock of the acquiring company. The recipients of the stock usually represent that the shares so taken are being taken for investment and not for distribution.

It has come to our attention in many cases that these so-called investment representations are regarded as a necessary part of a ritual which once completed leaves the owner free thereafter to sell the shares upon the occurrence of any event which can be asserted as a "change of circumstances." In many of these cases, a public distribution has occurred under conditions which lead us to the conclusion that the sellers should be regarded as statutory underwriters, that the securities should in fact have been registered and that the issuer had been placed in the position of having violated the law.

There is no insulating magic for an issuer in an investment letter of the character which we have seen in circulation if the transaction in fact is a first step in a public distribution of the issuer's shares. An issuer if it chooses to employ its shares as currency for purposes of an acquisition of a business in reliance on Section 4(1) should, to protect itself against the risk of a one-year put under Section 12(1) and against possible injunctive action, seek specific and clear-cut assurances as to the intention of the persons to whom shares are to be issued and provide by agreement for appropriate notice of an intent to sell and otherwise guard against the possibility that it may find itself involved in an illegal distribution.

One final bit of advice should be offered in concluding this review of SEC merger considerations. After you have worked your way through a complicated acquisition, prepared your proxy statement, held your meeting and won the overwhelming approval of your stockholders--before you put your files away and celebrate--please file your Form 8-K to report to an awaiting public the results of your endeavors.

Thank you.

#13 Sydney C. Orbach

March 6, 1962

Accounting Problems of First-Time Registration Statements

Abstract

The surge of new registrations between 1958 and 1962 brought increased problems in compliance with the Securities Act of 1933. "Going public" was not only a new experience for the companies but also for many accountants who had been dealing primarily with write-up work and taxes. Orbach details many of the pitfalls of S-1 filing. The problem of independence under Rule 2.01 is addressed as well as the need for certified statements for prior years.

"Going public" has become the publicized expression generally associated with a corporation that has been closely held either by a limited group of stockholders or a family group, and files a registration statement with the Securities and Exchange Commission for the first time for a proposed public offering of its

---

Presented before the Georgia Society of Certified Public Accountants.

securities.[1] As will be noted from the following statistics, the number of companies that have decided to "go public" shows no signs of slackening and in my opinion will continue or possibly increase in the foreseeable future.

In the four years that have elapsed from fiscal 1958 through 1961 the Securities and Exchange Commission has experienced a constantly increasing number of filings under the Securities Act of 1933 for the purpose of offering securities to the public. During the fiscal years 1958, 1959, 1960 and 1961 there were, respectively, 913, 1226, 1628 and 1830 registrations. In the first six months of this fiscal year 1224 registration statements were filed, being 515 more than the comparable period last year. In addition to the above, there is another statistic that is highly significant. In 1958, 1959, 1960 and 1961 the number of issues of companies which had not previously filed registration statements was 28%, 39%, 48% and 52%, respectively, of the total. In the first six months of the current fiscal year the percentage was 70%. It is this trend, I believe, that is particularly important to this audience, and I might add, creates greater problems for the staff of the Division

[1]The Securities and Exchange Commission, as a matter of policy, disclaims responsibility for any private publication by any of its employees. The views expressed herein are those of the author and do not necessarily reflect the views of the Commission or of the author's colleagues on the staff of the Commission.

of Corporation Finance than the company with public ownership that has previously filed with the Commission. The reasons for "going public" are varied. In a well-established company with many years of operations and profitability, the decision to "go public" may be based upon factors other than raising of new capital. Such factors could include a desire to establish a market valuation for estate planning or other purposes, older management seeking to create a company with eventual attraction for professional younger management, stock options or other benefits, and future growth possibilities through merger or acquisitions.

In the younger company the decision to "go public" is primarily a need for new capital resulting from growth and expansion and the realization that private resources and bank credit have their limitations and are not the answer to continued growth, particularly when the company has demonstrated a successful historical record of operations and an underwriting is feasible.

Although I have no statistics that are readily available, it seems to me that as the number of companies filing for the first time increases, the number of accountants who have had no previous experience with the Securities and Exchange Commission must of necessity increase also. Assuming that there may be quite a number of accountants in the audience in this category, I believe the remainder of this talk may serve to alert these particular members of the society to some of the problems they may encounter in a first-time registration statement. These deal with independence of accountants, auditing problems, rules and regulations of the Commission and their application, generally accepted accounting principles and the "Summary of Earnings."

Rule 2.01 of Regulation S-X defines the test of independence with respect to the certifying accountant. This rule prohibits any direct financial or any material indirect financial interest in the registrant, its parents and subsidiaries, or any connection as a promoter, underwriter, voting trustee, director, officer, or employee. In addition, the rule provides that appropriate consideration to all relevant circumstances of other relationships may be given.

I think most of our inquiries relate to the latter clause. "Write up" engagements which are common to smaller firms, close family relationship between the certifying accountants and the principal stockholders and/or management and financial dealings with same would ordinarily be the basis for raising questions as to the independence of the accountants.

If there are any possible circumstances that might raise a question as to the independence of the accountants, I would suggest that the accountants prior to any engagement upon a registration statement, recite the facts in a letter to the Commission and request a ruling. I can think of no more embarrassing situation between practitioner and client than to receive an adverse ruling, after the filing is made, which requires a new audit by a new firm of accountants.

The principal problem relating to auditing results from the fact that certified operating statements are required for at least the last three fiscal years of the registrant or the full life of the registrant if shorter.

Review of filings made by companies for the first time indicates that a great number have either had no prior audits or that the examinations made by the accountants in prior years have been so limited in scope as to preclude the expression of an opinion because inventories have not been observed nor receivables verified by independent confirmation in any period other than as of the last balance sheet date. The omission of verification of receivables in earlier periods generally poses no problem since subsequent verification at the balance sheet date and review of intervening transactions should provide the basis for a conclusion as to the validity of such accounts. However, inventories are another matter since the amounts reported in opening and closing inventories from year to year may have a drastic effect upon the earnings reported. Particular attention should be given to a review of accounting practices which may have resulted in "over-conservative" valuations in earlier periods with the resulting improvement in the last period reported upon.

Inquiries have been made as to the form of certification for the required three year period under such circumstances. When the accountant has followed alternative auditing procedures for earlier periods and concludes that an unqualified opinion is appropriate, a middle paragraph is generally included in the opinion. The following is one example:

"We observed the physical inventories as of 12/31/61 but did not observe the inventories (hereinafter referred to as the 'earlier inventories') inasmuch as these dates were prior to our engagement as auditors. We did, however, test-check the pricing and clerical accuracy of these inventories and also made certain analytical and statistical tests of related data, including review of gross profit ratios. As a result of these procedures, we have satisfied ourselves that the inventories used in the computation of cost of goods sold for the three years ended 12/31/61 are fairly stated."

In some cases, as a result of preliminary investigation by the accountants, it is readily apparent that an unqualified opinion for the three year period cannot be made because of inadequate or destroyed records or complete lack of any internal control. My recommendation in these cases is to wait until such time as properly certified statements can be presented.

Over the years the Commission has promulgated a number of forms for registration under the Securities Act of 1933, the most frequently filed being Form S-1, which form is used when no other form is authorized or prescribed. These forms contain instructions as to the financial statements required to be filed, whether parent company, consolidated, group or combination of statements, companies acquired through pooling of interests during the period covered and companies acquired by purchase after the balance sheet date, and the required dates and periods.

In addition to the different forms, the Commission's rules regarding certification, form and content of financial statements and supporting schedules required to be filed for most purposes under the Securities Act of 1933, the Securities Exchange Act of 1934, the Public Utility Holding Company Act of 1935 and the Investment Company Act of 1940, as well as minimum disclosure required in supplemental footnotes, are prescribed in Regulation S-X.

Although the various forms cover in general terms the type of financial statements required to be included in a registration statement, it is obviously impossible to write rules covering every type of situation that we run into in reviewing the financial statements. As a result, Item 13 of the Instructions as to Financial Statements of Form S-1 provides for the filing of other statements in addition to, or in substitution for, the statements required by the form where it is deemed necessary or appropriate for an adequate presentation of the financial statements. The following are some of the more common examples.

It seems to be quite common that, when a family controlled enterprise decides to "go public", such enterprise consists of a group of corporations under common stock onwership; presumably because as a closely held enterprise this arrangement had certain tax benefits. However, as the first step toward public ownership, these corporations must be put together in a parent subsidiary set-up or as a single entity. Quite frequently it happens that some of the separate corporations have different fiscal closings. Under these circumstances, the most satisfactory presentation is to recast all financial statements to a common fiscal date, generally that of the parent company or the one to be adopted by the successor entity. In certain instances, it may not be feasible to recast to a common date because of lack of accounting data with respect to inventories and/or other accounts. Under these circumstances, we have accepted combined statements in which 12 months operations for each separate company are included for each year reported upon and the interim results of those companies whose fiscal closings are either prior or subsequent to the balance sheet date are shown as direct debits or credits to retained earnings with appropriate explanation. Intercompany transactions should be eliminated for the period covered and the resulting summary should present either a corporate or consolidated operating statement which has reflected retroactively and properly "pooling of interests" accounting for all periods. In the usual case, the recapitalization takes place after the date of the balance sheet furnished. Although there may be some accountants who feel that the effect of a post balance sheet recapitalization must be discussed in a footnote, in the interest of simplicity, I can see no particular reason for not reflecting the recapitalization in the balance sheet proper provided it is so explained.

In some instances, a new corporate registrant has been organized to succeed to a partnership or group of partnerships. In reflecting the operating results for the required periods it is necessary to recast the partnership results to a pro-forma corporate basis by the introduction of additional items such as reasonable officers' salaries and corporate income taxes in order that the results be properly shown. Similar recasting would be required by a predecessor corporation or corporations which had availed themselves of the provisions of Sub-Caption S of the Internal Revenue Code. In addition, when a family group of corporations intends to merge into a single corporate entity the loss of the multiple surtax benefit in future operations would have to be explained and the effect on earnings specifically indicated. In this situation, it has been argued that there are usually offsetting benefits in a single corporation. I see no reason why a discussion along these lines should not be made, but any attempt to forecast future dollar savings is deemed in the nature of a projection and is generally disallowed.

In addition to the above, the following situations have become quite common.

A company acquired by a promotional group with a substantial step-up in fixed asset values and new debt structure would be required to show in addition to the historical operating results (generally with no per-share data) a pro-forma statement of income for the latest 12-month period or the latest fiscal period and interim period giving effect to new depreciation charges, interest charges and related tax reduction in order that per share data in the pro-forma statement correctly reflect the operating results of the company in terms of conditions existing at the time of the public offering. In addition to the above, quite frequently a registrant will acquire by purchase a material subsidiary or division close to the balance sheet date or after such date. If it appears that the historical operating results of the registrant could be materially affected by such acquisition, pro-forma operating statements would be required showing the operating results as if the acquisition had been made as of the beginning of the latest 12-month period.

The foregoing examples are to be contrasted with situations where the underwriter wishes to present an additional statement of financial condition giving effect to the results of the public offering, particularly when the historical balance sheet shows an unbalanced working capital position or excessive debt which will be materially changed as a result of the public offering and it is felt that the prospectus prose dealing with the application of proceeds is not as easily understood as statement presentation. The use of such a statement is limited to the underwriting conditions discussed in Rule 170 of the General Rules and Regulations under the Securities Act of 1933, the gist of such rules limiting its use to either a firm underwriting commitment or an "all-or-none" arrangement with full refund of subscriptions to stock if the underwriting is unsuccessful.

In the majority of cases of new registrants, comments by the accounting staff generally deal with revision of footnote disclosure furnished, request for additional footnotes specifically required by Regulation S-X and in certain instances revised presentation of the financial statements. However, in some filings, questions as to the application of generally accepted accounting principles have been raised by the staff even though the financial statements have been certified without qualification. This may result from any one of the following: (1) lack of knowledge of accounting bulletins promulgated by the American Institute of Certified Public Accountants, (2) unfamiliarity with accounting releases issued by the Securities and Exchange Commission, (3) conclusion that income tax rulings are necessarily acceptable for purposes of financial reporting, and (4) the use of a method of reflecting financial transactions which in our opinion may be subject to misinterpretation and have the capacity to mislead.

It is my understanding that most close corporations keep their records on a tax basis and while in the majority of cases no change is necessary, there are instances when such statements are not acceptable.

For example, statements have been presented in which all overhead has been omitted from inventories even though material in amount and have required correction to reflect such overhead in each of the years covered with provision made for the resulting tax liability.

The cash basis of accounting is acceptable for tax purposes when inventories are not a material factor but unacceptable for filing purposes and revision to accrual accounting would be required. There are a number of cases filed in which review and inquiry has revealed that losses inherent at the balance sheet date in the liquidation of certain assets has not been reflected in the accounts because of the belief that losses should be booked in the year of realization. This, of course, is contrary to generally accepted accounting principles which provide that known or anticipated losses be provided for, and in these cases correction is requested.

In some cases, a review of the accounting followed by the registrant would seem to indicate that a more realistic matching of costs and revenues might be attained if the registrant used a budgeted unit of production basis for amortization of certain deferred charges rather than an arbitrary five year time basis, particularly when the amounts involved are significant and could materially affect net income.

In addition to the above, there is another situation which has created a problem in the past. This relates to an acquisition by purchase in which an excess cost is not amortizable for tax purposes but considered as "good-will." Where it is clearly evident that such an item (even though deemed for tax purposes to be an intangible) is clearly related to an asset having a limited life, amortization of such intangible over the same life would be required.

Finally, there are some transactions which, if presented on a tax basis, seem to be in conflict with the economics involved and are in our opinion objectionable. The following two examples illustrate the point.

The use of the sale and lease-back technique has become quite common in industry. When in our opinion, a sale and lease-back is clearly a finance transaction, it would appear that the cash profit (net of the capital gains tax) would more properly be reflected as a deferred credit in the balance sheet and amortized to income as an offset to the new rental expense.

Occasionally, a registrant will set up certain financial arrangements for older management prior to filing. In general they follow a similar pattern, i.e., payment for so-called "advisory and consulting services" for ten years after retirement to the officer or to his estate and with certain vested rights prior to retirement. It seems to us that this type of financial arrangement is clearly in the nature of deferred compensation and should be provided for, net of future tax benefits, by charges to income over the period prior to estimated date of retirement.

The above cases illustrate the types of accounting which are subject to question. However, there are a good many more cases where financial statements presented to the public for the first time show evidence of drastic change from the method reflected in the accounts prior to the time public investment was considered. As mentioned before, close corporations generally follow tax accounting and since no company normally pays more in income taxes than is legally required, the resulting financial picture may not actually reflect the operating potential of the company. If, in our opinion, the revised statements show an attempt by the registrant to more clearly match costs and revenues or to follow an acceptable alternate method of accounting they of course can be presented as being in accordance with generally accepted accounting principles. Some of these concepts may not be familiar to all of you and therefore the following list of accounting concepts developed in certain industries should be of interest. Generally, the difference in accounting treatment is of more importance in smaller rapidly expanding companies than in older larger companies with relative stability in sales or revenue.

(1) Some companies with a heavy investment in machinery and equipment have felt it necessary to follow liberalized depreciation for tax purposes and straight line for financial purposes.

(2) The research and development costs of a particular product may be of such magnitude as to require capitalization of this item and subsequent amortization.

(3) Subscription income of publishing companies is required to be deferred over the life of the subscription. Related subscription expense has been capitalized and netted against the deferred income.

(4) Certain types of real estate developers who purchase acreage for the purpose of building a specified number of homes have felt it preferable to defer selling, general and administrative expenses connected with the development and amortize such costs as homes are sold.

(5) It is quite common for finance corporations to defer the first year of operating losses of newly opened offices and amortize such amounts over a period not in excess of three years.

(6) There is a trend in companies with multiple retail locations (particularly bowling and discount operations)

to defer certain of their pre-opening costs to be recovered against future operations.

(7) Newly organized companies may defer starting up costs prior to commercial operations to be amortized over a period not in excess of five years. In my opinion, the period of amortization may be accelerated to coincide with tax carry-forward benefits resulting from the same starting-up costs.

(8) Some companies engage in manufacturing or engineering under fixed price contracts have found that percentage of completion accounting presents a more realistic operating trend than completed contract accounting.

(9) Finally, a number of rather new companies engaged in leasing operations have presented their statements upon a finance company concept rather than as a company engaged in the rental of equipment. The financial presentation and accounting principles that I think are most realistic in this type of company would show the gross rental contract as an installment receivable, the unearned rental income as a deduction therefrom, the residual or salvage value of the equipment purchasable by the lessee at the expiration of the lease at the contract amount as an "other asset" and the rental income reflected in the accounts following "sum-of-the-digits" accounting in

order to match the related interest cost of borrowed money to finance these leases.

In all these cases, the companies follow a different basis for tax accounting and although the general effect of these different methods has been to improve the operating picture as compared with the results shown for tax purposes, they have been accepted on the premise that they more nearly match costs and revenues and hence the financial presentation is consistent with generally accepted accounting principles.

In addition to the instructions as to financial statements, Item 6 of Form S-1 covers the instructions as to the "Summary of Earnings," the preparation of which is of particular interest to the certifying accountants since it usually is covered by their certificate. In my opinion, it probably represents the most significant item in Form S-1 insofar as the company, the public investors and the underwriters are concerned. Item 21(b) of the form provides that in lieu of the summary there may be substituted the income statement in its entirety provided the first two years of the five year requirement of the summary (which periods may be presented upon an unaudited basis) are also included. In recent years, this optional presentation has been followed in the majority of filings and I believe is preferable since it eliminates duplication and simplifies the prospectus.

Because of the importance of the summary, particular attention is given to this item by both the group accountant and the group analyst. Particular reference is given in such review to the introductory paragraph of Item 6 which reads "In connection with such summary, whenever necessary, reflect information or explanation of material significance to investors in appraising the results shown, or refer to such information or explanation set forth elsewhere in the prospectus." The following illustrates some of the comments that are repeatedly cited.

When a company goes public for the first time it is quite common to enter into new salary arrangements with management or to set up new profit sharing arrangements or pension plans. In such cases, the additional costs which are not reflected in the five year summary may be material and should be brought to the attention of the reader. Since complete information of these arrangements is included elsewhere in the prospectus, a cross reference to this information in a note will ordinarily suffice.

When a company shows an erratic sales or net income picture for the period covered or where the gross-profit percentages show an abnormal relationship from year to year, it is customary to require a brief explanation of the factors that contributed to these results.

This is particularly important in the case where the latest period or periods show a marked increase in gross profit over earlier periods and the text in the prospectus covering the history and business of the company furnishes no clue as to the reason for such improvement.

In some filings, it may appear that certain sales and/or operating revenues, although properly included in the determination of net income for the period or periods are in the nature of non-recurring items and failure to discuss these items may result in misleading inferences. In this type of situation, discussion in the notes and, where material, the per share effect would ordinarily be required.

There have been a number of filings recently where there is a decided seasonal impact of the company's operations. When the filing coincides with the close of the fiscal year no particular emphasis is necessary as to the seasonal aspects of the operations. However, some of the filings have been made based upon special audits prior to the close of the fiscal year and generally after the peak season. Although it may be argued that comparable interim periods highlight the seasonal trend, I am not sure that such a conclusion is obvious. As a result, when prior historical results show that the balance of the year from the date of audit is normally a break-even on loss period, a specific statement to that effect is required.

In addition to the above, there are a number of repeated comments made by the staff which deal with the accounting aspects of the summary. The following illustrations are some of the more important.

When a company's income is derived from both sales and operating revenues, Rule 5-03 of Regulation S-X provides that both sales and operating revenues and related cost of goods sold and operating expenses be stated separately when either sales or operating revenues are in excess of 10% of the combined total. Inquiry by the staff in certain filings has revealed that combined amounts have been shown in the original filing although in violation of the rule. In such cases, correcting amendment has been requested.

The presentation of income tax provisions in a good many cases may raise questions. Accounting Series Release #85 issued by the Commission contemplated that where material, provision for deferred income taxes be shown separately and an appropriate discussion of the circumstances included in the related notes to the financial statements. This is particularly important in those companies that follow accrual accounting for financial statement purposes and cash collection for income tax purposes. In some cases, the percentage relationship of income taxes to income before taxes may be so unusual as to require further text explanation. This could be true in a specific type of industry, a multiple corporation set-up with surtax benefits per corporation, a company whose income is based in large measure upon the lower capital gains rates and consolidated income statements which include foreign subsidiaries such as Puerto Rican which enjoy tax relief over a limited period of years and which income statements do not provide for Federal income taxes if distributed. In this latter situation, disclosure of the circumstances and the amounts of income involved would be required.

Companies with volatile or erratic income results have an additional type of disclosure. When the last year or years of the summary have benefitted from the utilization of carry-forwards it seems clear that a misleading per share amount is presented unless a discussion is included as to the per share effect of the carry-forward benefit as well as the remaining unused amount and the year of expiration. In this connection, in a limited number of recent filings a different presentation was followed. In these cases, companies were either acquired by purchase in a tax free merger or acquired for taxable consideration and no value could be ascribed to a predecessor carry-forward benefit because of the amount of the consideration involved. In these situations, it seems to me that the fairest presentation is one in which the amount and per-share effect of such carry-forward benefits are reflected in the income statements as a special item after the determination of net income.

Because of the fact that price-earnings ratios have become such an important factor in the determination of the market value of common stock being offered, review by the staff of the method of computation of per-share earnings is done in all cases. In spite of the fact that Accounting Research Bulletin #49 issued by the American Institute of CPA's was an attempt to provide a working guide as to the methods to be followed, repeated comments for correction or expansion have been made. For instance:

Per share data should be adjusted retroactively for recapitalization after the balance sheet date, and for stock splits and stock dividends during the period covered; companies acquired by purchase for stock during the period covered by the summary should exclude the shares issued for the period prior to such acquisition in order to avoid an improper growth picture; per share amounts related to special items shown after the determination of net income should be shown separately and not included in a total with the per share amount of net income; and supplemental proforma computations of per share income for the latest period should be shown when there has been or will be a significant change in capitalization after the balance sheet date as a result of conversion of senior securities or where a material portion of the common stock sold will be used for the retirement of debt or the creation of normal working capital needs resulting in stock dilution.

In addition to the above, a number of companies filing for the first time have had recapitalizations in which the stock sold to the public will have prior dividend preferences whereas the stock retained by management will either have nominal subordinate divvidend rights or no dividend rights, in both cases with conversion rights over a period of years generally based upon fixed percentages. In such cases, earnings per share are required to be computed upon the total number of both classes of stock outstanding. However, when appropriate, no objection has been raised to showing separately as additional footnote disclosure the earnings coverage of the public class of stock as related to the dividend priority of such stock provided adequate disclosure is made as to the potential dilution of such coverage as a result of the convertible feature of such stock.

As a final thought, I would like to close with the following: When a close corporation "goes public" a new factor has been added, i.e., stewardship of public money. It is this area of accounting that I believe affords the certified public accountant his greatest opportunity for professional responsibility.

#14 Byron D. Woodside

June 23, 1964

Government-Industry Relations
Securities and Exchange Commission and
Corporate Securities Regulation

Abstract

This address is a series of comments on the "Special Study of Securities Markets." A Congressional resolution required the SEC to investigate the adequacy of the rules of national security exchanges and associations. Woodside's simplified conclusion is that: ...the Commission, the securities industry, and the issuers of publicly held securities, ...received something less than a 'clean certificate' and something more than a 'comfort letter'.

There occurs in every business a time for a thoughtful assessment of where you've been and where you're going. In most businesses, the close of the fiscal year represents a benchmark time--when it is convenient and appropriate to consider not only what the cold figures show concerning the past but also how the programs, the

---

Presented before the Forty-fifth Annual Conference of the National Association of Accountants.

plans, and the relationships with people so crucial to progress can best be explained in a periodic accounting--a report of stewardship. Today--just a week from the end of our fiscal year and before this audience in particular--is a good time in our business to have a look back to the near past and a look ahead in the general direction in which we seem to be moving.

Leaving aside some very important events which occurred but which may be viewed as aspects of ordinary operations and administration, the Special Study of the Securities Markets is the one event or activity which pre-empted our time, attention and energies during this past year. It is true, of course, that the Study had its origin in a joint resolution introduced in mid-1961. But it was almost the beginning of 1962 before the Special Study group of sixty-five people began to function as the well-knit, effective and coordinated investigative team it was destined to become.

At this time one year ago, the Commission had transmitted to the Congress the first installment of the report--five of thirteen chapters. The second installment of four chapters, to be transmitted in mid-July, and the final four chapters for delivery in August were still in various stages of preparation. Although there were certain unavoidable delays in printing, the entire report, consisting of thirteen chapters, together with a volume of the summaries and recommendations of the Study group and the various letters of transmittal are now public documents--available various letters of transmittal are now public documents--available for purchase from the Government Printing Office at nominal prices.

It has been recognized as a remarkable work--thorough, objective and comprehensive--a valuable addition to our financial literature. In the language one sees in the theatrical reviews, it has received critical acclaim. Every lawyer, accountant, or businessman concerned with securities practice or the securities business should have a set. Every business school and law-school library should include it among their reference works. I do not intend to try to summarize the report or its major conclusions. It speaks for itself. Rather, I want to offer some personal observations about the chain of significant events engendered by two terse sentences of Section 19(d) of the Exchange Act the new subsection added to the statute as a result of H. J. Resolution 438 in 1961.*

At the risk of oversimplification but to establish the general nature of the final conclusions of the Study group, couched in the language of your profession, I think it fair to say that the

*"The Commission is authorized and directed to make a study and investigation of the adequacy, for the protection of investors, of the rules of national securities exchanges and national securities associations, including rules for the expulsion, suspension, or disciplining of a member for conduct inconsistent with just and equitable principles of trade. The Commission shall report to the Congress on or before April 3, 1963, the results of its study and investigation, together with its recommendations, including such recommendations for legislation as it deems advisable."

Commission, the securities industry and issuers of publicly held securities, i.e., industry generally, received something less than a "clean certificate" and something more than a "comfort letter."

Again at the risk of oversimplification but to pay a tribute to the orginating resolution and the nature of our system, one of the prime benefits of the Special Study is not to be found in the report or in the content of any other document published before or after it. In brief, that benefit was and is simply that many thoughtful, experienced, caring people in many walks of life recognized the fact of the resolution and the Study as a demand for reassessment and a call to action. Thus, the Special Study prompted many special studies in many places around the country. Industry not only announced publicly its intention and desire to cooperate with the Study group; it discharged that commitment fully. Further, it anticipated some of the predictable critical conclusions later to be reached by the Special Study and recognized other subjects as likely candidates for identification as problem areas. Long before even the first chapters had been delivered to the Congress, there was an evident awareness on the part of the leaders of the securities industry and a swelling tide of sentiment among the self-regulatory instrumentalities that responsibilities must be re-thought and the public interest served. One illustration of the genuineness of that sentiment was the sustained and thorough efforts of industry leaders in mustering vigorous, articulate support of the members of the exchanges and the NASD for the Commission's legislative program now awaiting action in the House--a program fully supported and justified by the data compiled by the Special Study and the Commission's experience over the years. Another is the fact that many firms voluntarily reviewed and modified their internal procedures, and the NASD and the exchanges accelerated and improved some of their programs relating to qualification and supervision of personnel and the controls over sales practice and sales literature.

The conduct of the Special Study generated severe pressures on the limited personnel of the Study group, upon the senior members of our regular staff and upon the Commission itself. The magnitude of the effort, the volume of material handled, the tremendous amounts of reading and discussion and commentary, the flight of time and the scope of subject matter all tended to blur an extremely significant fact. The fact was and is that the Study was the finest opportunity in thirty years for the Commission and industry to discover and ponder many things about our securities markets and securities business. The Commission learned about many aspects of the business which it encounters rarely or not at all in its day-to-day work. The Commission was confronted with the manifold problems and responsibilities of the self-regulators in a manner and to a degree virtually impossible in the ordinary course of administration and enforcement of the securities laws. Equally important, industry had the opportunity to learn much about itself which had not been known generally. Thus, while some segments of the business knew their own fields very well, many knew little about the specialties of others. Only a relative few had the broad knowledge and experience flowing from familiarity with the whole sweep of the securities business which would encourage one to speak with assurance and authority for large industry groups.

The Special Study and the need to communicate concerning it--its specifics and its implications--initiated--in fact compelled--a tremendous education process within government, within industry and between government and industry. This process is one of the most important end products of the entire operation. It began early, has continued in good faith, and must continue long into the future. It reminds one constantly that for all our capability for instantaneous transmission of words, we have yet to solve the problem of effective and rapid communication of facts and ideas. The complexity of subject matter, the diversity of interests, the constant development and changes, the dispersion of the population concerned with the particular problem, all prompt concern whether communication results in comprehension. This is difficult at best when there is trust in motive and confidence in purpose. It becomes troublesome indeed if there exists distrust or doubt concerning what is said or what is done. But the process must go on. I--who am not one given to volubility--believe that we must keep talking. For reasons which are not always obvious to business or the ordinary citizen but which are important to our system of regulation, the various observations, conclusions and recommendations of the Special Study must receive the careful work and thought of those best able to judge them and their relation to the public interest. They may be accepted, modified, rejected, deferred or subjected to further study, but they must be dealt with. A record must be made and decisions reached. The Study deserves this. Common sense and good management call for it. Congress will demand it.

The Special Study criticized much of what it saw. One of its purposes was to probe, and probe deeply, to ascertain whether there was much or little which seemed to call for critical comment. But its main theme, in my judgment, cannot be characterized either as praise or censure. It was a sober, intellectually honest evaluation of what was recognized to be a most sensitive and efficient system of marketing and trading in securities--participated in by a whole people to a degree not known elsewhere and regulated by a system entirely unique. Certainly there can be no doubt that the Study group confirmed the wisdom and in general the effectiveness of the regulatory scheme reflected in the various securities acts adopted by the Congress beginning with the Securities Act of 1933. This confirmation, I believe, judging by the House and Senate Reports on the pending legislation, has been a source of no inconsiderable pride and satisfaction on the part of our legislative committees. This regulatory scheme, as you know, relies heavily on the discipline of public disclosure of business facts, the willingness of businessmen to establish their own standards of ethical conduct, and the willingness of businessmen to enforce not only their chosen ethical standards but also legal standards established in the statutes--through self-governing self-regulatory institutions. It is significant, I think, that the Study, in making recommendations designed to strengthen and broaden the concepts of disclosure and self-discipline, did not propose changes in the nature of the regulatory pattern which would in any real sense alter the character of the relationship in this field between business and government; i.e., the Commission, spelled out in the statutes thirty years ago. In other words, our regulatory tools are, on the whole, satisfactory. They must be employed wisely and as completely as the particular public interest requires. In many areas they must be employed more vigorously, or in a different way or with modified objectives. In some instances they must be employed to deal with subject matters not heretofore reached by the regulatory or self-regulatory restraint.

The Study group, in emphasizing throughout the report the self-regulatory aspects of our system, was merely reflecting with great magnification the specific provisions of the joint resolution. This emphasis produced, in my opinion, a side effect throughout the financial community which was to the good. We of course have known in a general way of the work done by the committees of the National Association of Securities Dealers, the Investment Bankers Association and the stock exchanges. But the Study, for the first time, I believe, gave the people intimately connected with the business and who knew at first hand the details and specifics of the problems of self-regulation as to which many were experts. More important, they spoke with an opportunity to be heard effectively--heard by government--heard by their fellows under circumstances which encouraged action.

Some were staff people attending to specific jobs. More often they were businessmen-volunteers who applied their time, judgment and experience to knotty problems of self-regulation--discipline of fellow businessmen, rule-making, policy matters, education, business standards, training of personnel, sales practices. They had convictions, ideas and concern about the securities business. They reflected an awareness of an aspect of their position which is receiving more attention around the country than ever before. The stock exchanges and, to a somewhat lesser degree, the NASD (the only registered securities association) are the possessors of delegated governmental powers of no mean scope. The Congress intended that that delegated power be used. There is nothing quite like Congressional oversight--the Special Study is a not so oblique species of that phenomenon--to cause the holders of government power and government responsibility to review their own conduct and their objectives. It seems to me that the membership has demonstrated a growing awareness that, as businessmen, they have a very special relationship to their government and to each other and a very special interest in seeing to it that this system of ours works and works well.

These volunteers, who served on business-conduct committees, for example, during the somewhat frenzied days of 1960 and 1961, developed, unaided by anyone in the Commission, firm convictions derived from their experiences in committee work that unlimited access to the securities business was not in the interest of the investor or the good name of their industry. The reaction of NASD Committee No. 12, as expressed in a formal resolution dated January, 1962, is eloquent. In part it states:

> "...We have had to deal with an increasingly high rate of influx of proprietors, officers, partners and other personnel who are unqualified by reason of lack of proper moral attitudes, inadequate training and experience and insufficient capital funds; ...the Business Conduct Committee in this District has found it increasingly difficult within the present framework to enforce high standards of commercial honor and just and equitable principles of trade in such manner as to adequately protect the public interest... this... Committee strongly urges the Board of Governors... to provide for the establishment of a more rigid set of qualification standards in the area of character, experience and financial responsibility, preferably as a prerequisite to membership and/or registration."

An important aspect of our pending legislative program responds to this plea. In fact, the principles underlying the pending bill, their virtually universal acceptance by the securities business, their time-tested soundness have been so well demonstrated that we have high hopes that the operation of the proposed legislative amendments will have a beneficial impact upon the securities business and the processes of regulation and self-regulation far greater than might at first glance appear.

It is easy for the scoffer to say that the SEC merely wants more reports and more power and thus brush the matter aside as another example of unwanted bureaucratic intrusion into private affairs. The Commission and the industry have been saying earnestly and with the voice of a joint, though somewhat different, experience that acceptance of this view would fail to grasp the magnitude of the potential for development of our securities markets. Essentially, the bill is aimed on the one hand at granting the NASD adequate authority to raise the quality and capability of those who seek to enter the securities business--to give an assist to a growing awareness of the need for a professionalism, if you please. On the other hand, the bill is aimed at making certain that a reliable security dealer can know his merchandise in the over-the-counter market, that he can have at hand reliable information as a foundation for reliable advice to his public customers.

One of the great opportunities and contributions of the Joint

Resolution and the Special Study was the search for the dimensions, characteristics and operational techniques of the over-the-counter market. I think, for the first time, we now have a solid basis of fact and informed judgment based upon a really comprehensive survey which can be employed to advantage to construct a more efficient, reliable and quality system in over-the-counter securities. It is interesting, I think, to note that those who worked on the Exchange Act in 1934 realized in a general way that over-the-counter securities somehow should receive a rough sort of equivalence of treatment with listed securities. This was reflected in the peculiar language of old Section 15, which in effect provided that it would be unlawful, in contravention of rules of the Commission to insure to investors protection comparable to that provided in the case of the exchanges, for a broker or dealer to make or create a market for an over-the-counter security or for any broker or dealer to use any facility of any such market. The section continued--authorizing such rules to provide for the regulation of all transactions by brokers and dealers on any such market--the registration of brokers and dealers making or creating such a market--and, please note, providing for the registration of the securities for which they make or create a market.

This section was dropped in its entirety when the Maloney Act was adopted in 1938 establishing the statutory basis for the development of the NASD as the great self-regulatory mechanism for the non-exchange part of the securities business. And of course there was no provision in those 1938 amendments for the registration of over-the-counter securities. But the principle was recognized in 1934 that regulation of the securities business could not proceed effectively and equitably with one part of the market carefully supervised from the point of view of the facts concerning the securities traded and the other part of the market free to operate in an informational dark of the moon. In looking back over the history of our legislation, it seems to me that the odd result reached in 1938 in this respect was probably due to two or three factors. I believe I am right in saying that there then was not nearly the activity or the interest in, or knowledge of, the over-the-counter market as compared with the exchanges. I think there probably were doubts as to just how to develop a suitable regulatory pattern for this then-little-known business. Finally, I think that this subject, like many others referred to in the '34 Act, was left for the Commission to learn from experience and to come forward when a need was established or a solution to a problem called for a legislative response.

Sixty-five years ago--thirty-five years before the Exchange Act--the New York Stock Exchange initiated a procedure requiring companies making applications for listing their securities to enter into a listing agreement with the Exchange by which they commit themselves to a code of performance after listing in respect of matters dealt with by the agreement. One of these, in the words of the Exchange, "represented the Exchange's effort to satisfy, by a formal requirement, a public need which it had long recognized, but which its previous unsupported efforts had been unable to fill--the need of investors for regular financial reports by the companies whose securities they held." A primary objective of the agreement was, again in the words of the Exchange, "Timely disclosure, to the public and to the Exchange, of information which may affect security values or influence investment decisions..."

This conclusion, so obviously right at the time of the Spanish-American War with respect to listed securities, is also obviously right in this day of Telstar, Polaris, backward-wave oscillators and yttrium iron garnet-tuned parametric amplifiers, with respect to the over-the-counter securities; if anything, more so.

The over-the-counter market has come of age; it is of tremendous size and importance; the public participation and direct and indirect public interest in it are growing. We depend on it for skillful, efficient marketing of new issues, for the seasoning process that every market must experience as a security finds its place among its fellows, to be judged in terms of price and volume by the flow of supply and demand.

The Special Study spells these matters out in detail, it arms the industry and the Commission with a sound knowledge, it confirms the wisdom and rightness of the Stock Exchange in 1899, the Congress in 1934 and the Commission's recommendations on the subject to the

Congress on three prior occasions. Today, with solid support from the entire securities industry, we stand on the verge of completing a program almost but not quite consummated thirty years ago.

We have high hopes for this two-pronged advance. A better and more comprehensive flow of timely and reliable financial information from over-the-counter companies is bound to be beneficial to the investor and would-be investor. It will enable the broker-dealer to do a better job. It will facilitate the enforcement efforts of the Commission, the self-regulatory institutions of industry and the state securities administrators. It will give greater meaning to the other effort being made--the development of a quality and professionalism in the business which I think will come to have growing significance.

The Special Study and our efforts flowing out of it come at a critical time in the development of our economy. The report touches subjects which clearly are undergoing or will call for great change.

The security-owning population is growing--it is anticipated it will exceed twenty-million before long. It will make a great difference how that growing population finds its way into such ownership--directly through ownership of corporate securities or indirectly through ownership of intermediary agencies which will hold the corporate securities.

It seems quite clear that new competitive forces are at work. The banks are pressing for participation in various aspects of the securities business. The insurance companies have already pressed forward. The competitive struggle between the institution and the broker dealer and the problems of the third market, it seems to me, are bound to intensify.

No one knows what automation will do in the securities business. The concensus seems to be that it will do much and its effects over a period of time will be far-reaching.

Indications point to tremendous growth in population in the years ahead, the need for a concomitant growth in industry and a corresponding capital market of quality, depth and receptivity to provide the monetary lubricant which keeps all this intricate economic machinery operating smoothly.

We cannot foretell precisely our own role or that of the securities industry in the evolution ahead, but our experience tells us that enforcement of the law, maintenance of public confidence and the flow of capital in both the new-issue market and the trading markets are best achieved with a market place bottomed on reliable information and operated by skilled, adequately capitalized, reliable investment houses.

A number of other developments are occurring which I think augur well for the future--developments which reflect an awareness on the part of various groups around the country of the importance of some of the matters I have mentioned to the well-being of the many aspects of our financial system.

The NASD and the exchanges have been working for some time to improve examination procedures, sales practices and sales literature and to establish qualifications for entry into the business which give recognition to functions.

Within the past year an advisory group of the Public Relations Society of America, Inc., has worked together and to some extent with our staff in a considerable effort to establish a Code of Financial Public Relations. In commenting to the president of the Society last December, our Chairman stated:

> "By adopting this Code, the Society--like a number of other unofficial self-regulatory groups in other areas--has expressed recognition of its responsibilities to the public. I am sure that the Society understands, however, that the new Code is merely the foundation for a program of self-regulation and not in itself a complete program. In the last analysis, the Code will have to be evaluated in the light of the level of conduct which it inspires or commands.

"I trust that the Society will build on this necessary foundation and enhance its efforts to achieve a level of practice in financial public relations consonant with the needs of investor protection."

The Financial Analysts Federation, an organization of some 7500 members in twenty-eight constituent societies in major cities of this country and Canada, has embarked on a very fine program which should receive the support and commendation it deserves. Under its auspices, the Institute of Chartered Financial Analysts was organized in 1959. It has fostered an educational program and established examination procedures by means of which those who qualify by study, and demonstrate fitness by meeting the required standards, can become Chartered Financial Analysts. The Federation, which has a real interest in the objectives of our legislative program, has given it their full endorsement and support.

Recently it came to my attention that a new organization has been formed which, in my opinion, has a real potential for public service. I refer to the recently organized Society of American Business Writers. This group, which was originally proposed some four or five years ago, is reported to have ninety charter members representing leading publications throughout the country. In my judgment, this group, which named as their first president one of our leading financial writers, should be encouraged and supported.

The state administrators continue their efforts to advance their programs of investor protection though they continue also to labor under severe handicaps of budget and personnel limitations. We have had occasion before to comment on the improvement in annual reports and corporate publicity.

In other words, there are a lot of people working in one way or another at various activities which are aimed at or collaterally affect the better working of our securities markets.

This leads me to observe that the Special Study did less than it might well have done in the matter of assessing the role of your profession in our business. I believe I am correct in saying that there is no specific reference or comment directed at the accountants. But in a real sense there is high praise in the report for the corporate financial officers and the independent public accountants, if you know where to look. The report made no particular effort to praise anyone. I think on this occasion I am permitted a freedom of expression above and beyond that usually found in "official" reports, and accordingly I will interpret.

In Chapter IX, the Special Study observes that "Disclosure is the cornerstone of Federal securities regulation; it is the great safeguard that governs the conduct of corporate managements in many of their activities; it is the best bulwark against reckless corporate publicity and irresponsible recommendation and sale of securities." In Chapter XII, the Special Study notes the Commission's "marked success" in administering the disclosure provisions for issuers.

Fair, adequate, understandable disclosures under these acts begin with the corporate accounting records and the financial statements synthesized from them. Almost everything else to be said about a company and its securities either affects or explains--finds cause or effect in the profit and loss statement and the statement of condition. In a very real sense the accountants are the unsung heroes of many a corporate drama and many an actor on the corporate stage cannot play his more dramatic part until the less spectacular work of the financial officer and accountant has arranged the scenery and perhaps established the basic theme.

Only we who live with these statutes can fully appreciate the extent to which, in the evolution of our regulatory scheme, we have relied upon the accounting profession to establish standards and to apply them or the extent to which the accountants' work has influenced administrative policies generally. This reliance furthermore has been at the profession's invitation.

With statutory authority reposing in the Commission to prescribe--to require--to dictate by rule how financial statements should be prepared and presented, the Commission very early in its life, at the request of the profession, stood aside and not only withheld governmental action but actively encouraged the full self-development of the initiative sought to be exercised. The wisdom of that regulatory decision and the soundness of the administrative trust thus demonstrated really have never been seriously questioned. For twenty-five years it has been the exceptional situation which prompted the Commission to speak directly by rule on matters of accounting principles.

The profession thus has performed an important role as a self-regulatory institution. Although it is not the holder of delegated governmental power, as is the NASD or the stock exchanges, its accomplishments are a credit to volunteer activity--shaped by general statutory principles--which achieve a species of compulsion without the customary trappings of the compulsory process.

We have a continuing interest in the viability of this effort--this process, or however it should be described. Speaking for myself, it is better, I think, to have some of the looseness--the creaking joint, if you will--some sacrifice of the ultimate in consistency and uniformity and acceptability under such a system than to seek the rule--government or industry inspired--which either binds people to a rigid conformity or sets up a standard from which departures multiply in achieving solutions to problems. How many remember the two dozen or more exceptions from the rule for the use of old Form A-2 under the Securities Act which evolved over a period of time until the form itself was abolished?

We thought the dismay with which our reaction to the investment credit episode seems to have been greeted, in some quarters, most unfortunate. We intend no rebuff to the profession or the Accounting Principles Board. On the contrary, we have encouraged and continue to encourage them in their work. We would caution, however, against the profession undertaking to do what you have always pleaded that we not do.

We know from long experience that even a relatively simple matter such as our Rule 14a-3, which in effect says a company's financial statements in its annual report to its stockholders should not be inconsistent in any material way with the financial statements filed with us, becomes an extremely difficult and protracted exercise in rule-making and in fact somewhat contentious. The task you set yourselves to force conformity on matters of accounting principle when there is not in fact acceptability of conformity, I think, is an impossible one. In any event, such a step calls for full exploration of problems and procedures. But this view in no sense reflects upon the efforts of those dedicated, highly intelligent and articulate public-minded members of the profession who vigorously urge more, and more penetrating, research and who constantly seek to narrow differences and, where possible, broaden the scope of that which is truly "the acceptable" of the profession. We salute them and their efforts.

Those who wish to compel conformity--or rather seek to have us compel conformity--for only we in the final analysis have the tools to enforce the law or to set enforcement in motion--will no doubt be less than happy with this approach. What then are we left with, say they, except education and persuasion?

The short answer in our field of activity, I think, is that these have been the principal tools by which so much has been and continues to be accomplished. They have been the genius of the administration of the disclosure provisions of the '33 and '34 Acts. With your continued assistance, I think they are likely, in major respects, to remain so.

#15 Manuel F. Cohen

October 26, 1968

Financial Executives Institute

Reporting for Diversified Companies

Abstract

With the growing numbers of conglomerates and the increased trading activity related to them, the SEC perceives the need for better disclosure. Skepticism is arising as to the sources of profitability; whether it is due to performance or acquisition activity, Cohen feels the need to reexamine the criteria for purchasing and pooling and to consider a line of business reporting for conglomerates.

I am pleased to be here this morning before so many representatives of our customers. I am particularly pleased to join Bob Haack and to congratulate the New York Stock Exchange community for the far-sighted action it has taken under his leadership. It was also with some anticipation that I looked forward to meeting Mr. Charles

---

Presented before the Financial Executives Institute, New York.

Bluhdorn about whom I have heard so much. He represents, in the view of many, a relatively new breed of businessmen. The financial press in recent times has given a great deal of attention to their feats of corporate legerdemain, and to their breathtaking balancing acts. The emphasis in the press and elsewhere on his activities, and those of several others similarly engaged has, however, diverted attention from what can only be described as a revolution in American business; I am talking about the tremendous increase in the number of public companies which have been diversifying into unrelated areas of operation. These highly publicized activities reflect, however, only a fraction of the increasing number of acquisitions and mergers involving companies in widely different lines of business. And, of course, many companies over the years have diversified through internal programs. This accelerating trend is changing the face of industry in the United States and abroad.

Now where does this trend leave the public investor without whom much of it would be impossible? All too often, he is left in the dark, particularly when these companies publish financial statements only on an overall company basis. It has been urged that investors and the marketplace need more detailed information, particularly concerning the relative contributions of the various lines of business, if meaningful investment decisions are to be made.

Not unexpectedly, some of those who may be called upon to furnish this information have quarreled with the idea of categorizing the diversified company into its principal business lines. In their view, the investor is (or should be) interested, not in information concerning the component parts, but only in the consolidated figures.

The Commission _too_ has recognized the importance of disclosure of overall operating results. I refer to the development, after a long struggle, of the requirement for consolidated statements in any presentation of the financial position of a corporation and its affiliated companies. But this development, in the context of the rapid changes in the last several years, has been a bit too successful.

A disclosure problem does arise when a company or group of affiliated companies in an integrated line of business decides to diversify into unrelated areas. The investor or his adviser, in such cases, no longer receives information previously available to him from the financial statements of the acquired companies. Presentation of information in consolidated form concerning the combined businesses may conceal significant information. The prospects of a conglomerate enterprise are not measured simply by a figure which reports the total profitability of the enterprise. The past history and changes in profitability of the significant segments are essential to any realistic evaluation of its recent experience and any assessment of its prospects.

Corporate earnings, unlike dollars, have a quality as well as a quantity. Few would suggest that a dollar per share earnings in a "Wildcat Oil Company", with a most erratic performance, and a dollar per share earnings in General Motors have the same worth and significance to investors. The value of earnings is based, at least in part on risk, profitability and growth potential of the business. A conglomerate company, is in fact, a number of disparate businesses each of which may represent different degrees of risk, profitability and opportunity for growth. In these circumstances, unless adequate information concernings these segments is provided, it is, at the very least, difficult to make meaningful investment judgments.

We have always recognized that a reasonable breakdown is essential to meaningful evaluation of past, and informed assessment of future, performance. Wholly apart from the importance of such information to investors, its disclosure is a potent stimulant to the improvement or elimination of substandard operations. The lack of relevant information and the attendant inventor frustration can result in a failure of confidence which could have serious consequences for the stability and credit standing of the company. In recent times, certain conglomerates have experienced such a failure, with consequent sharp declines in the market prices of their securities. Undoubtedly, other factors contributed to this result. I believe, however, that the lack of adequate and material information, suitably broken down for the separate business segments, has been an important factor.

Public skepticism about the performance of certain conglomerates has also been attributed to uncertainty whether reported earnings reflect increasing profitability of the company's operations or are merely the result of the accounting treatment accorded recent acquisitios. Whatever a breakdown may show about the profit or lack thereof of the separate business operations of the company, I suggest that history supports the view--already adopted as a matter of practice and law in certain foreign jurisdictions--that the diversified company can only gain public confidence when the material facts about its operations are fully disclosed. Last week I was privileged to discuss this very problem with the Society of Investment Analysts in London, many of whom expressed surprise that British practice was so much further advanced than ours (and that there was some opposition to the provision of relevant material information).

I have heard that some corporate officials feel the Commission's concern for improved disclosure is part of a government-wide effort to put a damper on the growth of diversified companies. I know of no such effort. There has, of course, been much interest expressed by certain government officials in the various branches of government in the increased pace and the newer forms of combinations. I must emphasize that the concern of the SEC in better disclosure, has no secondary anti-trust or tax enforcement motive. It is, solely and simply, a part of our continuing effort to provide meaningful information to the investing public. The fact that conglomerates are of growing importance, and are usually actively traded, emphasizes the necessity for such information.

I should note, as I have elsewhere, that improved disclosure in this area is not without its problems. Indirect costs of the enterprise must be allocated in such a manner as to make the separate profit and loss figures not misleading. However, whatever the problems of making equitable allocations of costs, they are not insoluble. Nor do they provide a reason for abandoning the effort for improved disclosure. I must repeat that, without adequate information concerning the separate business lines of a company--and I emphasize that we are not talking about each and every product--the investor or his adviser will be handicapped in his analysis of the company's prospects. With or without such information, he must still arrive at some judgment about the prospects of the enterprise, or give up the attempt. That, after all, is what investing or investment management is all about.

Of course, we have always had companies conducting widely different operations. And, as you know, the Commission has, for many years, required such companies to provide information in registration statements regarding the relative importance of each product or service or class of similar products or services which contributed 15% or more to the gross volume of business. It was over two years ago that the American Institute of Certified Public

Accountants' Committee on Relations with the S.E.C. and Stock Exchanges, at my request, made a survey of the disclosure problems of diversified companies. At the end of September 1966 the Committee issued its report. At about that time the F.E.I. proposed to the Commission that it initiate and finance a study. We agreed to defer action pending the completion of the report. In the meantime, I urged voluntary disclosure in numerous public statements, and the Accounting Principles Board, in a statement entitled "Disclosure of Supplemental Financial Information by Diversified Companies," issued in September, 1967, encouraged diversified companies to disclose voluntarily "supplemental financial information as to industry segments of the business."

These efforts to achieve voluntary disclosure have had mixed results. In a survey of 1966 reports to stockholders, we noted some progress. Our review of 1967 reports indicates additional progress, but not to the extent we hoped to see. Where improvements were made, we noted many examples of informative disclosures: relative contributions to net income; relative contributions to net income before allocation of corporate overhead, taxes and other items; and relative "operating profits" of the various divisions.

Our Division of Corporation Finance has also reported more informative disclosures in registration statements. Certain companies, for example, have given the approximate percentage of contributions to consolidated net income of each major product group. Others have presented tables showing sales and net income for significant segments of the business in actual dollar amounts. Still other companies have disclosed major differences between contributions to sales and earnings and have specifically mentioend material segments of the business which had operated at a loss. We believe much more can be done along these lines by many companies. It may not be amiss to note that the Companies Law in the United Kingdom was amended in 1967 to require such information and more. This followed the adoption of similar requirements by the London Stock Exchange.

In the two years since the F.E.I. proposed its study on disclosure, many worthwhile articles and statements on this subject have been prepared by professional groups and by individuals. In recent months three important studies have been published. The F.E.I.'s comprehensive study was published in June under the title Financial Reporting by Diversified Companies The proceedings of a two-day conference on the subject, held at Tulane University last fall, were published last spring as was the report of a study conducted by the National Association of Accountants. With all this material available, much of it stimulated by the Commission, our staff undertook to draft revisions to the description of business items in our registration forms as they relate to diversified companies. On September 4, the Commission published for public comment a proposal to amend the description of the business item in Forms S-1 and S-7 used for registration of securities under the Securities Act of 1933 and Form 10 for registration of securities under the

Securities Exchange Act of 1934. Comparable amendments of other disclosure requirements under the 1934 Act have been deferred pending the receipt of comments on these proposals as well as the completion, shortly, of the general study of our disclosure requirements under the Securities Exchange Act of 1934 currently under way in the Commission.

Prior to preparation and publication of the current proposal, the staff conferred with Dr. Mautz, who was responsible for the development of the F.E.I. study, and with the advisory committee that assisted him. Our proposal reflects many helpful suggestions received as a result of this effort and others. If adopted in the form published, it would require information concerning separate classes of related or similar products or services which, during either of the previous two fiscal years, contributed 10% or more to total sales and operating revenue, or to income before extraordinary items and income taxes have been deducted. For these business egments, disclosure would be required of the approximate amount or percentage that each contributed to revenues and to net income for each of the last five years. However, if this is not practicable, disclosure of the contribution most closely approaching net income would be required. Comparable data on revenues and earnings received from foreign sources, other than Canada, from government procurement or from any single customer are also to be reported. These latter sources of revenue and income are not dealt with in the F.E.I. report, but we currently obtain information in some form in these areas. Early comments indicate that some editing of the proposal may be necessary here. The proposal would also require companies registering securities to report, to the extent practicable, the approximate amount of assets employed in each segment of business.

For some time the staff has felt that the 15% test of materiality, used in our existing rules, was too high. Certain earlier proposals reflected this view. The F.E.I. study suggested retention of the 15% test. The proposal out for comment would drop the test to 10% of the volume of business or net income before extraordinary items and income taxes and extend the disclosure requirement from one to five years. The response of financial analysts in the F.E.I. study showed that the majority felt that 10% to 14% was a desirable balance between the need for information and the burden on management, and that the maximum number of segments of the business to be reported should be eleven or less. Setting the test at 10% would seem to meet these views. In this regard, we have noted many examples of companies which have voluntarily reported separately on segments that accounted for less than 15% of sales or earnings of the business.

I am aware that the managing director of the F.E.I., in a letter sent to members on September 17, took issue with this and certain other requirements in the proposal as not being in accord with the recommendations in Dr. Mautz's study. On this same date, our staff conferred with members of the F.E.I. Committee on Corporate Reporting regarding these and other possible areas of disagreement.

The reasons for the position taken in the proposal were explained and it was thought that there was an understanding of them by your committee. Your committee very recently submitted further comments reflecting its viewpoint. I should note also that others, outside the Commission, interested in this problem have not agreed with certain of the conclusions of the F.E.I. study. We will, of course, give very serious consideration to the comments of your committee and to others who write us concerning the proposed amendments.

I must reiterate that the SEC's interest in this reporting problem is, simply and solely, to secure additional disclosures helpful to investors and their advisers. We have not other motivation. Our experience in the past few years with voluntary disclosure shows that the problems involved in developing improved disclosure can be overcome. Nevertheless, there are some who do not favor additional disclosure. They argue that disclosure of the profitability of the various business lines of a diversified company will place the company at a disadvantage with respect to its customers and competitors. These protests are similar to those which greeted the required disclosure of sales and cost of goods sold when the Securities Acts were adopted and implemented over a generation ago.

To sum up, the need for improved disclosure is clear. The feasibility of improved disclosure has been demonstrated. It has been long delayed, but with the assistance and cooperation of business and profesisonal groups, such as the F.E.I., the

Commission hopes that improved disclosure for diversified companies will soon become a reality.

Finally, I believe it important to note that improved disclosure, as I have discussed it thus far, is not the answer to all the reporting problems of diversified companies. We have, to use but one illustration, noted recent instances in which companies, in the narrative sections of their reports and in the new media, have distorted their growth records by comparing current earnings--which included earnings derived from acquisitions and accounted for on a pooling-of-interests basis--with prior year earnings which had not been restated on a pooled basis. This, of course, was inconsistent with Accounting Principles Board Opinion Number 10. In a recent release (Securities Exchange Act Release No. 4910) the Commission indicated that it considered such comparisons misleading within the meaning of the relevant provisions of the Securities Acts. This release also indicated, as did the APB opinion, that if companies wish to reconcile restated figures with those previously reported, this may be done on a supplemental basis.

Although recent Accounting Principles Board accounting opinions have dealt with reporting for business combinations, there is an urgent need for re-examination of the basic criteria established by the profession for determining the applicability of purchase or pooling accounting in a combination. These standards have been seriously eroded over the years. This fact, along with the increased use of more complex securities, and differing methods for dealing with them, have brought about distortions of the pooling concept beyond its original purpose. Questions have arisen whether pooling accounting is used primarily to improve reported earnings figures, rather than to reflect the economic nature and effects of certain types of combinations. Where applicable accounting rules permit, the astute business manager still can increase a company's reported sales and earnings (if not apparent performance) by adding the sales and earnings of another company through merger or acquisition. Among the more serious problems flowing from the accelerating trend toward diversification, from a disclosure standpoint, is this tendency to distort the pooling concept.

The recently published Accounting Research Study on "Accounting for Goodwill" which also deals with accounting for business combinations may provide further stimulus for the development of new or improved standards in this area of accounting. It has evoked extensive comments from all members of the Project Advisory Committee. We hope to assist, by our comments, in the development of appropriate standards.

If you have followed our recent activities you know that we are ot really looking for business. We have enough to keep us busy for some time. It is also a measure of the importance with which we view these reporting matters that we take so much time at this juncture, to deal with them. Many think we are taking too much time. While I believe that our sense of priorities here is sound, it should not be interpreted as a reflection of a lack of urgency or importance of a reasonably prompt solution of these problems.

#16 James J. Needham

October 20, 1970

Some General Remarks about the SEC and the Accounting Profession

Abstract

Needham states that the relationship between the Commission and the profession is one to be envied by other professionals. He also discusses an expanded concept of independence related to a responsibility to the public interest, and he cautions the accountant not to exploit unsettled areas of accounting principles in favor of management's desire to report improved earnings.

Recently I read the papers and talks presented at the Seaview Symposium covering the topic "Corporate Financial Reporting: Conflicts and Challenges." One of the contributors at the Symposium predicted the Commission would usurp the authority of the Accounting Principles Board. It seems the profession has lived

Presented before a Joint Meeting of the Knoxville Chapter of the Tennessee Society of Certified Public Accountants, the National Association of Accountants, the National Association of Securities Dealers and the Knoxville Bar Association.

with this fear since 1936. The genesis of that fear is described in Jack Carey's recent book published by the Institute. Jack, in the section entitled "Honeymoon Ends," commented that after the Commission was established, several conciliatory speeches were made to the profession, until December 4, 1936, when in a speech made to the Investment Bankers Association, Chairman Landis said:

> The impact of almost daily tilts with accountants, some of them called leaders in their profession, often leaves little doubt that their loyalties to management are stronger than their sense of responsibility to the investor.

How well has the relationship faired since that indictment was expressed? Jack continues by saying the relationship between the profession and the Commission has ranged from praise to criticism. Sometimes seemingly unduly harsh; and, sometimes mingled with the thinly veiled threat the Commission might exercise its latent powers to prescribe accounting principles and methods.

The relationship was further discussed at the annual meeting of the American Institute of Certified Public Accountants in 1966, in a speech in which Chairman Cohen stated:

The Securities and Exchange Commission, as a matter of policy, disclaims responsibility for any speeches by any of its Commissioners. The views expressed herein are those of the speaker and do not necessarily reflect the views of the Commission.

> ...Congress gave us the final responsibility for insuring that adequate standards of disclosure are maintained and it is a responsibility that we take very seriously. However, we prefer--and I anticipate that the Commission will always prefer--to accomplish these objectives through cooperation as long as we are persuaded that it is an effective and expeditious way to achieve them.

The relationship between the SEC and the profession, Jack Carey concluded:

> ...prodded the profession to make improvements both in accounting and auditing that otherwise might have taken longer to achieve.

Personally, I see little possibility the relationship between the profession and the Commission will change materially; and while the "honeymoon" has ended, I trust the two groups can maintain some marital bliss. Like other groups which have their own personality and which must work continually in close proximity, some friction will develop; but, the beneficial results so far have made the relationship one to be envied by other professionals.

Mr. Landis' speech also raised the issue of independence. The term has reached its present definition in an evolutionary process like many of the other concepts in accounting. No one here needs to be reminded under existing Commission regulations an accountant is not considered to be independent if he has any direct financial interest or any material indirect financial interest in his client.

The members of the profession have no problem with this aspect of independence; but, independence has a broader meaning and imposes a positive duty upon the accountant about which Maurice Stans, now Secretary of Commerce, had this to say:

> With the addition of the qualifying adjective "public", to define an area of service and also a profession, there are added to accounting two connotations--one of service to a general clientele, the other of responsibility to the public interest. It is the second of these that is least understood.

I believe the obligation imposed upon the accountant within this meaning of independence is that he should use accounting to convey to the public the clearest picture of the financial condition and results of a business.

The real test of the accountant's independence often comes when he must make a decision with respect to an accounting treatment of a matter not covered by a specific APB Opinion. Too many times the accountant rationalizes or justifies his decision by pointing to the fact that his problem has not been specifically dealt with in accounting literature. This is the most specious form of reasoning.

I believe that too many times when confronted with close questions some accountants ignore one of the fundamentals of accounting--namely that substance shall triumph over form. This means that despite complicated legal instruments and whatever other documentation presented by a client, the accountant is charged, in the first instance, with the repsonsibility of seeing to it that the business impact of the transaction in question is reported rather than a literal reflection of a legal document.

Furthermore, structuring a "business deal" in an attempt to exploit unsettled accounting principles is unfair to everyone and at times can come perilously close to commercial fraud. Management, as well as accountants, has a responsibility to see to it that the real significance of financial transactions is set forth properly in financial statements.

Truly independent accountants are well aware of their responsibilities in this area. As a matter of fact, the vast majority discharge those responsibilities in keeping with their code of professional ethics. Nevertheless, too often the valuable time of the Commission and its staff is consumed in discussios with issuers and their professional advisers who are not motivated towards full and fair disclosure but more towards the reporting of improved earnings.

This practice is of real concern to the professional staff of the Commission. I urge the business community and its professional advisers to have this matter foremost in their minds.

In conclusion, I must confess the Securities and Exchange Commission has often been characterized in unflattering terms; but, on balance, I believe our reputation is best described by a recent writer who said:

> The Securities and Exchange Commission is known as a considerate agency of government, the guardian angel of widows and orphans and the polite policeman of those in the securities business. It is happily endowed with a competent staff which has traditionally displayed a benign understanding of the difficulties of compliance with all the niceties of federal securities regulation.

In all fairness, I must also tell you the writer then went on for three pages to expose our weaknesses.

Sadly, no government agency can expect to be loved by all of the people, all of the time--particularly an agency such as ours, which has such broad responsibilities. However, it is much more important that people, such as yourselves, understand the reason for our being and something of the problems we face.

I hope my remarks have contributed toward that end.

Contents of S.E.C. Speech Files

Accounting History Research Center

Georgia State University

ADDRESS before the New York State Society of CPA's
Landis............October 30, 1933

INTERPRETATIONS OF RULES & REGULATIONS before the New York State Society of CPAs
Landis............January 14, 1935

ADDRESS before the Illinois Society of CPAs
Mathews...........January 18, 1935

ADDRESS before the Milwaukee Chapter Wisconsin Society of Certified Public Accountants
Mathews............January 8, 1937

SOME ACCOUNTING PROBLEMS OF THE SECURITIES & EXCHANGE COMMISSION before the New York State Society of CPAs
Blough............January 11, 1937

ADDRESS at the Joint Spring Meeting of the Virginia Society and the North Carolina Association of Public Accountants
Cavanaugh.............May 21,1937

SOME PROBLEMS IN PRESENTATION OF FINANCIAL INFORMATION TO INVESTORS before the Controllers Institute of America
Blough.............October 5, 1937

ACCOUNTANTS' CERTIFICATES before the Boston Chapter of the Massachusetts Society of CPA's

Blough...........December 13, 1937

THE NEXT STEP IN ACCOUNTING before the American Accounting Association

Healy............December 27, 1937

ADDRESS before the Society for the Advancement of Management and the International Management Congress

Douglas.........September 21, 1938

ADDRESS before the Controllers Institute of America

Werntz..........September 27, 1938

ADDRESS before the Ohio Society of CPA's

Werntz...........September 7, 1939

SUBJECTS FOR ACCOUNTING RESEARCH before the American Institute of Accountants

Werntz..........September 20, 1939

WHAT IS EXPECTED OF THE INDEPENDENT AUDITOR: FROM THE VIEWPOINT OF THE INVESTOR before the American Institute of Accountants

Werntz..........September 21, 1939

ACCOUNTING FOR INVESTORS: THE FUNDAMENTAL IMPORTANCE OF CORPORATE EARNING POWER before the Controllers' Institute of America

Frank.............October 10, 1939

ACCOUNTING AND THE COMMISSION'S ENFORCEMENT PROGRAM before the Chi Chapter of Delta Sigma Pi Johns Hopkins University

Kline.............October 12, 1939

THE RELATION OF ACCOUNTING STATEMENTS AND REPORTS TO SECURITY ISSUES before the Third National Accounting Conference

Werntz...........November 15, 1939

INDEPENDENCE AND COOPERATION before the Controllers Institute of America

Werntz...............June 7, 1940

ACCOUNTING REQUIREMENTS OF THE SECURITIES AND EXCHANGE COMMISSION before the Texas Society of Certified Public Accountants

Werntz..............June 13, 1940

THE SIN OF PERFECTIONISM before the American Institute of Accountants

Frank............October 18, 1940

THE GOVERNMENT'S RESPONSIBILITY FOR THE REGULATION OF ACCOUNTING REPORTS before the Accounting Symposium Percentennial Conference of the University of Pennsylvania

Werntz..........September 16, 1940

STANDARDS OF DISCLOSURE IN FINANCIAL STATEMENTS before the Middle Atlantic States Accounting Conference

Cavanaugh............June 7, 1941

PROGRESS IN ACCOUNTING before the Fifty-Fourth Annual Meeting American Institute of Accountants

Werntz..........September 16, 1941

MEETING THE ACCOUNTING REQUIREMENTS OF THE SECURITIES AND EXCHANGE COMMISSION before the Pennsylvania Institute of CPA's

King.................June 24, 1947

FOOTNOTES TO FINANCIAL STATEMENTS before the Virginia Society of Public Accountants

King.............September 5, 1947

PLAIN TALK IN ACCOUNTING before the American Institute of Accountants

Caffrey...........November 5, 1947

SOME CURRENT ACCOUNTING PROBLEMS before the 22nd Michigan Annual Accounting Conference

King............November 15, 1947

SOME COMMENTS CONCERNING THE PRESENTATION AND INTERPRETATION OF CORPORATE FINANCIAL STATEMENTS before the New Jersey Society of CPA's
King............December 16, 1947

PRESENTATION OF PERTINENT DATA IN FINANCIAL STATEMENTS before the Ohio State University Tenth Annual Institute on Accounting
King.................May 21, 1948

GENERALLY ACCEPTED ACCOUNTING PRINCIPLES before the New Jersey Society of CPA's and the Wisconsin Society of CPA's
King..........October 5 & 15, 1948

ACCOUNTING KEEPS PACE WITH THE TIMES before the Delaware State Society of CPA's
King.............February 28, 1949

THE INVESTOR LOOKS AT ACCOUNTING before the Annual Reports Forum University of Michigan
McDonald........September 21, 1950

THE CONCEPT OF INDEPENDENCE IN ACCOUNTING before the American Institute of Accountants
Cook...............October 3, 1950

FINANCIAL STATEMENTS--THE BRIDGE BETWEEN DISCLOSURE AND INFORMATION before the American Institute of Accountants
McCormick..........October 3, 1950

DEFICIENCIES IN THE PRESENTATION OF INFORMATION REQUIRED BY FORM X-17A-5, UNIFORM QUESTIONNAIRE FOR BROKER-DEALERS before the 63rd Annual Meeting of American Institute of Accountants
LaPadula...........October 4, 1950

THE ACCOUNTANT'S LANGUAGE--THE WORLD'S BUSINESS before the Certified Public Accountants Association of Ontario
McDonald..........October 20, 1950

PROFESSIONAL ETHICS as Viewed by the S.E.C.
ADDRESS before the Annual Meeting of the American Institute of Accountants

King...............October 8, 1952

PROVIDING FUNDS FOR OUR ENTERPRISES BY THE ISSUE OF SECURITIES before the 1954 Eastern Spring Conference of the Controllers Institute of America

Demmler............March 22, 1954

THE ROLE OF ACCOUNTING IN THE REGULATION OF THE ISSUE AND MARKETING OF SECURITIES IN THE UNITED STATES before the American Institute of Accountants

Demmler...........October 16, 1954

CORPORATE ACCOUNTING STANDARDS UNDER FEDERAL SECURITIES LAWS before the 18th Annual Institute on Accounting of the Ohio State University

Armstrong............May 17, 1956

HIGHLIGHTS IN CURRENT FINANCIAL REPORTING before the 1957 Annual Meeting of the Illinois Society of CPA's

Armstrong............June 6, 1957

PARTICULAR S.E.C. MERGER CONSIDERATIONS before the Finance Orientation Seminar #121-91, "Organizing for, Appraising, and Financing Corporate Mergers and Acquisitions" American Management Association

Woodside......November 20-22, 1957

ACCOUNTING ASPECTS OF BUSINESS COMBINATIONS before the American Accounting Association

Barr...............August 27, 1958

THE CANADIAN ACCOUNTING PROFESSION AND THE S.E.C. before the 56th Annual Conference of The Canadian Institute of Chartered Accountants

Barr...........September 15, 1958

THE INDEPENDENT ACCOUNTANT AND THE S.E.C. before the Twenty-First Annual Ohio State University Institute on Accounting
Barr..................May 21, 1959

DISCLOSURE IN THEORY AND PRACTICE before the Certified Public Accountants of the Pacific Northwest
Barr.................June 27, 1959

THE ROLE OF THE ACCOUNTANT IN THE RESTORATION AND MAINTENANCE OF PUBLIC CONFIDENCE IN THE CAPITAL FORMATION PROCESS before the Hagerstown Chapter National Association of Accountants
Sargent...........October 15, 1959

ACCOUNTING--CHANGING PATTERNS--THE IMPACT OF REGULATORY AGENCIES before the Graduate School of Business University of Chicago
Barr.............November 11, 1959

ACCOUNTING RESEARCH Panel Discussion at the Annual Meeting of American Accounting Association--Ohio State University
Barr...............August 30, 1960

ACCOUNTING AND AUDIT PROBLEMS WITH PARTICULAR REFERENCE TO NEW REGISTRANTS WITH THE SECURITIES AND EXCHANGE COMMISSION before the Ohio Society of CPA's and The New York State Society of CPA's
Barr..............November 1, 1960

BUSINESS COMBINATIONS AND OTHER FINANCIAL REPORTING PROBLEMS before the Controllers Institute of America
Barr..............January 18, 1962

ACCOUNTING PROBLEMS OF FIRST-TIME REGISTRATION STATEMENTS before the Georgia Society of CPA's--Atlanta Athletic Club
Orbach...............March 6, 1962

FINANCIAL STATEMENTS--HOW RELIABLE? before the Alumni of the Graduate School of Business Administration of New York University and Long Island Chapter National Association of Accountants
Barr.....March 23 & April 16, 1963

THE S.E.C. AND CANADIAN OPERATIONS before the Tenth Annual Western Canada Conference on Financial Management and Petroleum Accounting --The Banff School of Fine Arts and Centre for Continuing Education

Barr..................May 16, 1963

ACCOUNTING TREATMENT OF INVESTMENT TAX CREDIT ON CORPORATE FINANCIAL STATEMENTS before the American Management Association Finance Briefing Session #1347-01 Final I.R.S./Treasury Department Corporate Tax Rules and Guidelines

Barr and Orbach......June 18, 1963

FINANCIAL REPORTING REQUIREMENTS IN REGULATION A FILINGS before the American Institute of CPA's

Epstein..............June 25, 1963

SOME COMMON DEFICIENCIES IN FIRST FILINGS AND PREPARATION FOR CONFERENCES WITH S.E.C. STAFF prepared by Sydney C. Orbach for a Course on Filings with the S.E.C. sponsored by the American Institute of Certified Public Accountants

Orbach..............June 24, 1963
Dunlap..............July 11, 1963
Barr................July 18, 1963

THE INFLUENCE OF GOVERNMENT AGENCIES ON ACCOUNTING PRINCIPLES WITH PARTICULAR REFERENCE TO THE SECURITIES AND EXCHANGE COMMISSION before the 37th Annual Michigan Accounting Conference

Barr.............October 18, 1963

GOVERNMENT-INDUSTRY RELATIONS before the Forty-fifth Annual Conference of the National Association of Accountants

Woodside...........June 23, 1964

CONSOLIDATED FINANCIAL STATEMENTS--QUESTIONS OF VALUATION--A discussion prepared for the "Arbeitskreis der Wirtschaftsprufunsgs-Aktiengesellschaften"

Barr................June 29, 1964

CURRENT DEVELOPMENTS AT THE S.E.C. before the 1964 Convention American Accounting Association--Indiana University
Cohen...........September 1, 1964

TRENDS IN FINANCIAL REPORTING before the Nineteenth Annual Conference of Accountants--University of Tulsa
Barr...............April 29, 1965

A REVIEW OF THE COMMISSION'S ADMINISTRATIVE POLICIES RELATING TO FINANCIAL REPORTING UNDER THE SECURITIES ACT before the Fourth Annual Accounting Forum of Hayden, Stone Incorporated
Woodside........November 18, 1965

ADDRESS before the Nineteenth Annual Conference of the Financial Analysts Federation
Cohen................May 24, 1966

ADDRESS before the American Institute of CPA's
Cohen.............October 5, 1966

ADDRESS before the American Institute of CPA's
Cohen.............October 5, 1966

THE S.E.C. AND THE ACCOUNTING PROFESSION--YESTERDAY AND TODAY before the Banking, Corporation and Business law Section of the New York State Bar Association
Barr.............January 26, 1967

TRENDS AND FUTURE REQUIREMENTS FOR CORPORATE FINANCIAL REPORTING before the Twentieth Annual Financial Management Conference
Barr..................May 1, 1967

CORPORATE FINANCIAL REPORTING: THE DEVELOPING DEBATE ON "LINE OF BUSINESS" DISCLOSURE before the National Association of Accountants
Barr................June 27, 1967

NEED FOR PRODUCT-LINE REPORTING before Symposium on Financial Reporting for Conglomerates
Barr............November 13, 1967

ADDRESS before the Financial Executives Institute
Cohen............October 26, 1968

REMARKS before a Joint Meeting of the Knoxville Chapter of the Tennessee Society of CPA's, the National Association of Accountants, the National Association of Securities Dealers, and the Knoxville Bar Association
Needham..........October 20, 1970

For Product Safety Concerns and Information please contact our EU
representative GPSR@taylorandfrancis.com
Taylor & Francis Verlag GmbH, Kaufingerstraße 24, 80331 München, Germany

www.ingramcontent.com/pod-product-compliance
Ingram Content Group UK Ltd.
Pitfield, Milton Keynes, MK11 3LW, UK
UKHW022214190926
475702UK00003B/356

* 9 7 8 0 3 6 7 5 1 5 8 9 8 *